Jeffrey Schwartz ■ Stanley B. Yeldell

Criminal Justice
INTERNSHIP MANUAL

THIRD EDITION

Kendall Hunt
publishing company

Kendall Hunt
publishing company

www.kendallhunt.com
Send all inquiries to:
4050 Westmark Drive
Dubuque, IA 52004-1840

ISBN 978-1-5249-9329-0

Published in the United States of America

DEDICATION OF HOPE

This Criminal Justice Internship Manual is dedicated to my daughters: Lauren and Brittany. It is my hope one day, whenever that might be, hearts and souls will be truly reunited. That day, however, cannot come soon enough.

DEDICATION OF INSPIRATIONS

This Criminal Justice Internship Manual is dedicated to my niece, Tamara Herald and her twins: Jamil and Jemal Herald, so proud of all of you.

CONTENTS

ACKNOWLEDGMENTS

We would like to express our appreciation to the criminal justice, security, professional, and criminal justice professors and students who have contributed to this manual. It is richer because of their personal sharing:

Val Andreassi, DMD, Rowan University alumn, contributing toward career goals and an explanation of the dynamic workplace.

David Ashworth, Rowan University student, successful completion of the Law and Justice Studies Department internship program, military professional; contributing toward the perspectives on networking, making the most out of the internship, and importance of continuing education.

Peg Brown, co-author of the First and Second Editions of this manual; her hard work and dedication as the former Rowan Law and Justice Studies Administrative Assistant, actively engaged in the internship program and always available to help students, contributed greatly throughout the manual.

William Cheety, Rowan University student, contributed toward a cohesive assembly of agencies in New Jersey.

Kenneth P. MacKenzie, highest ranking martial artist in Hapkido, world record holder for breaking, over 30 years creating and overseeing several martial art schools in New Jersey, Rowan University Alumni and the first student to have engaged in the formalized internship program at Rowan; contributed his personal story and perspectives on maximizing the internship experience.

Dirk Stephan, Security Professional, owner of INSECO Security Company; contributed perspectives on internship possibilities, lifelong learning and dedication to achieving goals.

PREFACE

The Criminal Justice Internship course is an interesting and diverse vehicle for students to examine the practical aspects of the criminal justice system prior to entering the actual employment arena.

Our interest in this manual evolved from teaching and/or advising criminal justice internship students over a duration of 20 or more years in the Law and Justice Studies Department at Rowan University. We have discovered there was more than ample need to design and craft a text targeted for the criminal justice students.

Our goal was to formulate and produce a manual that would satisfy the criminal justice market, as well as other disciplines. We envision that the manual will be utilized as the primary or required vehicle for criminal justice programs and closely-annexed programs.

Students will be able to examine each chapter to gain an understanding of how the supporting information will assist in guiding them to their desired internship.

The manual solicits the student to actively participate in the learning process, to continue to learn, and to realize that the skills gained in an internship may be used throughout life.

Many students will wish to exceed the basic information and utilize the Internet and related sources to pursue an internship. We have included some directories and specific links of interest.

Furthermore, it is our intended goal to produce a multifaceted, versatile manual that will be utilized by professors and practitioners within the criminal justice field. Also, we believe two-year programs, four-year programs and graduate programs will welcome the manual.

It is our hope that students will discover the Internship Manual to be an invaluable road map and an informative resource instrument in their pursuit for future employment.

ABOUT THE AUTHORS

Jeffrey L. Schwartz, Assistant Professor Rowan University Law and Justice Studies Department. Professor Schwartz, besides possessing a Ph.D., has numerous certifications and ongoing practical experience in the law enforcement field. He is a retired police officer, an approved instructor with numerous agencies, a licensed private detective, and an instructor trainer in many facets of policing. Further, Professor Schwartz is a subject matter expert in terrorism, use of force, supervision, and tactical training. He has instructed at various police academies, security training academies, consulted with public and private schools, as well as, consulted with numerous private businesses.

Professor Schwartz has published articles in professional journals, authored chapters in textbooks, and is an author of *The Criminal Justice Internship Manual* (2015), author of *The Invariable Evolution: Police Use of Force in America* (2017), author of *The Victimology Handbook* (2018), developed curriculum for several Universities, conducted major research for a level one trauma center in New Jersey, collaborated in research and policy with numerous police agencies, is co-advisor for internships at Rowan University and continues to mentor students on a daily basis. Professor Schwartz is the faculty advisor for the Criminal Justice Preparation Club, of which he is the founder at Rowan University. Professor Schwartz has lectured across the country as a use of force expert. He was a lecturer for the Federal Law Enforcement Training Center and conducted seminars on use of force in various venues. He consulted on anti-terrorism and other related issues for the Department of Defense with several federal defense contractors. Professor Schwartz continues to be a resource for many agencies in policy, diversity, recruiting, and training. Further, he continues research and publications.

Dr. Stanley B. Yeldell began his education at a four-room segregated school. With the ruling of Brown vs. the Board of Education, he and his classmates were transferred to Aura Elementary School. He played on the first African-American baseball team in Glassboro, the Lawns Red Legs Babe Ruth Team. Dr. Yeldell graduated from Bowie State University in 1969, with experience as the first African-American legislative intern for the late Senator Edward T. Conroy of Maryland. In 1972, he graduated with his J.D. from Howard University. For the past 40 years, he has been a respected and beloved faculty member of the Department of Law and justice Studies at Rowan University. He has had numerous publications and authored three text books.

Dr. Yeldell's work with students has been a hallmark of his career. As Internship Coordinator for Criminal Justice courses, he typically works with more than 100 students each semester to locate internships, match students so that their qualifications and interests fit the internship opportunities, and supervise them during their internship. In 2012, he received an award from the New Jersey College & University Public Safety Association for setting up a Student Patrol at Rowan University. Dr. Yeldell was the first of two inductees into the Law and Justice Hall of Fame at Rowan. Further, there is a Dr. Stanley B. Yeldell Scholarship to be awarded annually to a Law and justice major who demonstrates his or her academic excellence, leadership, and community service.

Chapter 1

INTRODUCTION

This manual provides an introduction to the ever-changing fields within the criminal justice system. It will serve as a practical resource that includes descriptions and numerous sources for students to investigate while pursuing an internship.

Although less than exhaustive in its treatment of competing positions, the manual's comprehensive view assists in clarifying and responding to numerous inquiries about the complexities of internships and their applications to career explorations.

The manual is practically useful, as well as, theoretically sophisticated. It includes significant descriptions of numerous resources. Each chapter reveals the authors' understanding of the integral obstacles, providing plain-spoken advice about what it takes to maximize an internship. In addition, it contains suggestions on how to cope with the dynamics of the criminal justice system.

FIGURE 1.1

The manual has been crafted so that the basic information or literature can be easily ascertainable in each chapter. Moreover, a succinct discussion of the major components of the criminal justice system is coupled with each component's conditions and requirements of employment. The vast opportunities for internships within the criminal justice system include the following criminal justice fields: Law Enforcement, Corrections, Courts, and Social Justice Organizations.

The manual consists of ten informative chapters. The manual commences with Chapter One, The Introduction, which introduces the theme of the manual with particular attention to the linkage between the major concepts and an overview of the criminal justice system.

Chapter Two, Criminal Justice Internships, examines the needs an internship fulfills for the student, the intern's career pursuits, and the utilization of the sources.

Chapter Three, Educational Requirements, articulates agency requirements, formulating learning objectives, and the roles of the supervisor and the university faculty advisors.

Chapter Four, Internship Portfolio, surveys the major components in the formulation of a resume, cover letter, exit letter/interview, and follow-up letter, as well as, securing meaningful recommendations.

Chapter Five, Law Enforcement Internships, describes and analyzes the educational requirements and conditions of employment as they relate to local, county, state and federal and special agencies.

Chapter Six, Correctional Internships, covers in detail the various levels of correctional institutions and their employment requirements.

Chapter Seven, Judicial Internships, introduces readers to the systematic levels of the judiciary and the variety of opportunities within.

Chapter Eight, Trends/Visions, focuses on how to identify the new emerging fields evolving into the future of criminal justice.

Chapter Nine, Criminal Justice Degree Programs, lists colleges and universities that offer a master's degree and/or Ph.D. program in criminal justice.

Chapter Ten, The Conclusion, provides an integrated synthesis of lessons about the need to follow the road map of an internship program as outlined in this manual. In addition, personal select stories from graduates of the internship program offer points of consideration and words of advice.

THE INTERNSHIP

The standard that must be utilized throughout an internship experience is the reasonable person concept. In the course of an internship, students may encounter complicated interpersonal or institutional matters that are difficult to navigate. The common sense approach mandates the attempt to use these encounters to enhance the student's understanding of complicated matters; the astute student of criminal justice will avoid the obvious pitfalls.

Any obstacles the intern faces will foster the learning process to develop the student's creative ability and skills. Ultimately, the real-world experience that an internship provides will strengthen the student's position to obtain employment or help the student to realize that this field is not a career path her or she wants to pursue. Either outcome, employment or a different career focus, provides one of the most useful life lessons one can hope to gain from a university degree program.

LAWJ 05356: CRIMINAL JUSTICE INTERNSHIP

The course is for an in-service to students (law enforcement, courts and corrections personnel) involving placement in a criminal justice related agency and an academic component.

In unusual circumstances other course work may be substituted for the internship; this requires the approval of the Internship Coordinator, who will then submit to the department chair. (Implemented Spring 2004)

LAWJ 05357: CRIMINAL JUSTICE INTERNSHIP II 3 S.H.

CJ Internship II course is not intended to replace Criminal Justice Internship I (LAWJ05356), but is intended to allow students additional opportunities for field experience.

Students must complete Criminal Justice Internship I (LAWJ05356) prior to enrolling in this course.

Students are to discuss this course with the academic advisor and then the Internship Coordinator prior to enrolling.

ROWAN UNIVERSITY LAW AND JUSTICE STUDIES DEPARTMENT

The Law and Justice Studies Department at Rowan University offers a unique program that allows students to be very hands-on in their respective fields before graduating. Our students enter the work force with experience on their resume, and full knowledge of what to expect in their respective fields.

ROWAN UNIVERSITY STUDENT PATROL PROGRAM

The Student Patrol Program at Rowan was crafted jointly by Professor Yeldell and Chief Security Officer Michael Funk as a response to an initiative to enhance campus security. It consists of a cooperative effort to place Law/Justice Internship students within the area of Rowan Public Safety, while providing a rigorous academic component. The Student Patrol Program is managed by Rowan Public Safety Police Officer Greg Farrar and assisted by Rowan Public Safety Police Officer Frank Agosta.

The Student Patrol Program at Rowan has been successful in identifying potential candidates for employment within the Public Safety Department at Rowan University.

Student Patrol members receive 30 hours of intense instruction on such diverse topics; as CPR, Homeland Security's Incident Command System, oral and written communications, and patrol tactics. Each Student Patrol member contributes 150 hours of patrol duty that includes; walking escort service, assistance with security functions, and student residence patrol.

As a measure of the program's success, 65% of the students who have participated in Student Patrol are now employed either directly or indirectly in full-time criminal justice.

The majority of the other graduates from the Student Patrol have either enrolled in various graduate schools or commissioned in the armed forces.

WHAT ARE THE BENEFITS OF AN INTERNSHIP?

The selection process for an internship is competitive. Therefore, being selected is an accomplishment. It is an opportunity to get work experience with an actual law enforcement agency. Also, the skills and knowledge that you will develop can be a beneficial attribute when competing for criminal justice job openings. Finally, it shows a true commitment to a career in law enforcement.

The competitive nature in obtaining an internship is akin to obtaining employment. In fact, some of the internships actually evolve into employment. When the student makes an impact on those in an agency (the professionals in the field), he or she has made invaluable contacts that can span an entire career.

Should the internship not directly lead to employment, for instance, the agency is not hiring at that time, a formalized process such as the Civil Service impedes direct hiring, or the intern decides the agency is not for them, the intern can nevertheless feel confident that the personnel in the agency will help with networking, securing interviews, distributing the intern's resume, providing letters of recommendation, informing the intern when hiring will occur, and many other related items.

FIGURE 1.2

FIGURE 1.3

There are certain procedures to follow if a job is under the Civil Service Commission.

In New Jersey - http://www.state.nj.us/csc/ The website will provide all information, descriptions and how to apply for civil service positions in New Jersey including many public safety jobs.

There are age requirements, physical requirements, educational, and other requirements. Consult the NJ Civil Service website for the specific information.

There are various exams to consider for the type of job announcement you are interested in applying. Be aware of posting dates for tests. There are fees to take the tests. Two guides provided by the NJ Civil Service Commission are free and accessible once you apply to take a posted exam. If you do not want to wait, several study guides and practice tests are available for purchase if you choose.

The Civil Service Commission gives preference to veterans. To be eligible you need to file Veterans Preference Claim Form to the Department of Military and Veterans Affairs.

For Law Enforcement positions, a person must pass a written exam called the Law Enforcement Examination (LEE). After someone passes, he or she will be on an eligibility list for two years. The next LEE exams are supposed to be in the Summer of 2016.

- Be sure to submit a complete job application to the New Jersey Civil Service Commission.
- Remember, it takes time to complete a profile and be able to submit an application.
- Review the online application guides prior to beginning anything on the website.
- Be sure to have a transcript handy to scan if you need to prove course history.
- Know all the dates and information for past employment.
- Provide an accurate resume.
- Follow the exact format for submitting any documents.

So, find the job announcement and make certain you meet the job requirements.

FEDERAL JOB WEBSITE

Usajobs.gov
This website provides all the information you need to apply for most federal jobs.

Federal job postings occur all the time, so be proactive. All the postings list needed qualifications, levels of experience, knowledge in the job area and any skills you may have that are applicable. Register on the site and upload your resume. You can also add a cover letter, which should be tailored to the specific job description posted, and speak to your experience as applicable to the required job skills.

Chapter 2

CRIMINAL JUSTICE INTERNSHIPS

INTRODUCTION

This chapter examines the importance of the internship, what needs it fulfills, and how these needs may change according to career pursuits. It defines the internship and discusses the objectives of an internship. The chapter provides an immediate challenge by requiring the student to assess his or her own critical needs coupled with how to examine and pursue various careers in the criminal justice field. The impact of technology enhances the student's options for exploring the numerous internships by utilizing Internet research avenues and the invaluable methods of networking.

© Grasko/Shutterstock.com

FIGURE 2.1

CHAPTER OUTLINE

1. Defining the Internship
2. Assessment of Needs
3. Career Pursuits
4. Internet Research
5. Networking

DEFINING THE INTERNSHIP

The internships are intended to actively remove the student from the academic classroom and place the student into a rich blend of practical laboratory and experiences yielded by the Criminal Justice Agencies.

The Internship Objectives:

a. Designed to supplement the formalized classroom theory with a supervised experience within the criminal justice system or related agencies or fields.

b. Will provide potential employers with the opportunity to observe and examine prospective employees.

c. Will emphasize an increasing need for field-related experiences and the enhancement of formalized theory through professional training within the criminal justice system.

d. Will foster a positive link between the university, college or community college, and related criminal justice agencies.

e. Enhance diversity within criminal justice agencies by providing potentially well qualified candidates, who can be readily assessed to fit the needs of the agency or organization.

f. Will aid in the determination of the student's career pursuit.

ASSESSMENT OF NEEDS

© Keepsmiling4u/Shutterstock.com

FIGURE 2.2

The internship is the most important experience that the student will encounter during his or her academic career. The student must examine his or her critical needs in order to decide what internship would satisfy his or her future career goals.

These needs and their internship-related counterparts are as follows:

a. Self-Actualization: Who am I? Opportunity for growth
b. Esteem: Self-worth and self-respect, and promotions
c. Social: Friends and human interaction
d. Security: Safe working conditions, good supervision, job security and training
e. Physical: Good working conditions, rest periods, sufficient income, heating/air conditioning

The internship has the potential to satisfy all five categories of human needs.

THE INTERNSHIP PROCESS

Every student who declares Law and Justice as their major will need to enroll and pass at least one Internship course in order to graduate. The student can enroll beginning their Junior year. It is well advised that the student does not wait until their last semester to enroll in the course. Students may take Internship I (150 hours and 3 s.h.) and Internship II (an additional 150 hours and earning an additional 3 s.h.)

Students should prepare themselves for the Internship process.

Resume/Cover Letter—Each student will be required to have a resume and cover letter the first week of the course. Therefore, it is recommended the student have both a resume and cover letter drafted already. There are many resources to help in the formulation of these documents in the Office of Career Advancement.

The student should proactively be engaged in obtaining an internship prior to enrolling in the Internship course. If the student has any questions if the agency or job will qualify for the Internship course, the student can always check with Professor Schwartz (Internship Coordinator).

The student at a minimum is expected to complete 150 hours at the internship site. This time usually equates to 10 hours per week during the regular academic semester. There are many ways to work around a student's school or existing work schedule (should the internship be at another agency/location). The start time and length of time to complete the necessary hours can all be worked with the Internship Coordinator.

The student, once successfully enrolled in the Internship course (whether online or in person) will be covered by Rowan's Certificate of Liability Insurance.

There are required forms that must be completed by the student prior to or in the beginning of the Internship course, as well as, during the course.

Depending upon the internship agency, the process may include drug screening and a more in-depth background check.

If the student has not secured an offer of internship placement, the student will identify which type of internship they are interested in. However, it is highly encouraged the student attempts to obtain an internship.

Depending on the agency, the background and other screening processes may need to be conducted prior to obtaining an interview with a prospective agency.

The textbook for the course contains all the forms needed by the student and the host agency to complete the requirements. The syllabus contained in the text will give students and host agencies an idea about the process involved.

There are several forms, no matter the internship, that are required to be completed.

- A letter of confirmation from the agency is required to be submitted to the Internship Coordinator prior to starting the internship experience, unless another arrangement is authorized by the Internship Coordinator.
- The student must submit a resume and cover letter as outlined in the text.
- The student must submit the **required Appendix (D, G, H, I, J, L)** in accordance with the instructions in the applicable pages of the text.
- The student is responsible for completing the internship application (Appendix A) and obtaining approval from the Internship Coordinator, unless other prior arrangements have been made with the Internship Coordinator.
- The student will complete and sign the Internship Agreement (Appendix C and F).

All guidelines from the University will be followed—discipline, honesty, attendance, etc. Please refer to the student handbook and course catalogs. This course is Pass/No Credit.

Remember, it is important to begin considering where the student will do an internship beginning their Junior year. The student needs to be proactive. The student must have a resume and cover letter. The student will need to ensure the internship they wish to secure is acceptable for the course. The student must complete the required forms and submit the required paperwork in order to pass the course.

CAREER PURSUITS

The internship is very important in satisfying your needs—not only your financial needs but also your identity and self-esteem needs. For these reasons, it is important to give careful thought to what career you will pursue. This manual will help you decide what you want to do with your career. You will have the opportunity to look at what is important to you and to ascertain what you have to offer potential employers during the internship. Conversely, you will be able to assess what the potential employers have to offer you.

Choosing a career has never been more difficult as it is today. With evolving technologies presenting new employment horizons, there are far more opportunities than ever before.

You must identify your career needs. Examine the list below and rank them according to importance, using one for the most important etc.:

_____ Degree of freedom you have on your job

_____ Number of fringe benefits

_____ Amount of feedback you receive about your performance

_____ Degree of employment security

_____ Amount of income

_____ Amount of praise for a job well done

_____ Opportunity for obtaining a promotion

_____ Opportunity to participate in making decisions

_____ Opportunity to create

_____ Opportunity to enhance self-worth or self-esteem

_____ Opportunity for development

_____ Available resources to complete assignments or projects

_____ Respect from others

_____ Work environment

INTERNET RESEARCH

The Internet offers a spectacular opportunity to learn about the criminal justice agency or related organizations you may consider by accessing the ever-increasing information that is available. Each site contains valuable information about the sponsoring agency or organizations that offer internship listings. Later, when preparing for your interview with a prospective agency, the knowledge you gain from research will set you apart from other candidates.

Consider:

1. The structure of the agency.
2. The function of the agency.
3. Identify who are the leaders in the agency.
4. Be able to explain why you choose this particular agency for your internship.
5. Explain your personal philosophy as compared with the mission statement of the agency.
6. Explain why you would want to work at this agency for a career.
7. Demonstrate how your skills or abilities work well with the agency.
8. Identify a challenge you faced and explain how you overcame the adversity.
9. Explain your strengths and areas which need improvement.
10. Explain how you are working to improve those areas you find lacking in your self-assessment.

While there exists an abundance of internship resources, their usefulness to you depends upon two aspects: 1) the geographical scope of your search and 2) which area of criminal justice you want to pursue.

It should come as no surprise that a nationwide internship database would not be the most effective instrument if you were hoping to find an internship in your current place of residence. When your search is locally focused, it is not worth spending too much time sorting through thousands of national listings. You can get lucky, of course, but your time would be better spent exploring local resources.

We, at Rowan University, along with the Gloucester County Prosecutor Office and Rowan University Department of Public Safety, have developed a process to enable "vetting" interns and (thus) provide a ready pool of interns for the 26 law enforcement agencies in Gloucester County. We are expanding the efforts to encompass all facets of the criminal justice system—our courts (local and superior), probation, parole, and many others within the Gloucester County area.

Should another university/college wish to obtain more information, most all is covered in this manual (with the exception of the Memorandum of Understanding).

The examination of the Internet for criminal justice internship information can be a frustrating task. To that end, we have assembled a list of web site addresses that you may find helpful. Special attention has been given to the New Jersey and Pennsylvania jurisdictions.

As you are researching, remember to note enough information to be useful should you obtain an interview. Items such as the type of organization, composition of the agency, the hierarchy and geographical locations of important areas within the jurisdiction, and knowledge of the population and history of the agency are just some examples of information that can help you prepare for the interview. Please review the section on what to consider as you are doing this research. Seek out your Internship Coordinator to help solidify any questions you may have. Investigate clubs in your university that help students prepare for employment. Take advantage of the University's Career Advancement Office and the resources offered.

NETWORKING

The networking process is a vital and central component of any effective internship search. This procedure will enable the student to continue his or her internship pursuit. The *American Heritage Dictionary* defines networking as:

> *An informal system whereby persons having common interests or concerns assist each other, as in the exchange of information or the development of professional contacts.*

Networking is the practice of utilizing your criminal justice contacts to discover potential internships. Effective networking will give the student an ever-building list of contacts, one of whom will be the individual who may offer you the position for which you have been searching. It can be a tiresome and frustrating process, but it is well worth the effort.

There are numerous reasons why some students resist the networking practice. First, some of them view networking as dishonorable because it seems to reward "you have to know someone," rather than the most qualified students. This is a very narrow and self-defeating position. Remember, networking can be the best way to contact that person.

FIGURE 2.3

You may be omitting a very important source—your criminal justice professor. The vast majority of individuals who teach criminal justice courses have extensive experience in their chosen fields, often with organizations located near their college or university. You need to ask your professors for advice and names of people to contact. They will be more than happy to assist you.

Another excellent starting point is your college or university's career center. In addition to employment listings, these career centers often collect contact information for alumni who are willing to talk to students about their professions. In addition, the career center can be instrumental in developing resumes and engaging in formal employment search engine databases.

The university or college may have a club or other resources who engage in bolstering student employability.

Rowan University has a Criminal Justice Preparation Club. Founded and advised by co-author Professor Jeffrey Schwartz, the Criminal Justice Preparation Club embodies all the facets mentioned in this manual by providing students with exposure to mock interviews, guest speakers and recruiters from many federal, state, and local agencies, along with a very practical way to network.

Friends and family represent a third source of professional contacts. For example, your Uncle Ted may have a very good friend who is a state trooper and an internship with that agency intrigues you. You need to pursue this contact and most important, be assertive and respectful; the results may surprise you.

Networking can also help you set up informational interviews, another valuable investment of your internship search time. Informational interviews are less formal talks during which you can ask questions about the agency or the organization. This type of internship exploration has a substantial amount of advantages. First, it will provide you with more information on which to base your career selection. Second, it gives you a chance to articulate your enthusiasm and qualifications to a potential employer even when there are no suitable positions available. Third, an informational interview gives your contact a better sense of your interests and skills, which will help them direct you to other contacts.

Finally, an often-overlooked advantage of networking is that it will help you uncover internships that have not been listed or advertised. Advance information through word-of-mouth is invaluable in giving you a head start over your competition. It not only puts you first in line for consideration, it also shows how resourceful you are. Remember, in order to network effectively, you must be organized.

Control networking and use it to your advantage and your efforts will result in an ever-growing web of people, organizations, and related agencies.

One important note—all agencies and organizations can utilize your social media footprint potentially for and against you. Trustworthiness, reliability, maturity, and other traits tha employers desire can be gleaned from a quick look at your social media. In fact, your e-mail address can immediately detract or even disqualify you from moving forward in an interview process. Names such as "Partyanimal@," "Gettinghigh@," "Nostudying@," etc. are examples that would not bode well.

Whatever you post on social media—pictures at parties with alcohol when you are under 21, suggestive or other inappropriate dress, comments attacking others point of view, comments about negative views on sexual preference, race, ethnicity or a host of related items—will not get you very far in an interview. It is perfectly legal for a potential employer to ask you to sign into Facebook right at the interview. During background checks, all your social media is accessed (with or without your knowledge at times). Your associates are critically important. If you know your friend Johnny is a gang member, you may rethink hanging around him anymore. Common sense will go a long way if you take a step back and examine your social media and your associates. Remember, it is you who will potentially lose a great career you dreamed about.

EXIT INTERVIEW AND FOLLOW UP LETTER/E-MAIL

The exit interview and follow up letter will be examined in detail later. It is important to know that networking while performing your internship will be extremely valuable. The process outlined later with the exit interview/follow up letter is an integral part of how the internship does not begin or end concurrent with the semester.

PERSONAL STORIES FROM ROWAN ALUMNI

We have decided to include only two personal stories about Rowan alumni in this Manual. We received hundreds of requests; therefore, to be fair we are including only the story from Kenneth MacKenzie, the first person to do the formalized internship program. The other story is unique. Although numerous internships have produced judges, prosecutors, Chiefs of Police, federal agents, lawyers, and a long list of professional careers, we chose the first story to represent how a career never stops evolving.

The student, who graduated with the highest honors, participated in an internship with a local police department. At that time, in the 1980s, the ride-along internship program with police agencies was just evolving. Not many departments wanted to participate. However, Professor Yeldell had personal relationships with many of the law enforcement agencies and paved the way for the ride along program.

The student did well and took Professor Yeldell's advice to network. The student followed the program: networking, getting to know the police officers, making sure the evaluations were completed and discussed with the police supervisor, and sending an exit letter, along with an exit interview. The student impressed the department and they offered a job to that student upon graduation from the university.

The student became a police officer and kept in contact with Professor Yeldell over the following years, proudly informing the professor about his education progress and progress within the police department. Professor Yeldell continued to remind his former student about the importance of continuing education and lifelong learning.

Keeping all the lessons in mind from the internship, the student asked Professor Yeldell about opportunities in the field of higher education. Professor Yeldell, with his wide network of contacts, secured an interview for the former student with the professor in charge of the criminal justice program in a nearby community college.

The former student, with all the lessons learned from the internship—networking, lifelong learning, and mentoring—did well in the interview. The former student became an adjunct professor for that particular community college.

Professor Yeldell continued to be in contact with the former student (who was now a police supervisor and adjunct professor). Professor Yeldell found out some opportunities existed in the adjunct pool at Rowan. So, with the former student's education and experience, Professor Yeldell recommended him to the Law and Justice Department's chairperson to be considered for an adjunct position.

The former student, drawing on his experiences in the internship program, excelled in the interview and was selected as an adjunct professor at Rowan. The former student, now colleague, collaborated with Professor Yeldell on projects and impressed the Law and Justice Department. So, when a position presented for a full time temporary professor, Professor Yeldell recommended this adjunct professor to be considered.

The adjunct professor did very well on the interviews and presentations. Now, the former intern, former student, former police officer, former adjunct at community colleges, former adjunct at Rowan was now on faculty within the Law and Justice Studies Department at Rowan. The now faculty member continues to work with Professor Yeldell on numerous initiatives and projects. In fact, he is now co-authoring this very manual (Jeff Schwartz).

The main point of this story and the reason the story is the importance of the internship experience. It's a unique story to end up a professor in the very university where one was a student and it shows how a career can (and will) evolve. Making the most out of every opportunity is key.

THE SECOND STORY FROM AN ALUMN*

Practical and hands-on experience in relationship to vocation are both invaluable and timeless. Because of this, my own chronology is somewhat irrelevant. It was however during the 1980s and the college was Glassboro State (aka GSC/Rowan University) in southern New Jersey. I was to become Dr. Stanley Yeldell's first Law & Justice student to step up and out, accepting an official external and for-credit internship.

*Contributed by Kenneth P. MacKenzie. Copyright © Kendall Hunt Publishing Company.

With 19 years of formal education under my belt, there were distinctly four teachers who had influenced my life in a positive and lasting way. First, there was Mrs. Ellie Jaffe, my fifth grade teacher who taught me that I had value. She showed me that if I dreamed big and acted big, the skies truly were the limit. Coach Nick Baker, my high school track and field coach taught me that there are no excuses. I will succeed or fail based on my vision and how hard I worked. A strong work-ethic is a rare and priceless commodity. Sometimes a nemesis and always a mentor, Dr. Herbert Douglas was one of my college professors. He taught me that there was more to "this" life and to "this" world than shown on the mural that "they" had painted for us. Lastly and most importantly, it was Dr. Stanley B. Yeldell who understood the power of joy and humor, and who encouraged me to step out into the unknown and to make my dreams happen. His classes, lessons on life, along with the internships that he facilitated set me on a course aimed for both adventure and success.

My college career had started at Drexel University in Philadelphia, Pa. Because I was interested in federal law enforcement at that time, I had selected accounting as my major. It was at a time and in an economy where financing higher education was a challenge. I decided after one year to move back home to New Jersey and to matriculate at Glassboro State College (GSC/RU), a much more affordable yet quality option.

While there, I participated as a member of the Swim Team, and enjoyed all aspects of college life. I worked at the YMCA in the early mornings and as a bouncer at a local nightclub by night. It was also that year that I opened my own Karate school—the first in the country dedicated to children's programs. Coming from a family who respected volunteerism, I also served with such organizations as the American Red Cross, the Big Brothers / Big Sisters, and the NRA in what spare time I could find. Having been asked by the Law and Justice department to fill a quota, I was accepted by "Together, Inc.'" into a certification course that would change my life. After months of additional evening classes and study, I was to be certified as a Youth Runaway, Drug, and Alcohol Counselor. Perhaps this was all too much…it was, however, my journey. My nature has always been to question the system, face fears, accept challenges, fully immerse myself, to be heard, and to keep my goals in the proverbial crosshairs at all times. Albert Einstein once pointed out that if a person lived to be 60 years old, and slept eight hours a night, he will have slept a total of 20 years. Not always the healthiest choice, but for me, sleep could wait.

Dr. Yeldell approached me one day after my Victimology class. He presented the idea of an internship to me. He told me that it needed to be a success, and that he wanted me to be the first intern. I was intrigued, honored, and far be it for me to turn down a challenge. What I was about to discover about myself was that I was a builder. The idea of participating in the development of the internship was exciting to me. I understood the gravity of the endeavor and was bound and determined to see both it and myself succeed.

I remember arriving 45 minutes early on the first day of my internship. I was wearing an ill-fitting suit, the only one that I owned, and a pair scuffed dress shoes that I had worn to my prom several years prior. The internship had been arranged and I would be spending three days per week at the West Jersey Hospital, now the much larger Virtua Health System in Camden City, NJ for the entire semester. My position was to be that of the Assistant to the Director of Security at the hospital. My supervisor was a well-dressed man who appeared to be in his mid-forties. He came off as a bit stiff, much like a military officer. I could see that my new position was not going to be a cake walk. On my second morning, the supervisor gave me a book, *Dress to Impress*. Reading it that night, I got the message. I immediately got my hair cut and picked up some more suitable clothes at the local second-hand shop. One of over twelve-hundred titles in my personal collection, that book is still in my library today.

Together the supervisor and I created my job title, along with priority lists for what I needed to accomplish daily, weekly, and by semester's-end. My responsibilities were to include but were not limited to evaluation of current security systems; documentation of upgrade recommendations and budget expectations; development of new and improved security systems for the hospital's building and grounds; updating of all security and safety policies; entry and exit stations to the facilities; surveillance systems; staff, patient and guest badging and log-books; security measures for keeping the nursing students at the adjoining nursing school safe; fire and emergency planning; evacuation planning; loss prevention; development of an official security manual (fire, evacuation, nursing school, etc.); and networking with local police, fire and emergency agencies and more.

The internship went so well that I was invited to tackle another one the following year. This time, and after intense training I would be spending the semester as a Juvenile Intake Officer with the Gloucester County Family Court. It was there that I continued to realize my knack for working with youth. It was through the positive professional relationships that I had made while serving the youth, families and courts of Gloucester County that I landed my final internship position (Note: Participating in more than one internship is highly unusual. Mine however were at a time in history where connections for the students of future generations and their potential internships were being set). This time I was attached to the Family Court of Camden County.

Later that year I was to achieve my B.A. Degree in Law and Justice. In doing so, I became the first male in my family graduate from college, thus setting a new minimum standard-of-excellence for my own future generations.

In those last two semesters working closely with juvenile offenders, my eyes opened to another option for working with youth…one that would launch me into a stellar and self-directed career as an entrepreneur. Working with families and kids (mostly teens) who were already "in the system" was emotionally draining. Granted, everyone has their own threshold, however I believed that my calling was to work with these people before they took a turn down the wrong path. I had a concept that would allow me to use one of my biggest passions, that of traditional Asian martial arts, as a vehicle for bettering youth. I knew from personal experience (I started my own training in martial arts in 1968 at the age of four) that the martial arts were a great way not only to build fitness and self-defense skills, but also to develop self-discipline, focus, self-respect (and that for others), and other such virtues. I was to work on the front end, preventing young people from making mistakes before they happened. The concept worked and thousands of martial arts schools across the United States and world have followed in suit.

Little did I know over 30 years ago at its inception that my school (aka *Dojang* in Korean), MacKenzie's TaeKwon-Do & Hapkido Institute (aka MacKenzie's Martial Arts) was to become the first all-children's martial arts school in the country. Today, with multiple locations throughout South Jersey, it offers its award-winning programs to folks of all ages. Specialized programs for law-enforcement, security, and military personnel have also emerged. For more see: www.MacKenziesMartialArts.com

Having produced hundreds of world-class Blackbelts, a disproportionate number of MacKenzie's Martial Arts students have gone on to greatness. They have represented and graduated from the best universities and have become leaders in their fields.

To think back and to consider that this journey of mine began with me as an intern puts a smile on my face. The self-discovery, practical experiences, and understanding of people that I gained during those times in the field has allowed me to serve over ten thousand students directly, and over a half-million other kids through motivational presentations.

Through the 1990s, I enjoyed success as a teacher, business owner, and competitor. In 1997, 1999 and 2002, I won the gold medal in full-contact fighting at the World-Championships in South Korea. Because of this, I was invited to serve as an Ambassador on a peace-exchange to Pyong-Yang in the DPRK (North Korea) in 2005. Resulting from that, I have been blessed with the opportunity to travel, train, teach, and compete in some 30 countries in Asia, Europe, Eastern Europe, North America, and Central. I have learned that "one door opens another"! In 2009, I was featured as the cover personality in *TaeKwon-Do Times* magazine's (second largest martial arts publication worldwide) November edition. In the next issue, I was honored with the distinction of "International Grandmaster of the Year." Since then, I have been on the cover of four major martial arts magazines, and write regular columns for several others.

The year 2010 was to bring the most unlikely honor of my life. I became the official "Inheritor" of the Korean martial art of Hapkido/Sinmoo Hapkido at the Sun-Moon University in Cheonan, South Korea, and the first American-born to achieve such distinction. It was my teacher, Hapkido-Founder "DoJuNim" Ji, Han Jae who bestowed the honor. Ji, Han Jae had formerly been the bodyguard to South Korean President Park Chung Hee for some 18 years. Featured in the film, *Game of Death*, he was also the last instructor to the late Bruce Lee. In 2011, and at the request of the United States State Department, I co-hosted the first ever North Korean TaeKwon-Do Team's Goodwill Tour here in the United States. Co-author of this book, long-time friend, fellow blackbelt and former college roommate, Professor Jeff Schwartz provided support and security teams for this historical event. In 2015 I hosted the first "Icons of the Martial Arts Hall of Fame." In 2015, I also hosted my first intern, a sports management and business student from Towson State.

The circle continues.

While I have on many occasions looked back upon my years studying under Dr. Yeldell, and the times both before and after, I stay forward-thinking. My suggestion to those reading this piece is that they take lessons and fond memories from the past, embrace the present, seize opportunity, and create a future to be proud of.

The Adventure Continues…

GM Kenneth P. MacKenzie
MacKenzie's Martial Arts, Owner
B.A., Law & Justice, Glassboro State College/Rowan University
America's first 10th Degree Blackbelt (10th Dahn), certified in Cheonan, South Korea in 2010.
World SinMoo Hapkido Federation, President
United States Team Member
United States Team Captain
Three-Time World Champion (Korea)
United States Team Coach
Hall of Fame Member

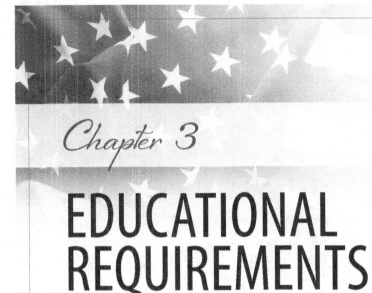

Chapter 3

EDUCATIONAL REQUIREMENTS

INTRODUCTION

The changing and complex criminal justice system will require enhanced skills and proficiencies. Many will require interns to possess certain educational requirements such as the completion of 60 college credits with a minimum grade point average. It is recommended that a formal internship process be incorporated into the university.

It is evident that attaining a college degree will increase your income potential. Education is the foundation for the work place. The ever-growing professional and technical areas of criminal justice will demand higher capabilities of the applicant. You must acquire new skills to keep up with modern technology. The future will belong to the knowledgeable employee, for one of the many benefits of an internship is that it instills the process to continue as a lifelong learner. Many agencies require continuing education and the background of an internship provides a solid foundation.

FIGURE 3.1

© VoodooDot/Shutterstock.com

You will find that the different agencies will not have uniform educational standards. In addition, the private and public sectors' educational requirements will not be the same.

CHAPTER OUTLINE

This chapter is designed to introduce students to the essential requirements of completing the internship. The chapter will discuss the following required components of the internship:

1. Internship Syllabus
2. Internship Application
3. Background Check
4. Drug Screen
5. Writing Sample
6. University Interview
7. Letter of Confirmation
8. Internship Agreement
9. Waiver and Release Agreement to coordinator and University
10. Waiver and Release Agreement to Agency
11. Confidentiality Agreement
12. Internship Portfolio
13. Code of Student Contact
14. Letter from University affirming student has no pending discipline or record

ACADEMIC COMPONENTS

- Part One of Research Paper: History of Agency and Student Learning Outcomes
- Evaluation Part 1: 40-Hour Evaluation
- Resume and Cover Letter
- Part Two of Research Paper: Duties and Activities
- Evaluation Part 2: 75-Hour Evaluation
- Part Three of Research Paper: Critical Analysis
- Part Four of Research Paper: Projects or Analysis
- Part Five of Research Paper: Internship Experience
- 150 Hour Evaluation
- Agency Assessment of Student Evaluation
- Student Evaluation of the Agency
- Exit Letter/Exit Interview
- Follow-up Letter
- Log book

PROJECTS AND ASSIGNMENTS EXPLAINED

Log Book:

1. Formulate the log book using the direction listed in the text.
2. Record your daily activities.
3. Be sure to collate with date, place, number of actual work hours and arrival and departure time.
4. Record your observations of how the agency functions.
5. Electronic submission of the log book is due by Tuesday 11:59 pm each week.
6. E-mail your Professor and "CC" your supervisor your weekly status reports of actual work hours, including arrival and departure times.

History of the Approved Agency:

1. The purpose for the agency's origination.
2. How was the agency promulgated?
3. The current function of the agency and is the mission different than the original intent.
4. Organizational chart of the agency (flow chart/chain of command).

Student Learning Outcomes:

1. Describe what you anticipate to learn in the agency.
2. Do you think you will be exposed to the different departments in the agency?
3. Do you believe you will discover the role the department plays in the overall organization?
4. Will the agency foster your career choice?
5. Will you gain a better appreciation of the agency's operations?

40-Hour Evaluation—Supervisor's Evaluation Form:

1. Complete the form—Name, Title and Placement Area.
2. Have the supervisor complete the evaluation of the student's performance.
3. Submit required comments from the supervisor; scan completed form and e-mail to Professor and "CC" supervisor in that e-mail.
4. The student must also include in the e-mail (from number 3) a summary of the discussion between the supervisor and student regarding the 40-hour evaluation.

Cover Letter:

1. Select a format from the types in the text.
2. Complete a cover letter from the type chosen for your approved agency.

Resume:

1. Select a format from the types in the text.
2. Construct your resume from the chosen type.

Duties and Activities (Part Two of the Research Paper):

1. List and describe your duties and activities.

75-Hour Evaluation:

1. Form completed by student, submit to Professor and "CC" supervisor in the submission e-mail.
2. Form completed by the supervisor, submitted to Professor and "CC" supervisor in e-mail, along with a summary of the discussion with the supervisor on student performance.

Critical Analysis (Part Three of the Research Paper):

1. Submit 10 strengths and 10 weaknesses of the agency.

Research Projects or Analysis of the Agency (Part Four of the Research Paper):

1. If research projects were assigned to student from agency, list and describe projects/outcomes.
2. If no research projects were assigned, then the student will complete a detailed analysis of the agency's internal operations.

Internship Experience (Part Five of the Research Paper):

1. Discuss duties and activities completed or observed.
2. Describe the value you received from the internship experience.

150-Hour Evaluation:

1. Form completed by the student.
2. Form completed by the supervisor submitted to Professor and "CC" supervisor in e-mail, along with a summary of the discussion with the supervisor on student performance.

Agency Assessment of Student Projects or Assignment—Agency Assessment of Student Performance:

1. Supervisor completes the form.
2. Form completed by the supervisor submitted to Professor and "CC" supervisor in e-mail, along with a summary of the discussion with the supervisor on student performance.

Student Evaluation of Agency—Student Evaluation of Internship Assignments:

1. Student completes the form.
2. Submit the form to the Professor.

Exit Letter/ Exit Interview:

1. Student expresses appreciation for being accepted into the agency.
2. The student discusses what was learned and how it enhanced their career choice.
3. Statement asking to be considered for employment.
4. Student requests exit interview appointment with supervisor. Student e-mails the Professor with the date/time/location of exit interview, "CC" the supervisor in the e-mail.
5. Original exit letter is given to the supervisor during exit interview appointment and a copy e-mailed to the Professor.

INTERNSHIP SYLLABUS

The syllabus will articulate the course requirements and the expectations that must be satisfied by the intern. The following is used by the author and has been refined over the last several decades. Therefore, this syllabus serves as an example that may be utilized by the university/college faculty/coordinator.

CRIMINAL JUSTICE INTERNSHIP SYLLABUS

Reference Number:

a. LAWJ 05356: Criminal Justice Internship I
b. LAWJ 05357: Criminal Justice Internship II

Dates: TBA (to be announced by Faculty/Coordinator of Internship)

Credits: Three (3) credits = 150 hours (must complete Internship I prior to Internship II)

Pre-Requisites: 24 s.h. (8 courses) in Law & Justice Studies—some are specifically designated:

a. Survey of Criminal Justice (LAWJ 05275)
b. Criminal Law (LAWJ 05255)
c. Criminal Justice Research (LAWJ 05380)

Additionally: College Comp II (COMP 01112)

Faculty/Coordinator of Internship: Dr. Stanley B. Yeldell

COURSE DESCRIPTION

The internship course will serve as the cornerstone of the student's academic experience. The course will remove the student from the academic theoretical classroom and put the student into a rich blend of practical laboratory and experiences yielded by the criminal justice agencies.

COURSE OBJECTIVES

1. The student will be able to identify the policies and procedures within a criminal justice agency.
2. The student will be able to explain the process the agency plays within the criminal justice system.
3. The student will explore and understand the history/evolution of the agency.
4. The student will develop critical outcomes for their experience within the agency.
5. The student will analyze and apply the outcomes in contrast to their original expectations.
6. The student will be equipped with real life experience and knowledge to further or solidify their career choice.

GENERAL EDUCATION GOALS

In addition to the above objectives, the more general goals of this course are to provide the student with the following tools to help develop his or her potential:

1. Development of the student's analytical thinking capabilities through comparison and contrast in the practical application of real world employment/exposure.
2. Enhancement of the student's critical thinking skills with assignments and the formulation of the internship objectives.
3. Utilization of research methods, including interviews and fact finding.
4. Understanding of the broader arena for implementation of interpersonal skills and practical knowledge.
5. Improvement in understanding human behavior and how various social and economic constraints impact people.
6. Increased student awareness of cultural and multi-cultural issues through study of social justice.
7. Preparation for employment, further education, and networking.

SUGGESTED OBSERVATION: THE STUDENT WILL BE REQUIRED TO OBSERVE THE SUBSEQUENT INTEGRAL FUNCTIONS OF THE CRIMINAL JUSTICE SYSTEM

a. Preliminary Hearing
b. Grand Jury Proceeding
c. Bail Hearings
d. Pre-trial Motion
e. Arraignment
f. Pre-Sentence Investigation Matters
g. Discovery
h. Plea Bargain Procedures
i. Role of Probation
j. Law Enforcement Roles in Criminal Cases
k. Pre-Trial Alternatives or Diversionary Programs

The previously discussed observational experience does not limit the student to said experiences. There are numerous experiences that have not been cited, but the previous listing will provide the student with the basic foundation of the criminal justice agencies.

REQUIREMENTS AND GRADING

a. The student must submit each part of the research paper in accordance with the written assignment rubric as guidance.
b. The student must submit the evaluations in accordance with the instructions in the applicable pages of the text.
c. The student must complete the discussion board in accordance with the instructions in the course, including providing scholarly research to support an opinion question. The premise of the discussion board is to facilitate discussion. However, it is imperative to provide academic information (not Wikipedia and related sites) to foster understanding of the topics.

d. The student must submit the exit letter and summary of exit interview, according to instructions.

e. The student will provide the Agency Assessment of Student Assignments to the proper supervisor. The supervisor will e-mail or fax the Assessment to the Professor/Department.

f. The student must submit the log book in accordance with the instructions.

g. The student must submit the resume in accordance with the instructions.

h. Unless the student has made arrangement due to exigent circumstances, no work will be accepted past the due date.

REQUIRED TEXTBOOK

Schwartz, Jeffrey, & Yeldell, Stanley B. (2016). *Criminal Justice Internship Manual, 3rd Edition*. Hoboken: Kendall Hunt Publishing Company. 978-1-4652-8996-4

EVALUATION

Research Paper (Five Parts each worth 7 points) – 35% of total grade

Evaluations (Five Parts each worth 5 points) – 25% of total grade

Discussion Board (Two Questions each week 1.5 points each) – 12 % of total grade

Student Log Book (12 points) – 12 % of total grade

Exit Letter/Exit Interview and Agency Assessment of Student Assignments (5 points each) –10% of total grade

Resume and Cover Letter (3 points each) – 6% of total grade

The course is on a Pass/No Credit basis. No grade will be allocated (Pass or No Credit only).

WRITTEN ASSIGNMENT RUBRIC

Instructor Grading Rubric for written assignments:

Note: These are only guidelines—exceptional work can earn a larger percentage while work below level may earn less.

a. Grammar/Spelling: 10 points
   • Proper use of grammar and punctuation
   • Proper spelling

b. Style: 15 points
   • Sentences are complete in thought
   • Sentences are concise, eliminating unnecessary words or phrases
   • Sentences vary in structure
   • Sentence transitions are present
   • Words used are precise, unambiguous, and used properly
   • An appropriate tone is used for the assignment

c. Organization: 15 points
  - The paper has a clear structure
  - There is a central theme or thesis to the paper
  - It is written for the appropriate audience
  - Ideas flow logically
  - Appropriate introduction to the paper or topics being covered
  - Logical conclusion that results from the thesis

d. Research/Format/Analysis of topic: 15 points
  - Orderly presentation of materials, thoughtful discussion, following general format requirements (margins, header, footer, font size, general amount of work)
  - Proper citations and references to resources, following APA or Blue Book format.
  - Use of headings, italics, and other aids (e.g., appendices, tables of contents), to improve the flow of the paper.

e. Content: 45 points
  - Purpose of the paper is clear
  - All questions/requirements of the assignment are answered in a substantive manner.
  - Major topics/theories are stated clearly and are supported by details and analysis.
  - Content is comprehensive, accurate, and/or persuasive integration of theory and practice.
  - Research is adequate and up-to-date

REQUIRED READINGS AND ASSIGNMENTS

The following is based upon an eight-week schedule (or half a semester/online format). The format can easily be transitioned into a normal 15-week schedule or whatever is the required number of week/contact hours.

Week 1: Chapter 1 and Chapter 2, Part One of Research Paper: History of Agency and Student Learning Outcomes, Log Book Entries, Discussion Board

Week 2: Chapter 3 and Chapter 4, 40-Hour Evaluation, Resume and Cover Letter, Log Book Entries, Discussion Board

Week 3: Chapter 5, Chapter 6, and Chapter 7; Part Two of Research Paper: Duties and Activities, Log Book Entries, Discussion Board

Week 4: Chapter 8, 75-Hour Evaluation, Log Book Entries, Discussion Board

Week 5: Chapter 9, Log Book Entries, Discussion Board

Week 6: Part Three of Research Paper: Critical Analysis and Part Four of Research Paper—Projects or Analysis, Log Book Entries, Discussion Board

Week 7: Chapter 10, Part Five of Research Paper: Internship Experience, 150-Hour Evaluation, Log Book Entries, Discussion Board

Week 8: Agency Assessment of Student Evaluation, Student Evaluation of the Agency, Exit Letter, Log Book Entries, Discussion Board

Late Policy: Late work is accepted with a 25% penalty per week an assignment is overdue unless exigent circumstances exist.

Student Accommodation: Your academic success is important. If you have a documented disability that may have an impact upon your work in this class, please contact your professor. Students must provide documentation of their disability to the Academic Success Center in order to receive official University services and accommodations. The Academic Success Center can be reached at 856-256-4234. The Center is located on the third floor of Savitz Hall. The staff is available to answer questions regarding accommodations or assist you in your pursuit of accommodations. We all look forward to working with you to meet your learning goals. (This is a Rowan University requirement and should be adapted to each academic institution's needs.)

Academic Dishonesty: The university's policies on academic dishonesty can be found in the latest Student Information Guide available on ine from Rowan University.

University Non-Discrimination Policy: Rowan University, as an equal opportunity and affirmative action employer, complies with all applicable state and federal laws regarding anti-discrimination, equal opportunity, and affirmative action:

> *It is the policy of the university that there shall be no unlawful discrimination against any person on the basis of race, sex, sexual orientation, age, height, weight, disability, color, religion, creed, national origin or ancestry, marital status, familial status, veteran status, or any other characteristic protected by federal or state laws.*

Rowan Success Network: Additional information about RSN may be found at www.rowan.edu/rsn." (Rowan University specific)

INTERNSHIP PROCESS OVERVIEW

UNIVERSITY/COLLEGE RESPONSIBILITIES

1. The university faculty/college coordinator serves as the student's advisor for the internship and as the link to the criminal justice agencies.
2. Authorizes students to complete internships without regard to race, religion, sex, age, national origin, or physical handicap.
3. Briefs the university/college faculty/coordinator regarding the evaluation requirements.
4. Ensures that each student receives the educational related internship assignments.
5. Maintains records of the student internship.
6. Notifies the university/college faculty/coordinator that the student intern has been dismissed from the internship because of unsatisfactory performance:
   a. Repeated absences without excuses.
   b. Failure to complete at least three assignments.
   c. Three late arrivals within a semester.
   d. Failure to comply with rules of University or the agency.
   e. General appearance is not acceptable to agency requirements.

AGENCY RESPONSIBILITIES

1. Accepts the policy of the department that students are assigned in accordance with the provisions of the Federal Civil Rights Act.

2. Adheres to the objectives of the department as contained in its course syllabus.

3. Accepts the conditions stipulated in the course syllabus.

4. Involves the students in meaningful agency programs by utilizing appropriate assignments or tasks.

5. Allows students to use their work product for academic discussion with the Faculty/Coordinator of the Internship Program, keeping in mind the need for confidentiality—therefore, some information will not be discussed.

6. Assures that each supervisor or site manager or designated representative will have adequate time within his/her work schedule to:

    a. Satisfy the educational objectives of the students through development of learning opportunities.

    b. Prepare for regularly scheduled conferences with students.

    c. Communicate with the Faculty/Coordinator of the Internship Program at periodic intervals to discuss learning opportunities and student performance.

    d. Prepare reports and evaluation as required by the department.

7. Permits the use of facilities by students of the department during the period of the placement, including:

    a. Space for students in an area sufficiently private for carrying on the assigned work or activity.

    b. Clerical services for those records and reports that are produced for the agency.

    c. Access to client and agency records as they relate to agency supervision.

4. Assures that the Faculty/Coordinator of the Internship Program is advised of policy and service changes and developments which may affect student learning or the department's curriculum.

5. Informs the Faculty/Coordinator of any early or immediate problems that may develop concerning a student's progress or performance.

6. Provides reimbursement of all student travel expenses on agency business.

7. Observes the University calendar with respect to student holiday and vacation periods.

8. Adheres to course objectives:

    _____

    _____

STUDENT RESPONSIBILITIES

1. Must complete all written assignments requested or required by the university/college regarding the internship.

2. Must maintain regular attendance at the criminal justice agency.

3. Repeated absences must be reported immediately to the university/college faculty/coordinator and the supervisor of the criminal justice agency.

4. Fulfill in a professional manner all the duties and responsibilities assigned by the agency's supervisor.

5. Adhere to the confidentiality and standards set by the University and the agency.

DISCHARGED, DESERTED OR DISMISSED

If the student has been discharged or dismissed by the agency prior to the completion of the internship, the university/college faculty/coordinator will record a No Credit Grade for the internship course.

The student must notify the university/college faculty/coordinator in writing within three days regarding the desertion. The failure to adhere to the previously articulated requirements will result in an automatic "No Credit" grade for said course.

CONFIDENTIALITY

Students may not disclose any written, verbal, or other form of privileged information obtained during and/or after the internship about clients (and/or their families), the agency and its employees and other associate organizations known to be confidential.

Maintaining confidentiality also refers to any carelessness in handling confidential information, or any release of information that would could compromise the agency.

Failure to maintain confidentiality can lead to:

- Dismissal from the program
- Legal action or liability
- Subsequent failing grade for the program

Be prepared to engage in a written confidentiality agreement with the agency.

FIGURE 3.2

© Wiktoria Pawlak/Shutterstock.com

CODE OF CONDUCT

As an intern, you are expected to meet certain obligations and expectations, as outlined below. Be prepared to enter into a written agreement with the University regarding the following in your internship:

During work hours, you are expected to:

- Arrive on time for all scheduled assignments.
- Dress professionally during work hours.
- Refrain from personal business during work hours.
- Conduct yourself in a professional manner.
- Maintain an accurate log book, accounting for hours you are on the internship site.
- Respect confidentiality and anonymity of some of the information you may come across in your internship.

FIGURE 3.3

© marinini/Shutterstock.com

- Follow through on all your commitments.
- Use good judgment when interacting with clients, colleagues, and supervisors.
- Seek feedback from your supervisor. Be willing to accept and respond to feedback as necessary in order to improve your performance.
- Remain drug and alcohol free; you are expected to follow the college's alcohol and drug policies while serving in your internship
- Notify both your Internship Coordinator and your immediate supervisor for any excusable absences from work hours. Every effort will be made to document the validity of the excuse.
- Violation of any of these standards may be responded to with a verbal or written warning, removal from the internship, and/or failure of the class.

WRITING SAMPLE

Prepare a writing sample to be submitted with the internship application. The writing sample should demonstrate in 500 words or less, your reasoning, drive, dedication, and interest in the internship you are seeking.

© Nonwarit/Shutterstock.com

FIGURE 3.4

1. What is the main reason you choose this particular field?
2. What reason did you choose this particular agency?
3. What motivates you to succeed in the internship?
4. How does the agency's mission statement match with your personal opinions/philosophy?
5. What separates you from others that may be seeking this same internship?
6. Specifically, why do you want to enter this field and how do you believe you are right for this internship?

SECURING AN INTERVIEW

Once you have consulted with the Internship Coordinator and you have completed the Internship Application, the Background Application and process, you will be able to secure an interview for an agency to consider you for the internship.

If you have already identified and obtained approval from an agency to secure an internship, then you will need to provide the letter of confirmation to the Internship Coordinator. The Internship Coordinator will approve or deny the suggested internship as qualifying.

© baranq/Shutterstock.com

FIGURE 3.5

If you are not interested in a law enforcement internship, then the background process will differ. All the procedures and applications remain the same, except you will not be required to satisfy the requirements as outlined in the Memorandum of Understanding with the Gloucester County Prosecutor's Office.

Should you be interested in an internship within law enforcement in Gloucester County, after the background process is complete, you will be placed in a pool of candidates from which agencies in Gloucester County will have access. Of course, you can approach an agency and inform them that you are on the approved list.

The letter of confirmation simply serves as a contract between the agency, yourself, and the University at which point the process for the Internship course can begin.

This manual provides various resources from which you can identify potential agencies for consideration as an internship. Federal, state, and local agencies are identified. Other internships including correctional, judiciary, law, and several others are discussed.

PROSPECTIVE INTERN QUESTIONS

Should I send my application in early?

Your application should be sent in as early as possible to ensure that all necessary documents are received by the appropriate deadline.

Does all the information in my application need to be sent in at the same time?

No, your recommendation letters may be sent in separately if so stated in your cover letter. However, to be eligible for consideration *all* required materials must be submitted.

What if my college schedule does not coincide with the internship schedule?

FIGURE 3.6

Other arrangements may be made. Please discuss this matter with the departmental intern supervisor when they contact you for an interview.

Is this a paid internship?

Internships are intended to provide a supplemental learning experience to a student's academic studies. Internships do not constitute permanent employment. However, paid internships are sometimes available.

What happens after I interview?

A letter of confirmation will need to be obtained. Please be patient as the interviewing process can be lengthy.

INTERNSHIP PROCESS

Once a site is identified and an offer of internship placement is received, students must meet with the Internship Coordinator to ensure the agency is an approved site; subsequently, students must fill out and bring in:

1. The Internship Application
2. Verification from the Dean of Students stating the student does not have any current or prior violations
3. A copy of your student transcripts (unofficial transcripts showing GPA and printed from online will suffice)
4. A copy of a photo ID (both a driver's license and student ID)
5. Letter of Confirmation (a copy of an e-mail, letter, etc)

Once approved, the student can register for the internship course.

The student will be required to submit the background check application.

Depending upon the internship agency, the process may include drug screening and a more in-depth background check.

If the student has not secured an offer of internship placement, the student will identify which type of internship they are interested.

Depending on the agency, the background and other screening processes may need to be conducted prior to obtaining an interview with a prospective agency.

The Internship Coordinator can assist in the process. This manual will be of great value in narrowing your internship choices and securing a letter of confirmation for the internship.

Once enrolled in the internship course, the Internship Coordinator will assist students throughout the completion of the internship and is available as a support resource.

© Mattz90/Shutterstock.com

FIGURE 3.7

FIGURE 3.8

The Internship Required Checklist

1. Internship Coordinator's Letter to Agency(s) discussing required course credits and mandatory hours
2. Letter of Confirmation
3. The student must obtain letter of confirmation from the agency
4. Internship Agreement
5. The agreement must be completed by student and agency

LEARNING OBJECTIVES

a. A. The student enrolled in the three (3) credit course must formulate five (5) learning objectives:

1. _____
2. _____
3. _____
4. _____
5. _____

b. The student enrolled in the six (6) credit course must formulate ten (10) learning objectives.

1. _____
2. _____
3. _____
4. _____
5. _____
6. _____
7. _____
8. _____
9. _____
10. _____

INTERNSHIP RESEARCH PAPER

The major components of the research paper will consist of:

1. Historical development of the agency or the organization.

_____
_____
_____
_____
_____
_____

FIGURE 3.9

© Kae Deezign/Shutterstock.com

2. How learning objectives will be satisfied.

_____
_____
_____
_____
_____

3. List and discuss duties and activities completed during the internship.

_____

_____

_____

_____

_____

4. Complete a critical analysis of the agency or organization. Discuss the strengths and weaknesses.

_____

_____

_____

_____

_____

5. Discuss any completed research projects submitted to the agency.

6. Summary.

The student must meet with agency supervisor to discuss how the following learning objectives are being satisfied:

1. _____
2. _____
3. _____
4. _____
5. _____
6. _____
7. _____
8. _____
9. _____
10. _____

JOURNALS

It is important to keep a journal to reflect your experiences at the internship site. The entries, besides the formal recording of time/attendance, should highlight what you are exposed to in the internship setting.

- Did you work with any employees?
- What type of work did you accomplish?
- Did you ask for responsibilities in your assignments?
- Did you go over and above to impress the agency?
- Describe a typical day in detail.
- Compare and contrast real life experiences/situations with what you have learned in classes.

FIGURE 3.10

Take the time to provide substance to your entries. These entries will help you formulate your research paper, your outcomes and (ultimately) serve as a reminder about your experience.

Remember to use the opportunity to learn about the agency, the agency's role, how the employees interact, how the agency interacts with the public, how you related to the supervisor and demonstrated a willingness to learn, as well demonstrated a willingness to accept responsibility and formulate valuable take away questions that can lead to your career path.

The journal is not a place to write frivolous material or to be complacent. Take the time to enrich your experience at the internship site.

FIGURE 3.11

Make sure to involve yourself with the agency to whatever extent is allowed. Learn the agency's role, learn the services or tasks most associated with the agency, make yourself known, and *be professional.*

When formulating your critical analysis of the agency, you will ask questions and provide insight from your experience. The journal will help you stay focused on the objectives. For example, when learning the history and organization of the agency, take the time to show an interest in the background. Most employees, especially supervisors, will enjoy talking about their agency and its

history. Take that time to interact and have some background information already. You can then interject or ask more specific questions; this demonstrates your commitment and professionalism.

Agency Role in the Criminal Justice System:

- What is the agency's main role?
- How do the employees go about fulfilling the mission of the agency?
- What did you observe?

- What did you participate in?
- In your internship experience, how does the agency impact the criminal justice system?
- What did you expect to find?
- Did you start with one concept? Did it change?
- What do the employees think about their roles?
- How satisfied do they seem to be?
- Is this a place where you would like to work? Explain your answer.

FIGURE 3.12

© scyther5/Shutterstock.com

SOCIAL MEDIA POLICY

Students using social media sites are expected to ensure that no information regarding clients or the agency is released. Students are not permitted to link to the social media profiles of clients or employees of the internship agency.

In the event that a student's social media profile or linkage is considered an invalid professional practice or an ethical violation, the student will be reviewed for unprofessional conduct.

Confidentiality and common sense are expected of student interns.

Act professionally and your social media should never reflect negatively on the agency or the University.

Chapter 4

INTERNSHIP PORTFOLIO

INTRODUCTION

This chapter is designed to enhance the student's skills in the formulation of a resume and cover letter, as well as in the organization of a follow-up letter. After reading this chapter, the student should be able to understand the purpose of a resume, the steps to creating a resume, and know how to prepare for the interview. Perhaps the most important aspect of formulation of the portfolio is that the student must understand the various types of interviews and how to handle the interview. Finally, the student will learn how to close the interviews, how to handle references and recommendations, and how to evaluate reviews of the Intern Performance Rating documents.

FIGURE 4.1

© HuHu/Shutterstock.com

CHAPTER OUTLINE

1. The Cover Letter
2. The Formulation of the Resume
3. Interviews
4. Closing the Interview
5. Follow-up Letter

THE COVER LETTER

You should never submit a resume alone. All resumes and other documents must be accompanied by a cover letter, even if it is very brief. Keep in mind the sequence below when composing the cover letter.

1. Address your cover letter to a specific individual, using their correct title in the agency.

2. If you have obtained the recipient's name through networking, be sure to open your cover letter with an acknowledgement of the source (e.g., Dr. Jones suggested you would be an excellent contact person).

3. A cover letter should be brief; normally a single page.

4. Conduct research about the internship prior to writing the cover letter.

5. A cover letter/resume is an employer's first opportunity to evaluate your writing ability.

© Rafal Olechowski/Shutterstock.com

FIGURE 4.2

COVER LETTER INFORMATION

YOUR NAME
YOUR PRESENT ADDRESS
CITY, STATE, ZIP CODE

Date of Correspondence

    Name of Individual
    Title
    Name of company/organization
    Address
    City, State, Zip Code

Dear Mr./Mrs./Ms. (Last Name):

    Explain why you are writing and about which position.

    Describe your experiences, along with any relevant information; such as, team sports, your interests in the field, course work, projects, or other items.

    Close by indicating you have included a resume and would look forward to an opportunity to speak in person about the position.

Sincerely,

Name

THE FORMULATION OF THE RESUME

The resume is very important to you because it can assist you in getting you into the door for an interview.

The creation of the resume is like crafting a beautiful artistic piece of sculpture. From the the conception of the idea to the completion of the masterpiece, you need to follow specific steps:

1. Secure all relevant information
2. Select the most appropriate type of resume
3. Select a format
4. Compose the initial draft
5. Edit the initial draft
6. Evaluate and revise the resume
7. Print the final draft

FIGURE 4.3

© Andrey_Popov/Shutterstock.com

RESUME CHECKLIST

- Information should neatly on one page.
- Use plain typeface with straight lines, around 10–14 point font.
- Omit shading or graphics.
- Name, address, telephone number, and e-mail address should centered at top, with name in bold or larger font.
- Highlight your skills and experience.
- Make your resume relevant and use the format that best fits for the job description
- Your objective should clearly state your intentions and provide a tie in with the agency's mission or goals.
- Education category should list GPA, expressed in tenths, if 3.0 or above. Example:

  Bachelor of Arts, Communication May 2016
  Specialization: Public Relations
  Rowan University, Glassboro, New Jersey
  GPA 3.4, Dean's List

  Rowan University, Glassboro, New Jersey, expected May 2016
  Bachelor of Science, Business Administration
  Specialization: Finance
  GPA 3.9, Dean's List
  Summa Cum Laude Honors anticipated
- List several jobs or activities, if applicable, in a consistent format in the Experience category.
- Job descriptions/accomplishments should be in bulleted statements.
- Avoid using pronouns "I" and "me."
- Use a variety of wording and try not to repeat the same in the other statements.

Remember, the resume might be the only chance you have to make yourself unique and marketable to a potential employer.

INTERVIEWS

The interview can be stressful. However, with proper planning and preparation, you will be successful.

The interview provides the agency with the opportunity to observe you. Make sure to know the following:

1. The history of the agency.
2. The role of the agency.
3. The organization and makeup of the agency.
4. The names of the people in charge. For example, in a local police department know not only the Chief, but also who comprises the local government. For a state agency, know the director, the mission, and other vital statistics.

FIGURE 4.4

Doing your homework on the potential employer is a key to success in the interview. Knowing how to respond to questions about yourself is another key to success.

Practice stating your strengths, your weaknesses, how would you improve yourself, some challenges you faced and how you overcame them, as well as be prepared to say why do you want to work at that particular agency, what value do you bring to the agency, and similar personality questions. Having the knowledge and practicing interviewing will help you in so many ways.

CLOSING THE INTERVIEW

Close the interview by asking how you can proactively go to the next step. Be sure to thank the interviewer for the opportunity to interview.

Regardless of the words you choose, make sure you deliver the message, "I will be an asset to the organization and looking forward to starting." You can also elaborate about the agency being your career choice and say that having a chance to demonstrate your value is all you have been looking for.

THE FOLLOW-UP E-MAIL

The follow-up letter/e-mail is an excellent opportunity to demonstrate your commitment to the internship. You should write your follow-up e-mail two or three days after the interview.

A follow-up e-mail should sell you, separate you from your competition, and state a next step. The objective is to keep the communication or the dialogue going. The follow-up is one way that student interns bolster their chances. Remain relevant but don't become a persistent annoyance.

FIGURE 4.5

SAMPLE FOLLOW-UP E-MAIL

To: Mr. John Smith
Ref: Internship Interview
From: John Q. Public
Date: March 2, 2016

Dear Mr. Smith:

Thank you for the opportunity to participate in the selection process for the position of security officer as an internship from Rowan University. I appreciate your taking the time from busy schedule to have personally conducted the interview. It was a pleasure to meet you and get to know even more about your company's vision.

I remain extremely interested in the position. I believe my drive, maturity, and personal values fit well in your organization. Please call if you need any further information.

Very sincerely,

John Q. Public

REFERENCES

The organization or agency will want to check your references.

You need to have references that represent a variety of reputable individuals. You should try to have business, academic and professional references.

Do not wait until you have to produce the references to attempt to gather them. Start as soon as possible. All along your life in high school, college, work; you should be collecting references.

Having experience and an explanation about how your experience impacted the person who is providing the reference is important. Consider the following as important aspects for a reference to include in their letter:

- Dependable
- Reliable
- Works well with others
- Takes direction well
- Offers suggestions for improvement
- Willing to help others
- Has drive and motivation to do a complete job
- Possesses leadership qualities
- Contributions you have made

REVIEW OF INTERN PERFORMANCE

The faculty/coordinator of the internship course must review the student's performance rating completed by the agency/organization supervisor. The student should request a copy of the supervisor's evaluation and especially the specific comments that earmark the student's strengths. The strengths are documented statements or actual testimonials of the student's capabilities. Also, the student should attach the evaluation to the student portfolio for further references.

Chapter 5

LAW ENFORCEMENT INTERNSHIPS

FIGURE 5.1

FIGURE 5.2

FIGURE 5.3

FIGURE 5.4

INTRODUCTION

This chapter will discuss the largest and most visible component of the criminal justice system—law enforcement. It begins with a brief discussion regarding the conditions and employment outlook in the field, and an examination of the various educational requirements. The law enforcement profession is a diverse profession, especially with the recent increase of females and minorities entering the field.

The law enforcement internships consist of the subsequent agencies and programs.

1. Local or municipal law enforcement agencies
2. County law enforcement agencies
3. State law enforcement agencies
4. Federal and special programs

CHAPTER OUTLINE

1. Conditions and Employment
2. Educational Requirements
3. Law Enforcement Internships
   a. Local: Chiefs of Police and City Sheriffs
   b. County
   c. State
   d. Federal and Special Programs

CONDITIONS AND EMPLOYMENT

The student must ask the basic question: Is law enforcement for me?

The student should make a rationale decision regarding his or her career. Some things to consider:

- Do you possess the personal attributes needed to be a law enforcement officer?
- Can you give orders?
- Can you take orders?
- Can you remain calm under stress?
- Can you treat people professionally and apply the law equally?
- Can you work the hours under the conditions required by the job?
- Can you control innate and required drives and impulses under various environmental situations, some of which may be ambiguous?

The student needs to be objective and reasonable in rendering decisions that affect those he/she encounters. The job in law enforcement is unique in that a law enforcement professional has the ability to take away someone's freedom and potential their life.

Unlike some other industries, the need for law enforcement professionals cannot be explained by the simple rules of supply and demand. Within the law enforcement field itself, however, job availability can vary greatly depending on a number of factors, the most obvious of which is a high incidence of crime. We shall see how crime waves change from street crime to technology related offenses—computer and Internet offenses.

The projected disparity in the job growth between public and private law enforcement professionals indicates especially increased demand in the private sector. The demand for guards and other private security personnel is expected to increase much faster through the year 2017.

The career outlook for criminal justice graduates is increasing every year. Various available positions come from a broad spectrum and employees are required to have a variety of educational and professional backgrounds.

The available roles in the criminal justice field are unlimited. Criminal justice careers are also very resilient during a suffering economy and many jobs benefit from tough economic conditions.

From technology and travel, healthcare to hospitality, within the both private and public sectors of almost every industry, criminal justice professionals are in very high demand.

As technology continues to advance and continue to change many aspects of everyday life, there will be an increase for criminals to find opportunities to steal from unsuspecting victims; thus, creating more opportunities for the criminal justice field.

Various criminal justice careers offer their employees' health insurance and vacation time, but the amount is dependent on the employer.

Most criminal justice careers require a variety of hours and graduates may expect to make on average $43,050 annually according to the U.S. Bureau of Labor Statistics (2013).

EDUCATIONAL REQUIREMENTS

The large increase of entry levels of law enforcement has been the result of attractive salaries and benefits. The number of qualified candidates exceeds the number of employment openings in federal law enforcement and in most state, local and special departments—resulting in the increase of hiring standards and the selectivity by employers. The federal law enforcement departments are requiring the prospective employees to possess a four-year degree and applicants to the state law enforcement departments must possess a two-year or associate degree.

FIGURE 5.5

http://www.internships.com/student
A variety of internships are listed

https://www.usajobs.gov/JobSearch/Search/GetResults?Internship=Yes
Federal Government Internship are listed

https://www.usajobs.gov/StudentsAndGrads
Federal Government Internships are listed

http://careers.state.gov/intern/student-internships
Department of State Internships are listed

https://www.looksharp.com/s/student-internships/washington-dc
Internships in Washington, DC are listed

http://www.dm.usda.gov/employ/sip/
USDA Internships are listed

http://www.gao.gov/careers/student.html
US Government Accounting Office are listed

http://www.epa.gov/careers
Environmental Protection Agency Internships

http://www.secretservice.gov/join/diversity/students/
Secret Services Internships

https://www.dhs.gov/homeland-security-careers/students
Department of Homeland Security Internships

http://ojp.gov/about/jobs.htm
Office of Justice Programs Internships

https://www.fletc.gov/fletc-college-intern-program
Federal Law Enforcement Training Center Internships

http://www.cbp.gov/careers/outreach-programs/youth/students-recent-grads
Customs and Border Patrol Internships

https://www.ice.gov/careers/internships
Immigration and Customs Enforcement Internships

https://www.atf.gov/careers/internships
Bureau of Alcohol, Tobacco, Firearms and Explosives Internships

https://www.nsa.gov/ia/academic_outreach/student_opportunities/
National Security Agency Internships

https://www.justice.gov/interpol-washington/internships
INTERPOL Internships

http://www.nleomf.org/about/employment/
National Law Enforcement Memorial Fund Internships

http://www.iacp.org/internships
International Association of Chiefs of Police Internships

http://policecomplaints.dc.gov/page/internship-program
Washington, DC Office of Police Complaints Internships

http://www.nj.gov/oag/dcj/Undergraduate-Law-Internship.html
New Jersey Division of Criminal Justice Internships

http://www.panynj.gov/careers/summer-internship-program.html
Port Authority of NY and NJ Internships

http://www.state.nj.us/governor/admin/law_intership.html
NJ Governor Legal Internships

http://www.dea.gov/careers/student-entry-level.shtml
DEA Internships

https://www.justice.gov/legal-careers/volunteer-legal-internships
Volunteer Legal Internships Department of Justice

https://www.fbijobs.gov/students
FBI Internships
The Federal Bureau of Investigation (FBI) seeks students at both the undergraduate and graduate level and offers a number of programs:
https://www.fbi.gov/about-us/otd/internships

Volunteer Internship Program
Honors Internship Program
Cyber Internship Program
Visiting Science Program
http://govcentral.monster.com/education/articles/1819-fbi-academy-internships

FBI Volunteer Internship Program
The FBI Volunteer Internship Program is an unpaid internship program for undergraduates in their junior or senior year, as well as, graduate and post-graduate students.
To qualify for the FBI Volunteer Internship Program, interns must meet certain requirements.
Further, students must meet all FBI employment standard entry requirements to qualify for an internship.

FBI Honors Internship Program
The FBI Honors Internship Program is a highly-competitive, paid summer internship program.
The FBI Honors Internship Program is held for ten weeks during the summer months.
Interns through the Honors Internship Program are chosen based on their academic course of study, their potential contribution, and the need of the agency.

FBI Cyber Internship Program
Students in the FBI Cyber Internship Program work alongside experts who examine information based on computer investigations.
Students in the Cyber Internship Program are either based in the FBI Headquarters in Washington, D.C. or at various FBI Field Offices for 10 weeks during the summer months.
The FBI Cyber Internship Program is a paid internship.
All candidates must apply for the Cyber Internship Program through USAJObs.gov. There are requirements and restrictions.

Honesty is required when completing any application or background form. In addition to ethical implications of lying, dishonesty on the forms is a federal offense, and a basis for finding you unfit for federal government employment.

Sometimes, simply waiting a year before applying will often solve any problem since the government is less concerned with past incidents than with your behavior in school and current situations.

Most positions in the federal government require U.S. citizenship.

SECURITY/SUITABILITY REVIEW

Many students apply for summer and permanent positions with various agencies in the U.S. government.

The security clearance is an evaluation of whether an individual is a security threat.

The suitability review is an evaluation of a person's "character."

All volunteers and summer interns, undergo a suitability review.

This review consists of filling out a Standard Form for background check/suitability. You will have to get fingerprint checks, and consent to a credit background check.

The questionnaires will vary with the division and the type of employment.

The adjudicative guidelines are:

- Allegiance to the United States
- Lack of foreign influence
- Your personal conduct
- Your credit history
- Drug and alcohol use
- Mental health check
- Criminal background check

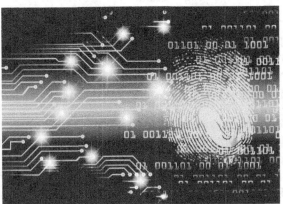

FIGURE 5.6

SECURITY CLEARANCE PROCESS

The internship clearance process can take anywhere from three to six months.

The length of the investigation depends on your background.

To review the security forms, go to www.opm.gov/forms. Look at the tab General Services Administration, then look for Standard and Optional Forms. Under the Standard Forms tab click on the form you want to view.

FIGURE 5.7

PENNSYLVANIA SPECIFIC OPPORTUNITIES

Abington Township Police Department
1166 Old York Road
Abington, PA 19001
Contact: Officer Roger Gillispie, Community
Policing Division Coordinator
(267) 536-1100
www.abingtonpd.org

American Civil Liberties Union/Foundation of
Pennsylvania
PO Box 40008
Philadelphia, PA 19106
(215) 592-1513
www.aclupa.org/takeaction/volunteerintern

FIGURE 5.8

© Filip Bjorkman/Shutterstock.com

Chester County Adult Probation
201 W. Market Street, Suite 2100
Post Office Box 2746
West Chester, PA 19380-0989
(610) 344-6290
www.chesco.org
Internship Application: www.chesco.org/DocumentCenter/View/1296

Office of the District Attorney Delaware County Courthouse
201 W. Front Street
Media, PA 19063
(610) 891-4161
www.co.delaware.pa.us

Darby Township Police Department
Chief Brian Patterson, Contact Person
2 Studevan Plaza
Sharon Hill, PA 19079
(610) 583-3245
www.police.darbytwp.org

Montgomery County Adult Probation
100 Ross Road, Suite 120
King of Prussia, PA 19406
(610) 992-7777
www.adultprobation.montcopa.org/adultprobation/cwp/view,a,1503,q,43982.asp#student

Delaware County Internship Program
Government Center Building
Media, PA 19063
(610) 891-4667
www.co.delaware.pa.us/planning/sidebarpages/internships.html

Delaware County Juvenile Court
Jeremy Damia, Contact Person
201 West Front Street
Media, PA 19063
(610) 891-4721
www.co.delaware.pa.us/planning/sidebarpages/internships.html

Domestic Violence Center of Chester County
PO Box 832
West Chester, PA 19381
(610) 431-3546
volunteer@dvccc.com
www.dvccc.com/youcanhelp/becomeavolunteer.html

Domestic Abuse Project of Delaware County
14 West Second Street
Media, PA 19063
(610) 565-6272
(610) 497-6737(Chester office)
www.dapdc.org/employment.html

Families of Murder Victims
Philadelphia District Attorney's Office
Tracy Simmons, MS, Program Director
2000 Hamilton Street, Suite 304
Philadelphia, PA 19130
(215) 567-6776
www.avpphila.org/families-of-murder-victims-fmv
fmv@avpphila.org

Montgomery County Office of the Coroner
Contact: Rosanna Avraham, Forensic Technician
RAvraham@montcopa.org
1430 DeKalb Street
Norristown, PA 19404
(610) 278-3057
(610) 278-3547 (fax)
www.montcopa.org/index.aspx?nid=196

Montgomery County Office of the District Attorney
Montgomery County Courthouse
Kevin R. Steele, Deputy District Attorney
Kelly Lloyd, Assistant DA (klloyd@montcopa.org)
2 East Airy Street
Norristown, PA 19404
(610) 278-3895
www.montcopa.org/index.aspx?nid=102

Montgomery County Public Defender's Office
Montgomery County Courthouse
2 East Airy Street
Norristown PA 19404
(610) 278-3000

Montgomery County Victim Services Center (VSC)
Contact: Jessica Rice, Community Education Programs Supervisor
325 Swede St., 2nd Floor
Norristown, PA 19401
(610) 277-0932 x232
www.victimservicescenter.org

Norristown Police Department
235 E Airy Street
Norristown, PA 19401
(610) 270-0977
Contact Person: Gina P. Davies
(610) 270-0490
gdavies@norristown.org
www.norristown.org/norristown-police-department.html

Pennsylvania Board of Probation and Parole
State Office Building
1400 Spring Garden Street
Philadelphia, PA 19130
www.pbpp.state.pa.us
www.portal.state.pa.us/portal/server.pt/document/1203520/intern_application_web_pdf

Philadelphia Adult Probation and Parole Department
1401 Arch Street
Philadelphia, PA 191072
(215) 683-1000
www.courts.phila.gov

Philadelphia Office of the District Attorney
Three South Penn Square
Juniper and South Penn Square
Philadelphia, PA 19107-3499
(215) 686-8000

General Info: www.phila.gov/districtattorney
Internship Application and Deadlines:
www.phila.gov/districtattorney//careers_UndergraduateInternships.html
E-mail cover letter and resume to da.undergrads@phila.gov

Philadelphia Family Court Juvenile Branch
1801 Vine Street
Philadelphia, PA 19149
(215) 686-4000
www.courts.phila.gov/common-pleas/family/juvenile

Radnor Township Police - Contact: Cpl. Kevin Gallagher
301 Iven Ave, Radnor, PA 19087
(610) 688-0503
kgallagher@radnor.org
www.radnor.com/department/division.php?fDD=15-92

United States Secret Service (Wilmington, DE)
Department of the Treasury
Wilmington, DE 19801
(302) 573-6188
www.secretservice.gov/opportunities_interns.shtml

Whitemarsh Police Department
Siobhan Klinger, Contact Person
616 Germantown Pike
Lafayette Hill, PA 19444
(610) 825-5078
sklinger@whitemarshpd.org

https://www.americajobs.com/federal/doj-pathways-internship-program-bureau-of-prisons-student-trainee-information-technology-student-trainee/1241288/

http://www.phila.gov/districtattorney/careers_UndergraduateInternships.html

http://www.aclupa.org/takeaction/volunteerintern/

http://www.woar.org/volunteer-intern/undergraduate-internships.php

http://www.onedayonejob.com/jobs/juvenile-law-center/

LOCAL: CHIEFS OF POLICE AND CITY SHERIFFS

ALABAMA

Anniston
1200 Gurnee Ave
Calhoun County 36201
(256) 238-1800

Auburn
141 N Ross St
Lee County 36830
(334) 501-3100

Bessemer
23 N 15th St
Jefferson County 35020
(205) 425-2411

Birmingham
1710 1st Ave N
Jefferson County 35205
(205) 328-9311

Decatur
402 Lee St
Morgan County 35602
(256) 341-4600

© Greg Browning/Shutterstock.com

FIGURE 5.9

© Barry Blackburn/Shutterstock.com

FIGURE 5.10

Dothan
210 N St Andrews St
Houston County 36303
(334) 615-4630

Florence
702 S Seminary
Lauderdale County 35630
(256) 760-6500

Homewood
1833 29th Ave S
Jefferson County 35209
(205) 332-6204

Hoover
100 Municipal Dr
Jefferson & Shelby Counties 35216
(205) 444-7700

Huntsville
815 Wheeler Ave
Madison County 35804
(256) 722-7100

Madison
100 Hughes Rd
Madison County 35758
(256) 772-5675

Mobile
2460 Government Blvd
Mobile County 36606
(251) 208-1701

Montgomery
320 N Ripley
Montgomery County 36101
(334) 241-2651

Northport
1910 Lurleen B Wallace Blvd N
Tuscaloosa County 35476
(205) 339-6600

ALASKA

Anchorage
4501 Elmore Rd
99507
(907) 786-8900

Fairbanks
911 Cushman St
99701
(907) 459-6500

Juneau
6255 Alaway Ave
99801
(907) 586-0600

ARIZONA

Apache Junction
11485 W Civic Center Dr
Pinal County 85323
(480) 982-8260

Avondale
519 E Western Ave
Maricopa County 85323
(623) 333-7000

Bullhead City
1255 Marina Blvd
Mohave County 86442
(928) 855-1171

Chandler
250 E Chicago St
Maricopa County 85225
(480) 782-4000

Flagstaff
911 E Sawmill Rd
Coconino County 86001
(520) 779-3646

Gilbert
85 E Civic Center Dr
Maricopa County 85296
(480) 503-6500

Glendale
6835 N 57th Dr
Maricopa County 85301
(623) 930-3000

Lake Havasu City
2360 McCulloch Blvd
Mohave County 86403
(520) 680-5403

Mesa
130 N Robson St
Maricopa County 85201
(480) 644-2211

Navajo
PO Box 3360
Window Rock
Apache County 86515
(520) 871-6581

Opelika
501 S 10th St
Lee County 36803
(334) 705-5200

Oro Valley
11000 N La Canada Dr
Pima County 85737
(520) 229-4900

Peoria
8351 W. Cinnabar Ave
Maricopa County 85345
(623) 773-7096

Phoenix
620 W Washington St
Maricopa County 85003
(602) 262-7626

Phoenix City
1111 Broad St
Russell County 36967
(334) 298-0611

Prattville
101 W Main St
Autauga County 36067
(334) 595-0200

Prescott
222 S Marina
Yuvapai County 86303
(928) 777-1988

Prichard
216 E Prichard Ln
Mobile County 36610
(251) 452-2211

Scottsdale
8401 E. Indian School Rd
Maricopa County 85251
(480) 312-5000

Sierra Vista
911 Coronado Dr
Cochise County 85635
(520) 452-7500

Surprise
14250 W. Statler Plaza, Suite #103
Maricopa County 85374
(623) 222-4000

Tempe
120 E 5th St
Maricopa County 85281
(480) 350-8311

Tucson
270 S Stone Ave
Pima County 85701
(520) 791-4444

Tuscaloosa
3801 Mill Creek Ave
Tuscaloosa County 35401
(205) 349-2121

Yuma
1500 S 1st Ave
Yuma County 85364
(928) 373-4656

ARKANSAS

Conway
1105 Prairie St
Faulkner County 72032
450-6120

El Dorado
402 NW Ave
Union County 71730
(870) 881-4800

Fayetteville
100-A W Rock St
Washington County 72701
(479) 587-3555

Fort Smith
100 S 10th St
Sebastian County 72901
(479) 785-4221

Hot Springs
641 Malvern
Garland County 71902
(501) 321-6789

Jacksonville
1412 W Main St
Pulaski County 72076
(501) 892-3191

Jonesboro
410 W Washington
Craighead County 72401
(870) 935-5562

Little Rock
700 W Markham St
Pulaski County 72201
(501) 371-4829

North Little Rock
200 W Pershing Blvd
Pulaski County 72114
(501) 758-1234

Pine Bluff
200 E 8th Ave
Jefferson County 71601
(870) 543-5100

Rogers
1905 S Dixieland Rd
Benton County 72756
(479) 636-4141

Russellville
115 West H
Pope County 72801
(479) 968-3232

Springdale
201 N Spring St
Washington County 72764
(479) 751-4542

Texarkana
100 N State Line
Miller County 75504
(903) 798-3130

West Memphis
626 E Broadway
Crittenden County 72301
(870) 732-7555

CALIFORNIA

Alameda
1555 Oak St
Alameda County 94501
(510) 337-8340

Alhambra
211 S First St
Los Angeles County 91801
(626) 570-5151

Anaheim
425 S Harbor Blvd
Orange County 92805
(714) 765-1900

Antioch
300 L St
Contra Costa County 94509
(925) 778-2441

Bakersfield
1601 Truxtun Ave
Kern County 93302
(661) 327-7111

Berkeley
2100 M.L.K. Jr Way
Alameda County 94704
(510) 981-5900

Brea
1 Civic Center Cir
Orange County 92821
(714) 990-7911

Burbank
200 N Third St
Los Angeles County 91502
(818) 238-3000

Chula Vista
315 Fourth Ave
San Diego County 91910
(619) 691-5151

Citrus Heights
6315 Fountain Square Dr
Sacramento County 95621
(916) 727-5500

Compton
301 S Willowbrook Ave
Los Angeles County 90220
(310) 605-6500

Concord
1350 Galindo St
Contra Costa County 94520
(925) 671-3220

Corona
730 Public Safety Way
Riverside County 92880
(951) 736-2330

Costa Mesa
99 Fair Dr
Orange County 92626
(714) 754-5280

Daly City
333 90th St
San Mateo County 94015
(650) 991-8000

Downey
PO Box 7016
10911 Brookshire Ave
Los Angeles County 90241
(562) 861-0771
El Cajon
100 Civic Center Way
San Diego County 92020
(619) 579-3311

El Monte
11333 Valley Blvd
Los Angeles County 91731
(626) 580-2110

Escondido
1163 Centre City Parkway
San Diego County 92026
(760) 839-4722

Fairfield
1000 Webster St
Solano County 94533
(707) 428-7300

Fontana
17005 Upland Ave
San Bernardino County 92335
(909) 350-7740

Fremont
2000 Stevenson Blvd
Alameda County 94538
(510) 790-6800

Fresno
2323 Mariposa St
Fresno County 93721
(559) 621-7000

Fullerton
237 W Commonwealth Ave
Orange County 92832
(714) 738-6800

Garden Grove
11301 Acacia Pkwy
Orange County 92840
(714) 741-5704

Glendale
131 North Isabel Street
Los Angeles County 91206
(818) 548-4840

Hayward
300 W Winton Ave
Alameda County 94544
(510) 293-7272

Huntington Beach
2000 Main St
Orange County 92648
(714) 960-8843

Inglewood
One W Manchester Blvd
Los Angeles County 90301
(310) 412-5211

Irvine
1 Civic Ctr Plz
Orange County 92606
(949) 724-7000

Long Beach
400 W Broadway
Los Angeles County 90802
(562) 570-7260

Los Angeles
100 W 1st St
Los Angeles County 90012
(213) 486-1000

Modesto
600 10th St
Stanislaus County 95354
(209) 572-9500

Oakland
455 7th St
Alameda County 94607
(510) 777-3333

Oceanside
3855 Mission Ave
San Diego County 92058
(760) 435-4900

Ontario
2500 S Archibald Ave
San Bernardino County 91761
(909) 395-2001

Orange
1107 N Batavia St
Orange County 92867
(714) 744-7444

Oxnard
251 South C St
Ventura County 93030
(805) 385-7600
Pasadena
207 Garfield Ave
Los Angeles County 91101
(626) 744-4501

Pomona
490 W Mission Blvd
Los Angeles County 91766
(909) 620-2155

Redding
1313 California St
Shasta County 96001
(530) 225-4200

Rialto
128 N Willow Ave
San Bernardino County 92376
(909) 820-2578

Richmond
1701 Regatta Blvd
Contra Costa County 94804
(510) 233-1214

Riverside
4102 Orange St
Riverside County 92501
(951)826-5700

Sacramento
5770 Freeport Blvd., Suite 100
Sacramento County 95822
(916) 264-5471

Salinas
222 Lincoln Ave
Monterey County 93901
(831) 758-7090

San Bernardino
710 North D St
San Bernardino County 92401
(909) 384-5742

San Diego
1401 Broadway
San Diego County 92101
(619) 531-2000

San Francisco
850 Bryant St # 545
San Francisco County 94103
(415) 553-1091

San Jose
201 W Mission St
Santa Clara County 95110
(408) 277-8900

San Mateo
200 Franklin Parkway
San Mateo County 94403
(650) 522-7710

Santa Ana
60 Civic Center Plaza
Orange County 92701
(714) 245-8665

Santa Barbara
215 E Figueroa St
Santa Barbara County 93101
(805) 897-2300

Santa Clara
601 El Camino Real
Santa Clara County 95050
(408) 615-4700

Santa Monica
333 Olympic Drive
Los Angeles County 90401
(310) 395-9931

Santa Rosa
965 Sonoma Ave
Sonoma County 95404
(707) 543-3600

Simi Valley
3901 Alamo St
Ventura County 93063
(323) 563-5400

South Gate
8620 California Ave
Los Angeles County 90280
(209) 937-8218

Stockton
22 E Market St
San Joaquin County 95202
(209) 937-8218

Sunnyvale
700 All America Way
Santa Clara County 94086
(408) 730-7100

Torrance
3300 Civic Center Dr
Los Angeles County 90505
(310) 328-3456

Vacaville
660 Merchant St
Solano County 95688
(707) 449-5200

Vallejo
111 Amador St
Solano County 94590
(707) 648-4321

Ventura
1425 Dowell Dr
Ventura County 93003
(559) 734-8116

Visalia
303 S Johnson St
Tulare County 93291
(559) 738-3215

West Covina
1444 W Garvey
Los Angeles County 91790
(626) 939-8500

Westminster
8200 Westminster Blvd
Orange County 92683
(714) 898-3315

Whittier
13200 Penn St
Los Angeles County 90602
(562) 567-9200

COLORADO

Arvada
8101 Ralston Rd
Jefferson County 80002
(720) 898-6900

Aurora
15001 E Alameda Dr
Arapahoe County 80012
(303) 739-6050

Boulder
1805 33rd St
Boulder County 80301
(303) 441-3333

Colorado Springs
705 S Nevada Ave
El Paso County 80903
(719) 444-7000

Denver
1331 Cherokee St
Denver County 80202
(720) 913-6010

Fort Collins
2221 S Timberline Rd
Larimer County 80525
(970) 221-6540

Greeley
875 W 10th St
Weld County 80634
(970) 350-9627

Lakewood
445 S Allison Pkwy
Jefferson County 80226
(303) 987-7111

Loveland
410 E 5th St
Larimer County 80537
(970) 962-2212

Pueblo
200 S Main St
Pueblo County 81003
(719) 553-2538

Thornton
9551 Civic Center Dr
Adams County 80229
(720) 977-5124

Westminster
9110 Yates St
Adams County 80031
(303) 658-2400

CONNECTICUT

Branford
33 Laurel St
New Haven County 06405
(203) 481-4241

Bridgeport
300 Congress St
Fairfield County 06604
(203) 581-5100

Bristol
131 N Main St
Hartford County 06010
(860) 584-3011

Cheshire
500 Highland Ave
New Haven County 06410
(203) 271-5500

Danbury
375 Main St
Fairfield County 06810
(203) 797-4611

East Hartford
31 School St
Hartford County 06108
(860) 528-4401

East Haven
471 N High St
New Haven County 06512
(203) 468-3820

Enfield
293 Elm St
Hartford County 06082
(860) 763-6400

Fairfield
100 Reef Rd
Fairfield County 06430
(203) 254-4800

Glastonbury
2108 Main St
Hartford County 06033
(860) 633-8301

Greenwich
11 Bruce Place
Fairfield County 06830
(203) 622-8000

Groton (Town of)
68 Groton Long Point Rd
New London County 06340
(860) 441-6712

Hamden
2900 Dixwell Ave
New Haven County 06518
(203) 230-4000

Hartford
253 High St
Hartford County 06103
(860) 757-4000

Manchester
239 E Middle Turnpike
Hartford County 06045
(860) 645-5500

Meriden
50 W Main St
New Haven County 06451
(203) 630-6201

Middletown
222 Main St
Middlesex County 06457
(860) 638-4000

Milford
430 Boston Post Rd
New Haven County 06460
(203) 878-6551

Naugatuck
211 Spring St
New Haven County 06770
(203) 729-5222

New Britain
10 Chestnut St
Hartford County 06051
(860) 826-3000

New Haven
596 Winchester Ave
New Haven County 06511
(203) 946-7572

New London
5 Governor Winthrop Blvd
New London County 06320
(860) 447-5281

Newington
131 Cedar St
Hartford County 06111
(860) 666-8445

Norwalk
1 Monroe St
Fairfield County 06854
(203) 854-3000

Norwich
70 Thames St
New London County 06360
(860) 886-5561

Shelton
85 Wheeler St
Fairfield County 06484
(203) 924-1544

South Windsor
151 Sand Hill Rd
Hartford County 06074
(860) 644-2551

Southington
69 Lazy Ln
Hartford County 06489
(860) 378-1600

Stamford
805 Bedford St
Fairfield County 06901
(203) 977-4444

Stratford
900 Longbrook Ave
Fairfield County 06614
(203) 385-4130

Torrington
576 Main St
Litchfield County 06790
(860) 489-2007

Trumbull
158 Edison Rd
Fairfield County 06611
(203) 261-3665

Vernon
725 Hartford Turnpike
Tolland County 06066
(860) 872-9126

Wallingford
135 N Main St
New Haven County 06492
(203) 294-2800

Waterbury
255 E Main St
New Haven County 06702
(203) 574-6920

West Hartford
103 Raymond Rd
Hartford County 06107
(860) 523-5203

West Haven
200 Saw Mill Rd
New Haven County 06516
(203) 937-3900

Wethersfield
250 Silas Deane Hwy
Hartford County 06109
(860) 721-2900

Windsor
340 Bloomfield Ave
Hartford County 06095
(860) 688-5273

DELAWARE

Dover
400 S Queen St
Kent County 19904
(302) 736-7111

Newark
220 Elkton Rd
New Castle County 19711
(302) 366-7111

Wilmington
300 N Walnut St
New Castle County 19801
(302) 654-5151

DIST OF COLUMBIA

Washington
300 Indiana Ave NW Rm 5080, 20001
(202) 727-4218

FLORIDA

Boca Raton
100 NW Boca Raton Blvd
Palm Beach County 33432
(561) 338-1234

Boynton Beach
100 E Boynton Beach Blvd
Palm Beach County 33435
(561) 742-6100

Cape Coral
1100 Cultural Park Blvd
Lee County 33990
(239) 574-3223

Clearwater
645 Pierce St
Pinellas County 33065
(727) 562-4420

Coral Springs
2801 Coral Springs Dr
Broward County 33065
(954) 344-1800

Davie
1230 S Nob Hill Rd
Broward County 33324
(954) 693-8200

Daytona Beach
129 Valor Blvd
Volusia County 32114
(386) 671-5100

Delray Beach
300 W Atlantic Ave
Palm Beach County 33444
(561) 243-7810

Fort Lauderdale
1300 W Broward Blvd
Broward County 33312
(954) 828-5700

Gainesville
413 NW 8th Ave
Alachua County 32601
(352) 334-2400

Hialeah
5555 E 8th Ave
Dade County 33013
(305) 953-5300

Hollywood
3250 Hollywood Blvd
Broward County 33021
(954) 967-4411

Jacksonville
501 E Bay St
Duval County 32202
(904) 630-0500

Lakeland
219 N Massachusetts Ave
Polk County 33801
(863) 834-6900

Largo
201 Highland Ave
Pinellas County 33770
(727) 587-6730

Lauderhill
6279 W Oakland Park Blvd
Broward County 33313
(954) 497-4700

Margate
5790 Margate Blvd
Broward County 33063
(954) 972-7111

Melbourne
650 N Apollo Blvd
Brevard County 32935
(321) 608-6731

Miami
400 NW 2nd Ave
Dade County 33128
(305) 603-6640

Miami Beach
1100 Washington Ave
Dade County 33139
(305) 673-7900

Miramar
3064 N Commerce Pkwy
Broward County 33025
(954) 602-4000

North Miami
700 NE 124th St
Dade County 33161
(305) 891-0294

Orlando
100 S Hughey Ave
Orange County 32801
(407) 246-2470

Palm Bay
130 Malabar Rd SE
Brevard County 32909
(321) 952-3464

Pembroke Pines
9500 Pines Blvd
Broward County 33024
(954) 431-2200

Pensacola
711 N Hayne St
Escambia County 32501
(850) 435-1900

Plantation
451 NW 70th Terrace
Broward County 33317
(954) 797-2100

Pompano Beach
2421 NW 16th St
Broward County 33069
(954) 831-5900

Port St Lucie
121 SW Port St Lucie Blvd
St Lucie County 34984
(772) 871-5000

St Petersburg
1300 1st Ave N
Pinellas County 33705
(727) 893-7780

Sarasota
2071 Ringling Blvd
Sarasota County 34237
(941) 861-5800

Sunrise
10440 W Oakland Park Blvd
Broward County 33351
(954) 746-3370

Tallahassee
234 E 7th Ave
Leon County 32303
(850) 891-4200

Tampa
411 N Franklin St One Police Ctr
Hillsborough County 33602
(813) 276-3200

West Palm Beach
600 Banyan Blvd
Palm Beach County 33401
(561) 822-1900

GEORGIA

Albany
201 West Oglethorpe Boulevard
Dougherty County 31702
(229) 431-2100

Alpharetta
2565 Old Milton Pkwy
Fulton County 30009
(678) 297-6300

Atlanta
226 Peachtree St SW
Fulton County 30303
(404) 614-6544

College Park
3717 College St
Fulton County 30337
(404) 761-3131

Dalton
301 Jones St
Whitfield County 30720
(706) 278-9085

East Point
2727 E Point St
Fulton County 30344
(404) 559-6226

Fort Benning
Wold Ave Bldg 215
Muscogee County 31905
706) 545-2011

Hinesville
123 East M L King Jr Dr
Liberty County 31313
(912) 368-8211

Jonesboro
170 S Main St
Clayton County 30236
(770) 478-7407

La Grange
911 1st St, Macon
Troup County 30241
706-883-2603

Macon
700 Poplar St
Bibb County 31201
478-751-7500

Marietta
240 Lemon St
Cobb County 30060
(770) 794-5300

Newnan
1 Joseph-Hannah Blvd
Coweta County 30263
(770) 254-2355

Peachtree City
350 Old State Hwy 74
Fayette County 30269
(770) 487-8866

Rome
5 Government Plz Ste 300
Floyd County 30161
706) 238-5111

Roswell
39 Hill St
Fulton County 30075
(770) 640-4100

Savannah
323 E Oglethorpe Ave
Chatham County 31412
912-651-6675

Smyma
2646 Atlanta Rd
Cobb County 30080
(770) 434-9481

Summerville
170 Cox St
Chattooga County 30747
(706) 857-0912

Valdosta
500 N Toombs St
Lowndes County 31601
(229) 242-2606

Warner Robins
100 Watson Blvd
Houston County 31093
478) 302-5378

HAWAII

Hilo
349 Kapiolani St
Hawaii County 96720
808-935-3311

Honolulu
801 S Beretania St
Honolulu County 96813
808-529-3111

Lihue
3990 Kaana St #200
Kauai County 96766
808-241-1711

Wailuku
55 Mahalani St
Maui County 96793
(808) 244-6400

IDAHO

Boise
7200 Barrister Dr
Ada County 83704
208-337-6790

Caldwell
605 Main St
Canyon County 83605
(208) 455-3122

Coeur D'Alene
3818 N Schreiber Way
Kootenai County 83815
(208) 769-2320

Idaho Falls
605 N Capital Ave
Bonneville County 83402
208-529-1200

Lewiston
1224 F St
Nez Perce County 83501
(208) 746-0171

Meridian
1401 E Watertower St
Ada County 83642
(208) 888-6678

Nampa
820 2nd St S
Canyon County 83651
(208) 465-2257

Pocatello
911 N Seventh
Bannock County 83201
208-234-6100

Twin Falls
356 Third Ave E
Twin Falls County 83201
208-735-4357

ILLINOIS

Arlington Heights
200 E Sigwalt St
Cook County 60005
(847) 368-5300

Aurora
350 N River St
DuPage County 60506
(630) 801-6500

Berwyn
6401 31st St
Cook County 60402
(708) 795-5600

Bloomington
305 S East St
Mc Lean County 61701
309-434-2700

Bolingbrook
375 W Briarcliff Rd
Will County 60440
(630) 226-8600

Calumet City
1200 Pulaski Rd
Cook County 60409
(708) 868-2500

Champaign
82 E University St
Champaign County 61820
208-529-1200

Chicago
3510 S Michigan Ave
Cook County 60605
(312) 747-5501

Cicero
4901 W Cermak Rd
Cook County 60804
708-652-2130

Decatur
707 W. South Side Drive Decatur
Macon County 62521
(217) 424-2711

Des Plaines
1420 Miner St
Cook County 60016
(847) 391-5400

Elgin
151 Douglas Ave
Kane County 60120
(847) 289-2700

Evanston
1454 Elmwood Ave
Cook County 60201
(847) 866-5000

Joliet
150 W Washington St
Will County 60432
(815) 724-3100

Markham
16313 Kedzie Pkwy
Cook County 60428
(708) 331-2171

Mount Prospect
112 Northwest Hwy
Cook County 60056
(847) 870-5656

Naperville
1350 Aurora Ave
DuPage County 60540
(630) 420-6197

Oak Lawn
9446 Raymond Ave
Cook County 60453
(708) 422-8292

Oak Park
1234 Madison St
Cook County 60302
(708) 383-6400

Palatine
595 N. Hicks Road Palatine
Cook County 60067
(847) 359-9000

Peoria
600 SW Adams St
Peoria County 61605
(309) 673-4521

Rockford
420 W State St
Winnebago County 61101
(815) 966-2900

Schaumburg
1000 W Schaumburg Rd
Cook County 60194
(847) 882-3534

Skokie
7300 Niles Center Rd
Cook County 60077
(847) 982-5900

Springfield
800 E Monroe St #345
Sangamon County 62701
(217) 788-8360

Waukegan
420 Robert V Sabonjian Pl
Lake County 60085
(847) 360-9000

Wheaton
900 W Liberty Dr
DuPage County 60187
(630) 260-2161

INDIANA

Anderson
1040 Main St
Madison County 46016
(765) 648-6700

Bloomington
220 E 3rd St
Monroe County 47408
(812) 339-4477

Carmel
3 Civic Square
Hamilton County 46032
(317) 571-2500

Columbus
123 Washington St Ste 11
Bartholomew County 47201
(812) 376-2600

East Chicago
2301 E Columbus Dr
Lake County 46312
(219) 391-8331

Elkhart
175 Waterfall Dr
Elkhart County 46516
(574) 295-7070

Evansville
15 NW M L King Blvd
Vanderburgh County 47708
(812) 436-7896

Fishers
4 Municipal Dr
Hamilton County 46038
(317) 595-3300

Fort Wayne
1 E Main St
Allen County 46803
(260) 427-1222

Gary
555 Polk St
Lake County 46402
(219) 881-1214

Greenwood
186 Surina Way
Johnson County 46143
317-346-6336

Hammond
509 Douglas St
Lake County 46320
(219) 853-6544

Hobart
705 E 4th St
Lake County 46342
(219) 942-1125

Indianapolis
50 N Alabama St
Marion County 46204
(317) 327-3811

Jeffersonville
2218 E 10th St
Clark County 47130
(812) 283-6633

Kokomo
100 S Union St
Howard County 46901
(765) 459-5101

Lafayette
20 N 6th St
Tippecanoe County 47901
(765) 807-1200

Lawrence
9001 E 59th St #200
Marion County 46216
317-545-7575

Merrillville
7820 Broadway #1
Lake County 46410
(219) 769-3722
Michigan City
102 W 2nd St
La Porte County 46360
(219) 874-3221

Mishawaka
200 N Church St
St Joseph County 46544
(574) 258-1678

Muncie
300 N High St Ste 215
Delaware County 47305
765.747.4838

Munster
1001 Ridge Rd
Lake County 46321
(219) 836-6600

New Albany
311 Hauss Square # 131
Floyd County 47150
(812) 948-5300

Noblesville
135 S 9th St
Hamilton County 46060
(317) 773-1300

Portage
2693 Irving St
Porter County 46368
(219) 762-3122

Richmond
200 E Main St
Wayne County 47374
(765) 973-9393

Schererville
25 E Joliet
Lake County 46375
(219) 322-5000

South Bend
701 W Sample St
St Joseph County 46601
(574) 235-9201

Terre Haute
1211 Wabash Ave
Vigo County 47807
(812) 238-1661

West Lafayette
711 W Navajo St
Tippecanoe County 47906
(765) 775-5200

IOWA

Ames
515 Clark Ave
Story County 50010
(515) 239-5133

Bettendorf
1609 State St
Scott County 52722
(563) 344-4023

Burlington
424 N 3rd
Des Moines County 52601
(319) 753-8355

Cedar Falls
220 Clay St
Black Hawk County 50613
(319) 273-8612

Cedar Rapids
505 1st St SW
Linn County 52404
(319) 286-5491

Clinton
113 6thAve S
Clinton County 52733
(563) 243-1455

Council Bluffs
227 S 6th St
Pottawattamie County 51503
(712) 328-4701

Davenport
416 N Harrison St
Scott County 52803
(563) 326-7979

Des Moines
25 E 1st St
Polk County 50309
(515) 283-4800

Dubuque
770 Iowa St
Dubuque County 52004
(319) 589-4410

Fort Dodge
702 1st Ave S
Webster County 50501
(515) 573-1426

Iowa City
410 E Washington St
Johnson County 52240
(319) 356-5275

Marshalltown
22 N Center St
Marshall County 50158
(641) 754-5725

Mason City
78 S Georgia
Cerro Gordo County
(641) 421-3636

Muscatine
312 E 5th St
Muscatine County 52761
(563) 263-9922

Sioux City
601 Douglas St
Woodbury County 51101
(712) 279-6440

Urbandale
3740 86th St
Polk County 50322
(515) 278-3938

Waterloo
715 Mulberry St
Black Hawk County 50703
(319) 291-4340

West Des Moines
250 G M Mills Civic Pkwy
Polk County 50265
(515) 222-3320

KANSAS

Dodge City
110 W Spruce St
Ford County 67801
(620) 225-8126

Garden City
304 N 9th St
Finney County 67846
(620) 276-1300

Grand Island
111 Public Safety Dr
Fayette County 68801
(308) 385-5400

Hutchinson
210 W 1st Ave
Reno County 67501
(620) 694-2819

Kansas City
700 Minnesota Ave
Wyandotte County 66101
(913) 573-6100

Lawrence
11 E 11th St
Douglas County 66044
(785) 830-7400

Leavenworth
601 S 3rd St #2055
Leavenworth County 66048
(913) 651-2260

Leawood
4201 Town Center Dr
Johnson County 66209
(913) 642-5555

Lenexa
12500 W 87th St Pkwy
Johnson County 66215
(913) 477-7300

Olathe
501 Old 56 Highway
Johnson County 66061
(913) 971-7500

Overland Park
12400 Foster
Johnson County 66213
(913) 895-6300

Salina
5850 Renner Rd
Saline County 66217
(785) 826-7210

Shawnee
6535 Quivira Rd
Johnson County 66216
(913) 631-2155

Topeka
320 S Kansas Ave Ste 100
Shawnee County 66603
(785) 368-9551

Wichita
455 N Main St
Sedgwick County 67202
(316) 268-4158

KENTUCKY

Bowling Green
911 Kentucky St
Warren County 42101
(270) 393-4244

Covington
1 Police Memorial Dr
Kenton County 41014
(859) 292-2230

Elizabethtown
300 S Mulberry St
Hardin County 42701
(270) 765-4125

Frankfort
300 W 2nd St
Franklin County 40601
(502) 875-8523

Henderson
1990 Barrett Cir
Henderson County 42420
(270) 831-1295

Hopkinsville
112 W 1st St
Christian County 42217
(270) 890-1500

Jeffersontown
10410 Taylorville Rd
Jefferson County 40299
(502) 267-0503

Lexington
150 E Main St
Fayette County 40507
(859) 258-3600

Louisville
633 W Jefferson St
Jefferson County 40202
(502) 574-7660

Owensboro
222 E Ninth St
Daviess County 42303
(270) 687-8888

Paducah
1400 Broadway
McCracken County 42001
(270) 444-8550

Raceland
711 Chinn St
Greenup County 41169
(606) 836-8621

Richmond
1721 Lexington Rd
Madison County 40475
(859) 623-8911

LOUISIANA

Alexandria
1000 Bolton Ave
Rapides Parish 71301
(318) 441-6401

Baton Rouge
704 Mayflower St
E Baton Rouge Parish 70401
(225) 389-3802

Bossier City
620 Benton Rd
Bossier Parish 71111
(318) 741-8605

Hammond
120 S Oak St
Tangipahoa Parish 70401
(504) 542-3500

Houma
500 Honduras St
Terrebonne Parish 70360
(504) 873-6300

Jeanerette
1437 Main St
Iberia Parish 70544
(337) 276-6323

Kenner
500 Veterans Memorial Blvd
Jefferson Parish 70062
(504) 468-7270

Lafayette
900 E University Ave
Lafayette Parish 70503
(337) 291-8600

Lake Charles
830 Enterprise Blvd
Calcasieu Parish 70601
(337) 491-1456

Monroe
700 Wood St
Ouachita Parish 71201
(318) 329-2600

New Iberia
457 E Main St Rm 104
Iberia Parish 70560
(337) 369-2307

New Orleans
715 S Broad St Ste 501
Orleans Parish 70119
(504) 821-2222

Ruston
501 N Trenton St
Lincoln Parish 71270
(318) 255-4141

Shreveport
1234 Texas Ave Rm 8
Caddo Parish 71101
(318) 673-6900

Slidell
2112 Sgt Alfred Dr
St Tammany Parish 70458
(985) 643-3131

MAINE

Bangor
240 Main St
Penobscot County 04401
(207) 947-7384

Lewiston
171 Park St
Androscoggin County 04240
(207) 795-9010

Portland
109 Middle St
Cumberland County 04101
(207) 874-8479

MARYLAND

Annapolis
199 Taylor Ave
Anne Arundel County 21401
(410) 268-9000

Baltimore
1034 N Mount St
Baltimore City 21202
(410) 396-2477

Frederick
100 W Patrick St
Frederick County 21701
(301) 694-2100

Gaithersburg
14 Fulks Corner Ave
Montgomery County 20877
(301) 258-6400

Germantown
20000 Aircraft Dr
Montgomery County 20874
(240) 773-6200

Hagerstown
50 N Burhans Blvd
Washington County 21740
(301) 790-3700

Rockville
1451 Seven Locks Rd
Montgomery County 20854
(301) 279-1591

Salisbury
699 W Salisbury Pkwy
Wicomico County 21801
(410) 548-3165

Silver Spring
1002 Milestone Dr
Montgomery County 20904
(240) 773-6800

Wheaton/Glenmont
2300 Randolph Rd
Montgomery County 20902
(240) 773-5500

MASSACHUSETTS

Boston
40 Sudbury St
Suffolk County 02114
(617) 343-4240

Brockton
7 Commercial St
Plymouth County 02302
(508) 941-0200

Brookline
350 Washington St
Norfolk County 02445
(617) 730-2222

Cambridge
5 Western Ave
Middlesex County 02139
(617) 349-3378

Chicopee
110 Church St
Hampden County 01020
(413) 592-6341

Fall River
685 Pleasant St
Bristol County 02721
(508) 676-8511

Framingham
1 William Welch Way
Middlesex County 01702
(508) 872-1212

Haverhill
40 Bailey Blvd
Essex County 01830
(978) 373-1212

Lawrence
90 Lowell St
Essex County 01840
(978) 794-5900

Lowell
50 Arcand Dr
Middlesex County 01852
(978) 937-3200

Lynn
18 Sutton St
Essex County 01902
(781) 595-2000

Malden
200 Pleasant St
Middlesex County 02148
(781) 397-7171

Medford
100 Main St
Middlesex County 02155
(781) 391-6755

New Bedford
572 Pleasant St
Bristol County 02740
(508) 991-6340

Newton
1321 Washington St
W Newton, Middlesex County 02465
(617) 796-2100

Plymouth
20 Long Pond Rd
Plymouth County 02360
(508) 830-4218

Quincy
1 Sea St
Norfolk County 02169
(617) 479-1212

Somerville
220 Washington St
Middlesex County 02143
(617) 625-1600

Springfield
130 Pearl St
Hampden County 01105
(413) 787-6310

Waltham
155 Lexington St
Middlesex County 02452
(781) 642-6166

Westford
53 Main St
Middlesex County 01886
(978) 692-2161

Weymouth
140 Winter St
Norfolk County 02188
(781) 335-1212

Worcester
9-11 Lincoln Sq
Worcester County 01608
(508) 799-8466

MICHIGAN

Ann Arbor
100 N Fifth Ave
Washtenaw County 48125
(734) 994-2848

Battle Creek
20 N Division St
Calhoun County 48204
(269) 966-3305

Canton
1150 S Canton Center Rd
Wayne County 48188
(734) 394-5400

Dearborn
16099 Michigan Ave
Wayne County 48126
(313) 943-2240

Dearborn Heights
25637 Michigan Ave
Wayne County 48127
(313) 277-6770

Detroit
12000 Livernois Ave
Wayne County 48226
(313) 596-1000

East Lansing
409 Park Ln
Ingham County 48823
(517) 351-4220

Farmington Hills
31655 W 11 Mile Rd
Oakland County 48336
(248) 871-2600

Flint
210 E 5th St
Genesee County 48502
(810) 237-6800

Grand Rapids
1 Monroe Center St NW
Kent County 49503
(616) 456-3403

Kalamazoo
150 E Crosstown Pkwy
Kalamazoo County 49001
(269) 337-8120

Lansing
120 W Michigan Ave
Ingham County 48933
(517) 483-4600

Livonia
15050 Farmington Rd
Wayne County 48154
(734) 466-2400

Novi
45125 W Ten Mile Rd
Oakland County 48375
(248) 348-7100

Pontiac
110 E Pike St
Oakland County 48342
(248) 857-7890

Redford Township
25833 Elsinore
Wayne County 48239
(313) 387-2500

Roseville
29753 Gratiot Ave
Macomb County 48066
(586) 447-4475

Royal Oak
221 E 3rd St
Oakland County 48067
(248) 246-3530

Saginaw
1315 S Washington Ave
Saginaw County 48601
(989) 399-1311

St Clair Shores
27665 Jefferson Ave
Macomb County 48081
(586) 445-5300

Southfield
26000 Evergreen Rd
Oakland County 48076
(248) 796-5500

Sterling Heights
40333 Dodge Park Rd
Macomb County 48313
(586) 446-2800

Taylor
23515 Goddard Rd
Wayne County 48180
(734) 374-1420

Troy
500 W Big Beaver Rd
Oakland County 48084
(248) 524-3443

Warren
29900 Civic Center Blvd
Macomb County 48093
(586) 574-4700

Waterford
5150 Civic Center Dr
Oakland County 48329
(248) 674-0351

West Bloomfield
4530 Walnut Lake
Oakland County 48323
(248) 975-9200

Westland
36701 Ford Rd
Wayne County 48185
(734) 722-9600

Wyoming
2300 De Hoop Ave SW
Kent County 49509
(616) 530-7300

MINNESOTA

Apple Valley
7100 147th St W
Dakota County 55124
(952) 953-2700

Blaine
10801 Town Square Dr NE
Anoka County 55449
(763) 785-6168

Bloomington
2215 W Old Shakopee Rd
Hennepin County 55431
(952) 948-3900

Brooklyn Center
6645 Humboldt Ave N
Hennepin County 55430
(763) 569-3333

Burnsville
100 Civic Center Pkwy
Dakota County 55337
(952) 895-4600

Coon Rapids
11155 Robinson Dr
Anoka County 55433
(763) 767-6481

Cottage Grove
12800 Ravine Pkwy S
Washington County 55016
(651) 458-2850

Crystal
4141 Douglas Dr N
Hennepin County 55422
763) 531-1014

Duluth
2014 W Superior St
St Louis County 55806
(218) 730-5565

Eagan
3830 Pilot Knob Rd
Dakota County 55122
(651) 675-5700

Eden Prairie
8080 Mitchell Rd
Hennepin County 55344
(952) 949-6200

Edina
4801 W 50th St
Hennepin County 55424
(952) 826-1610

Fridley
6431 University Ave NE
Anoka County 55432
(763) 572-3629

Inner Grove Heights
8150 Barbara Ave
Dakota County 55077
(651) 450-2525

Lakeville
9237 183rd St.
Dakota County 55044
(952) 985-2800

Mankato
710 S Front St
Blue Earth County 56001
(507) 387-8793

Maple Grove
12800 Arbor Lakes Pkwy N
Hennepin County 55369
(763) 494-6100

Maplewood
1830 E Cnty Rd B
Ramsey County 55109
(651) 777-8191

Minneapolis
19 N 4th St
Hennepin County 55401
(612) 673-5701

Minnetonka
14600 Minnetonka Blvd
Hennepin County 55345
(952) 939-8500

Moorhead
915 9th Ave N
Clay County 56560
(218) 299-5118

Oakdale
1584 Hadley Ave N
Washington County 55128
(651) 739-5086

Plymouth
3400 Plymouth Blvd
Hennepin County 55447
(763) 509-5160

Richfield
6700 Portland Ave S
Hennepin County 55423
(612) 861-9898

Rochester
101 SE 4th St
Olmsted County 55904
(507) 328-6810

Roseville
2660 Civic Center Dr
Ramsey County 55113
651) 792-7008

St Cloud
101 11th Ave N
Stearns County 56303
(320) 251-1200

St Louis Park
3015 Raleigh Avenue South
Hennepin County 55416
(952) 924-2600

St Paul
367 Grove St
Ramsey County 55101
(651) 266-5588

White Bear Lake
4701 Hwy 61
Ramsey County 55110
(651) 429-8511

Winona
201 W Third St
Winona County 55987
(507) 457-6302

Woodbury
2100 Radio Dr
Washington County 55125
(651) 714-3600

MISSISSIPPI

Biloxi
170 Porter Ave
Harrison County 39530
(228) 392-0641

Clinton
305 Monroe St
Hinds County 39056
(601) 924-5252

Columbus
523 Main St
Lowndes County 39701
(662) 328-7021

Greenville
216 Main St
Washington County 38701
(662) 378-1515

Gulfport
2220 15th St
Harrison County 39502
(228) 868-5900

Hattiesburg
701 James St
Forrest County 39401
(601) 544-7900

Jackson
327 E Pascagoula St
Hinds County 39205
(601) 960-1234

Meridian
2415 6th St
Lauderdale County 39301
(601) 485-1847

Pascagoula
611 Live Oak St
Jackson County 39567
(228) 762-2211

Southaven
8691 Northwest Dr
De Soto County 38671
(662) 393-5283

Starkville
101 Lampkin St
Oktibbeha County 39759
(662) 323-4134

Tupelo
118 Lemons Dr
Lee County 38801
(662) 841-6491

Vicksburg
820 Veto St
Warren County 39180
(601) 636-2511

MISSOURI

Ballwin
300 Park Dr
St Louis County 63011
(636) 227-9636

Blue Springs
903 W Main St
Jackson County 64015
(816) 228-0110

Cape Girardeau
205 Caruthers Ave
Cape Girardeau County 63701
(573) 335-4040

Chesterfield
690 Chesterfield Pkwy W
St Louis County 63017
(636) 537-3000

Columbia
600 E Walnut St
Boone County 65201
(573) 874-7404

Ferguson
222 S Florissant Rd
St Louis County 63135
(314) 522-3100

Florissant
1700 N Hwy 67
St Louis County 63033
(314) 831-7000

Gladstone
7010 N Holmes St
Clay County 64118
(816) 436-3550

Grandview
1200 Main St
Jackson County 64030
(816) 316-4900

Hazelwood
415 Elm Grove Ln
St Louis County 63042
(314) 838-5000

Independence
223 N Memorial Dr
Jackson County 64050
(816) 325-7300

Jefferson City
401 Monroe St
Cole County 65101
(573) 634-6400

Joplin
303 E 3rd St
Jasper County 64801
(417) 623-3131

Kansas City
1200 Linwood Blvd, Kansas City
Jackson County 64109
(816) 234-5510

Kirkwood
131 W Madison Ave
St Louis County 63122
(314) 822-5858

Lee's Summit
10 NE Tudor Rd
Jackson County 64086
(816) 969-1700

Maryland Heights
11911 Dorsett Rd
St Louis County 63043
(314) 298-8700

O'Fallon
100 N Main St
St Charles County 63366
(636) 240-3200

Raytown
10000 E 59th St
Jackson County 64133
(816) 737-6016

St Charles
1781 Zumbehl Rd
St Charles County 63303
(636) 949-3300

St Joseph
501 Faraon St
Buchanan County 64501
(816) 271-4777

St Louis
315 S Tucker Blvd
St Louis County 63102
(314) 444-5630

St Peters
1020 Kimberly
St Charles County 63376
(636) 278-2222

Springfield
321 E Chestnut Expy
Greene County 65802
(417) 864-1810

University City
6801 Delmar Blvd
St Louis County 63130
(314) 725-2211

MONTANA

Bozeman
615 S 16th
Gallatin County 59715
(406) 582-2000

Great Falls
12 1st Ave S
Cascade County 59401
(406) 771-1180

Missoula
435 Ryman St
Missoula County 59802
(406) 552-6300

NEBRASKA

Bellevue
1510 Wall St
Sarpy County 68005
(402) 293-3100

Grand Island
111 Public Safety Dr
Hall County 68801
(308) 385-5400

Kearney
2025 Ave A
Buffalo County 68848
(308) 237-2104

Lincoln
575 S 10th St
Lancaster County 68508
(402) 441-7204

Omaha
505 S 15th St
Douglas County 68102
(402) 444-5600

NEVADA

Elko
1401 College Ave
Elko County 89801
(775) 777-7310

Henderson
223 Lead St
Clark County 89015
(702) 565-8933

North Las Vegas
1301 E Lake Mead Blvd
Clark County 89030
(702) 633-9111

Reno
455 E 2nd St
Washoe County 89505
(775) 334-2175

Sparks
1701 E Prater Way
Washoe County 89434
(775) 353-2231

NEW HAMPSHIRE

Concord
35 Green St
Merrimack County 03301
(603) 225-8600

Derry
1 Municipal Dr
Rockingham County 03038
(603) 432-6111

Dover
46 Locust St
Strafford County 03820
(603) 742-4646

Manchester
405 Valley St
Hillsborough County 03103
(603) 668-8711

Merrimack
31 Baboosic Lake Rd
Hillsborough County 03054
(603) 424-2222

Nashua
0 Panther Dr
Hillsborough County 03062
(603) 594-3500

Portsmouth
3 Jenkins Ave
Rockingham County 03801
(603) 427-1500

Rochester
23 Wakefield St
Strafford County 03867
(603) 330-7127

Salem
9 Veterans Memorial Pkwy
Rockingham County 03079
(603) 893-1911

NEW JERSEY

Bayonne
630 Ave C
Hudson County 07002
(201) 858-6900

Brick Township
401 Chambers Bridge Rd
Ocean County 08723
(732) 477-8300

Camden
800 Federal St
Camden County 08103
(856) 757-7400

Cherry Hill
820 Mercer St
Camden County 08034
(856) 488-7828

Clifton
900 Clifton Ave
Passaic County 07013
(973) 470-5900

Dover Township
37 N Sussex St
Toms River, Ocean County 07801
(973) 366-0302

East Brunswick
1 Civic Center Dr
Middlesex County 08816
(732) 390-6900

East Orange
15 S Munn Ave
Essex County 07018
(973) 266-5000

Edison
100 Municipal Blvd
Middlesex County 08817
(732) 248-7400

Elizabeth
1 Police Plz
Union County 07201
(908) 588-2000

Evesham Township
984 Tuckerton Rd
Marlton, Burlington County 08053
(856) 983-2900

Gloucester
1261 Chews Landing
Blackwood, Camden County 08012
(856) 228-4500

Hamilton
1270 White Horse Ave
Mercer County 08619
(609) 581-4016

Irvington
561 Nye Ave
Essex County 07111
(973) 373-0010

Jersey City
576 Communipaw Ave
Hudson County 07304
(201) 547-5450

Lakewood
231-3rd St
Ocean County 08701
(732) 363-0200

Middletown Township
1 Kings Hwy
Monmouth County 07748
(732) 615-2100

Newark
22 Franklin St
Essex County 07102
(973) 733-6068

Old Bridge Township
1 Old Bridge Plaza
Middlesex County 08857
(732) 679-3400

Passaic
330 Passaic St
Passaic County 07055
(973) 365-3900

Paterson
111 Broadway
Passaic County 07505
(973) 321-1111

Perth Amboy
365 New Brunswick Ave
Middlesex County 08861
(732) 442-4400

Piscataway Township
555 Sidney Rd
Middlesex County 08854
(732) 562-1100

Trenton
225 N Clinton Ave
Mercer County 08609
(609) 989-4170

Union
981 Caldwell Ave
Union County 07083
(908) 686-6709

Union City
3715 Palisade Ave
Hudson County 07087
(201) 865-1111

Vineland
111 N 6th St
Cumberland County 08360
(856) 691-4111

Wayne
475 Valley Rd
Passaic County 07470
(973) 694-0600

Wildwood Crest
6101 Pacific Ave
Cape May County 08260
(609) 522-2456

Woodbridge
1 Main St
Middlesex County 07095
(732) 634-7700

NEW MEXICO

Albuquerque
400 Roma Ave NW
Bernalillo County 87102
(505) 768-7100

Las Cruces
217 E Picacho
Dona Ana County 87701
(575) 528-4200

Rio Rancho
500 Quantum Rd
Sandoval County 87174
(505) 891-5900

Roswell
128 W 2nd
Chaves County 88201
(575) 624-6770

Santa Fe
2515 Camino Entrada
Santa Fe County 87505
(505) 428-3710

NEW YORK

Albany
165 Henry Johnson Blvd
Albany County 12202
(518) 462-8013

Amherst
500 John James Audubon Pkwy
Erie County 14228
(716) 689-1322

Binghamton
38 Hawley St Government Plaza
Broome County 13901
(607) 723-5321

Buffalo
74 Franklin St
Erie County 14202
(716) 851-4444

Cheektowaga
3223 Union Rd
Erie County 14227
(716) 686-3500

Clarkstown
20 Maple Ave
New City, Rockland County 10956
(845) 639-5800

Clay
4483 Rt 31
Onondaga County 13041
(315) 652-3846

Colonie
312 Wolf Rd
Latham, Albany County 12110
(518) 783-2744

Greece
400 Island Cottage Rd
Rochester, Monroe County 14612
(585) 865-9200

Hamburg Town
6100 S Park Ave
Erie County 14075
(716) 649-3800

Hempstead
99 Nicholas Ct
Nassau County 11550
(516) 483-6200

Irondequoit
1300 Titus Ave
Rochester, Monroe County 14617
(585) 336-6000 X:305

Islip Township
401 Main St
Suffolk County 11751
(631) 224-5303

Mount Vernon
Roosevelt Sq N
Westchester County 10550
(914) 665-2500

New Rochelle
475 North Ave
Westchester County 10801
(914) 654-2300

New York City
30-10 Starr Ave, Long Island City
New York County 11101
(718) 610-0570

Niagara Falls
1925 Main St
Niagara County 14305
(716) 286-4547

Ramapo
237 Rt 59
Suffern, Rockland County 10901
(845) 357-2400

Rochester
185 Exchange Blvd
Monroe County 14614
(585) 428-1315

Schenectady
531 Liberty St
Schenectady County 12305
(518) 382-5200

Syracuse
511 S State St
Onondaga County 13202
(315) 442-5250

Tonawanda
200 Niagara St
Kenmore, Erie County 14150
(716) 692-2121

Troy
55 State St
Rensselaer County 12180
(518) 270-4411

Utica
413 Oriskany St W
Oneida County 13502
(315) 735-3301

Yonkers
104 S Broadway
Westchester County 10701
(914) 377-7900

NORTH CAROLINA

Asheville
100 Court Plaza
Buncombe County 28802
(828) 259-5880(828) 252-1110

Burlington
267 W Front St
Alamance County 27215
(336) 229-3500

Camp Lejeune
MP Company Hdqtrs Marine Corp Base
Onslow County 28542
(910) 451-3193

Cary
120 Wilkinson Ave
Wake County 27513
(919) 469-4012

Chapel Hill
828 Martin Luther King Jr Blvd
Orange County 27514
(919) 968-2760

Charlotte
601 E Trade St
Mecklenburg County 28202
(704) 336-8301

Concord
30 Market St SW
Cabarrus County 28026
(704) 783-2207

Durham
510 S Dillard St
Durham County 27701
(919) 560-0897

Fayetteville
467 Hay St
Cumberland County 28301
(910) 433-1529

Gastonia
200 E Long Ave
Gaston County 28052
(704) 810-0376

Goldsboro
204 S Center St
Wayne County 27530
(919) 705-6572

Greensboro
300 W Washington St
Guilford County 27401
(336) 373-2287

Greenville
500 S Greene St
Pitt County 27835
(252) 329-4315

Hickory
347 Second Ave SW
Catawba & Burke Counties 28602
(828) 328-5551

High Point
1009 Leonard Ave
Guilford County 27260
(336) 883-3224

Jacksonville
206 Marine Blvd
Onslow County 28040
(910) 455-4000

Kannapolis
314 S Main St
Cabarrus & Rowan Counties 28081
(704) 920-4000

Kinston
205 E King St
Lenoir County 28501
(252) 939-3220

Raleigh
218 W Cabarrus St
Wake County 27601
(919) 996-3855

Rocky Mount
330 S Church St
Nash County 27804
(252) 972-1450

Salisbury
130 E Liberty St
Rowan County 28144
(704) 638-5333

Wilmington
615 Bess St
New Hanover County 28401
(910) 343-3600

Wilson
120 N Goldsboro St
Wilson County 27893
(252) 399-2323

Winston-Salem
725 Sr1725
Forsyth County 27101
(336) 773-7700

NORTH DAKOTA

Bismarck
700 S 9th St
Burleigh County 58504
(701) 223-1212

Fargo
222 4th St N
Cass County 58102
(701) 235-4493

Grand Forks
122 S 5th St
Grand Forks County 58201
(701) 787-8000

Minot
515 2nd Ave SW
Ward County 58701
(701) 852-0111

OHIO

Akron
217 S High St
Summit County 44308
(330) 375-2552

Canton
218 Cleveland Ave SW
Stark County 44702
(330) 489-3100

Cincinnati
310 Ezzard Charles Dr
Hamilton County 45214
(513) 352-3505

Cleveland
1300 Ontario St
Cuyahoga County 44113
(216) 623-5000

Cleveland Heights
40 Severance Cir
Cuyahoga County 44118
(216) 291-4987

Columbus
120 Marconi Blvd
Franklin County 43215
(614) 645-4600

Cuyahoga Falls
2310 2nd St
Summit County 44221
(330) 928-2181

Dayton
345 W. Second St
Montgomery County 45422
(937) 225-5005

Elyria
18 W Ave
Lorain County 44035
(440) 323-3302

Euclid
545 E 222nd St
Cuyahoga County 44123
(216) 731-1234

Green Township
6303 Harrison Ave
Cincinnati, Hamilton County 45247
(513) 574-0007

Hamilton
331 S Front St
Butler County 45011
(513) 868-5811

Kettering
3600 Shroyer Rd
Montgomery County 45429
(937) 296-2555

Lakewood
12650 Detroit Ave
Cuyahoga County 44107
(216) 521-6773

Lorain
200 W Erie Ave
Lorain County 44052
(440) 204-2100

Mansfield
30 N Diamond St
Richland County 44902
(419) 755-9724

Mentor
8500 Civic Center Blvd
Lake County 44060
(440) 974-5760

Middletown
1 Donham Plaza
Butler County 45042
(513) 425-7766

Parma
5555 Powers Blvd
Cuyahoga County 44129
(440) 887-7300

Springfield
130 N Fountain Ave
Clark County 45502
(937) 324-7685

Toledo
525 N Erie St
Jefferson County 43624
(419) 245-3340

Union Township
4312 Glen Este-Withamsville Rd
West Chester, Butler County 45245
(513) 752-1230

Warren
141 South St SE
Trumbull County 44483
(330) 841-2536

Youngstown
116 W Boardman St
Mahoning County 44503
(330) 742-8900

OKLAHOMA

Ardmore
23 S Washington St
Carter County 73401
(580) 223-1212

Bartlesville
100 E Hensley Blvd
Washington County 74003
(918) 338-4001

Broken Arrow
1101 N 6th St
Tulsa County 74012
(918) 259-8400

Edmond
23 E First St
Oklahoma County 73034
(405) 359-4420

Enid
301 W Garriott Rd
Garfield County 73701
(580) 242-7000

Lawton
10 SW 4th St
Comanche County 73501
(580) 581-3200

Midwest City
100 N Midwest Blvd
Oklahoma County 73110
(405) 739-1306

Moore
117 E Main St
Cleveland County 73160
(405) 793-5171

Norman
201 W Gray St
Cleveland County 73069
(405) 321-1600

Oklahoma City
219 E Main St
Oklahoma County 73104
(405) 297-1180

Ponca City
200 E Oklahoma Ave
Kay County 74601
(580) 767-0371

Shawnee
16 W 9th St
Pottawatomie County 74801
(405) 273-2121

Stillwater
723 S Lewis
Payne County 74074
(405) 372-4171

Tulsa
175 E 2nd St
Tulsa County 74103
(918) 596-9288

Yukon
100 S Ranchwood Blvd
Canadian County 73099
(405) 354-1711

OREGON

Albany
1117 Jackson St SE
Linn County 97321
(541) 917-7680

Beaverton
4755 SW Griffith Dr
Washington County 97005
(503) 526-2264

Bend
555 NE 15th St
Deschutes County 97701
(541) 693-6911

Corvallis
180 NW 5th St
Benton County 97339
(541) 766-6924

Eugene
777 Pearl St Rm 107
Lane County 97401
(541) 682-5111

Gladstone
535 Portland Ave
Clackamas County 97027
(503) 655-8211

Gresham
1333 NW Eastman Pkwy
Multnomah County 97030
(503) 618-2313

Hillsboro
250 SE 10th ave
Washington County 97123
(503) 681-6190

Keizer
930 Chemawa Rd NE
Marion County 97303
(503) 390-3713

Lake Oswego
380 A Ave
Clackamas County 97034
(503) 635-0250

Medford
411 W 8th St
Jackson County 98501
(541) 774-2250

Portland
1111 SW 2nd Ave
Multnomah County 97204
(503) 823-0000

Salem
555 Liberty St SE Rm 130
Marion County 97301
(503) 588-6123

Springfield
344 A St
Lane County 97477
(541) 726-3714

Tigard
13125 SW Hall Blvd
Washington County 97223
(503) 639-6168

PENNSYLVANIA

Abington
1166 Old York Rd
Montgomery County 19001
(215) 885-4450

Allentown
544 N 6th St
Lehigh County 18101
(610) 437-7751

Altoona
1106 16th St
Blair County 16601
(814) 949-2491

Bensalem Township
2400 Byberry Rd
Bucks County 19020
(215) 639-3700

Bethlehem
434 W Broad St
Northampton County 18018
(610) 865-7187

Bristol Township
2501 Bath Rd
Bucks County 19007
(215) 785-4040

Erie
626 State St
Erie County 16501
(814) 870-1125

Harrisburg
123 Walnut St
Dauphin County 17101
(717) 255-3131

Haverford Township
1010 Darby Rd
Havertown, Delaware County 19083
(610) 853-1298

Lancaster
39 W Chestnut St
Lancaster County 17602
(717) 735-3300

Lower Merion Township
75 Lancaster ave
Ardmore, Montgomery County 19003
(610) 642-4200

Millcreek Township
3608 W 26th St
Erie, Erie County 16506
(814) 833-7777

Penn Hills
12245 Frankstown Rd
Penn Hills, Allegheny County 15235
(412) 793-2035

Philadelphia
8th & Race St Franklin Sq
Philadelphia County 19106
(215) 686-3280

Pittsburgh
100 Grant St
Allegheny County 15219
(412) 255-2814

Reading
815 Washington St
Berks County 19601
(610) 655-6116

Scranton
100 S Washington Ave
Lackawanna County 18503
(570) 348-4130

State College
243 S Allen St
Centre County 16801
(814) 234-7150

Upper Darby Township
7236 W Chester Pike
Delaware County 19082
(610) 734-7693

RHODE ISLAND

Coventry
1075 Main St
Kent County 02816
(401) 826-1100

Cranston
5 Garfield Ave
Providence County 02920
(401) 942-2211

Cumberland
1380 Diamond Hill Rd
Providence County 02864
(401) 333-2500

East Providence
750 Waterman Ave
Providence County 02914
(401) 435-7600

Johnston
1651 Atwood Ave
Providence County 02919
(401) 231-4210

Lincoln
100 Old River Rd
Providence County 02865
(401) 333-8281

Newport
120 Broadway
Newport County 02840
(401) 847-1306

North Providence
1967 Mineral Spring Ave
Providence County 02904
(401) 233-1433

Pawtucket
121 Roosevelt Ave
Providence County 02860
(401) 727-9100

Providence
325 Washington St
Providence County 02903
(401) 272-3121

Warwick
99 Veterans Memorial Dr
Kent County 02886
(401) 468-4200

West Warwick
1162 Main St
Kent County 02893
(401) 821-4323

Westerly
60 Airport Rd
Washington County 02891
(401) 596-2022

Woonsocket
242 Clinton St
Providence County 02895
(401) 766-1212

SOUTH CAROLINA

Aiken
251 Laurnes
Aiken County 29801
(803) 642-7620

Anderson
401 S Main St
Anderson County 29624
(864) 231-2277

Charleston
180 Lockwood Blvd
Charleston County 29403
(843) 577-7434

Columbia
1 Justice Square
Richland County 29201
(803) 545-3500

Florence
324 W Evans St
Florence County 29501
(843) 665-3191

Goose Creek
519 N Goose Creek Blvd
Berkeley County 29445
(843) 572-4300

Greenville
4 McGee St
Greenville County 29601
(864) 271-5333

Greenwood
520 Monument St
Greenwood County 29648
(864) 942-8405

Mount Pleasant
100 Ann Edwards Ln
Charleston County 29464
(843) 884-4176

Myrtle Beach
1101 Oak St
Horry County 29577
(843) 918-1300

North Charleston
2500 City Hall Ln
Charleston County 29419
(843) 740-2800

Rock Hill
120 E Black St
York County 29730
(803) 329-7200

Spartanburg
145 W Broad St
Spartanburg County 29306
(864) 596-2035

Summerville
300 W 2nd N St
Dorchester County 29483
(843) 871-2463

Sumter
107 E Hampton Ave
Sumter County 29150
(803) 436-2700

SOUTH DAKOTA

Aberdeen
114 2nd Ave SE
Brown County 57401
(605) 626-7000

Rapid City
300 Kansas City St
Pennington County 57701
(605) 394-4131

Sioux Falls
320 W 4th St
Minnehaha County 57104
(605) 367-7212

TENNESSEE

Bartlett
3730 Appling Rd
Shelby County 38133
(901) 385-5555

Chattanooga
3410 Amnicola Hwy
Hamilton County 37406
(423) 643-5000

Clarksville
135 Commerce St
Montgomery County 37040
(931) 648-0656

Cleveland
100 Church St NE
Bradley County 37311
(423) 476-1121

Collierville
156 N Rowlett St
Shelby County 38017
(901) 457-2520

Columbia
707 N Main St
Maury County 38401
(931) 388-2727

Cookeville
10 E Broad St
Putnam County 38503
(931) 526-2125

Germantown
1930 S Germantown Rd
Shelby County 38183
(901) 754-7222

Hendersonville
3 Executive Park Dr
Sumner County 37075
(615) 822-1111

Jackson
234 Institute St
Madison County 38301
(901) 425-8400

Johnson City
601 E Main St
Washington County 37605
(423) 434-6160

Kingsport
200 Shelby St
Sullivan County 37660
(423) 229-9300

Knoxville
800 Howard Baker Jr Blvd
Knox County 37927
(865) 215-7000

Memphis
201 Poplar Ave St 12-05
Shelby County 38103
(901) 636-3700

Murfreesboro
302 S Church St
Rutherford County 37130
(615) 849-2685

Nashville
200 James Robertson Pkwy
Davidson County 37201
(615) 862-7400

Oak Ridge
200 S Tulane Ave
Anderson County 37830
(865) 425-4399

Smyrna
400 Enon Springs Rd E
Rutherford County 37167
(615) 459-6644

TEXAS

Abilene
450 Pecan
Taylor County 79602
(325) 673-8331

Amarillo
200 SE Third Ave
Potter County 79101
(806) 378-9452

Arlington
620 W Division St
Tarrant County 76004
(817) 459-5700

Baytown
3200 N Main St
Harris County 77521
(281) 422-8371

Beaumont
255 College
Jefferson County 77704
(409) 832-1234

Bedford
2121 L Don Dodson Dr
Tarrant County 76021
(817) 952-2440

Brownsville
600 E Jackson St
Cameron County 78520
(956) 548-7000

Bryan
303 E 29th St
Brazos County 77805
(979) 209-5300

Carrollton
2025 E Jackson Rd
Dallas County 75006
(972) 466-3290

College Station
2611 A Texas Ave
Brazos County 77840
(979) 764-3600

Corpus Christi
321 John Sartain St Rm 525
Nueces County 78469
(361) 886-2600

Dallas
9801 Harry Hines Blvd
Dallas County 75201
(214) 670-6178

Denton
601 E Hickory St Ste E
Denton County 76205
(940) 349-8181

El Paso
911 N Raynor St
El Paso County 79903
(915) 564-7000

Fort Worth
1000 Throckmorton St
Tarrant County 76102
(817) 392-6700

Galveston
601 54th St
Galveston County 77550
(409) 765-3702

Garland
1891 Forest Ln
Dallas County 75040
(972) 485-4840

Grand Prairie
801 Conover Dr
Dallas County 75051
(972) 237-8710

Houston
1200 Travis 16th Fl
Harris County 77002
(713) 884-3131

Irving
305 N O'Connor
Dallas County 75061
(972) 273-1010

Killeen
402 N 2nd St
Bell County 76541
(254) 501-8830

Laredo
4712 Maher Ave
Webb County 78041
(956) 795-2800

Lewisville
1187 W Main St
Denton County 75067
(972) 219-3600

Longview
302 W Cotton
Gregg County 75601
(903) 237-1199

Mc Allen
1121 S 16th St
Hidalgo County 78501
(956) 972-7412

Mesquite
777 N Galloway Ave
Dallas County 75149
(972) 285-6336

Midland
601 N Loraine St
Midland County 79702
(432) 685-7108

North Richland Hills
7301 NE Loop 820
Tarrant County 76180
(817) 427-7000

Odessa
205 N Grant Ave
Ector County 79761
(432) 333-3641

Pasadena
1201 Davis St
Harris County 77506
(713) 477-1221

Plano
909 14th St
Collin County 75086
(972) 424-5678

Port Arthur
645-4th St
Jefferson County 77640
(409) 983-8600

Richardson
140 N Greenville
Dallas County 75081
(972) 744-4800

Round Rock
2701 N Mays St
Williamson County 78664
(512) 218-5500

San Angelo
401 E Beauregard St
Tom Green County 76903
(325) 481-2696

San Antonio
800 Dolorosa #402
Bexar County 78207
(210) 207-7365

Sugar Land
1200 Hwy 6
Fort Bend County 77487
(281) 275-2500

Temple
209 E Avenue A
Bell County 76501
(254) 298-5500

Tyler
711 W Ferguson St
Smith County 75702
(903) 531-1090

Victoria
306 S Bridge St
Victoria County 77901
(361) 572-3221

Waco
300 Austin Ave
Mc Lennan County 76701
(254) 750-5600 .

Wichita Falls
610 Holiday St
Wichita County 76301
(940) 760-5000

UTAH

Bountiful
805 S Main St
Davis County 84010
(801) 298-6000

Clearfield
55 S State St
Davis County 84015
(801) 525-2806

Layton
429 Wasatch Dr
Davis County 84041
(801) 336-3520

Logan
62 W 300 N
Cache County 84321
(435) 716-9300

Midvale
7912 Main St
Salt Lake County 84047
(801) 256-2500

Murray
5025 S State St
Salt Lake County 84107
(801) 264-2673

Ogden
2186 Lincoln Ave
Weber County 84401
(801) 629-8221

Orem
95 E Center St
Utah County 84057
(801) 229-7070

Pleasant Grove
87 E 100 S
Utah County 84062
(801) 785-3506(

Provo
48 S 300 W
Utah County 84603
(801) 785-3506

Roy City
5051 S 1900 W
Weber County 84067
(801) 774-1063

St George
265 N 200 E
Washington County 84770
(435) 627-4301

Salt Lake City
475 S 300 E
Salt Lake County 84111
(801) 799-3100

Sandy
10000 S Centennial Pkwy
Salt Lake County 84070
(801) 568-7200

South Jordan
1600 Towne Center Dr
Salt Lake County 84095
(801) 254-4708

West Jordan
8040 S Redwood Rd
Salt Lake County 84088
(801) 569-2000

West Valley City
3575 S Market St
Salt Lake County 84119
(801) 963-3300

VERMONT

Burlington
1 North Ave
Chittenden County 05401
(802) 658-2704

VIRGINIA

Alexandria
3600 Wheeler Ave
22314
(703) 746-4444

Blacksburg
200 Clay St SW
Montgomery County 24060
(540) 961-1150

Charlottesville
315 E High St
22902
(434) 970-3777

Chesapeake
1209 20th St
23320
(757) 382-6556

Danville
427 Patton St
24541
(434) 799-5111

Hampton
40 Lincoln St
23669
(757) 727-6530

Harrisonburg
101 N Main St
22801
(540) 434-4436

Leesburg
65 Plaza St
Loudoun County 20176
(703) 771-4500

Lexington
11 Fuller St, Lexington
24450
(540) 463-3705

Lynchburg
905 Court St
24505
(434) 455-6050

Manassas
9518 Fairview Ave
20110
(703) 257-8000

Newport News
9710 Jefferson Ave
23607
(757) 928-4100

Norfolk
100 Brooke Ave
23510
(757) 664-3277

Petersburg
8 Courthouse Ave
23803
(804) 733-2369

Portsmouth
801 Water St
23704
(757) 393-5300

Prince William
8900 Freedom Center Blvd
Prince William County 22192
(703) 792-5111

Richmond
2501 Q St
23223
(804) 646-3602

Roanoke
348 Campbell Ave SW
24016
(540) 853-2212

Salem
36 E Calhoun St
24153
(540) 375-3078

Staunton
116 W Beverley St
24402
(540) 332-3842

Suffolk
150 N Main St
23434
(757) 514-7840

Virginia Beach
2509 Princess Anne Rd
23456
(757) 385-4377

Williamsburg
425 Armistead Ave
23185
(757) 220-2333

Auburn
101 N Division
King County 98001
(253) 931-3080

Bellevue
450 110th Ave NE
King County 98004
(425) 452-6917

Bellingham
505 Grand Ave
Whatcom County 98225
(360) 778-8800

Bothell
18916 N Creek Pkwy #103
King County 98011
(425) 486-1254

Bremerton
1025 Burwell St
Kitsap County 98337
(360) 473-5220

Des Moines
21900 11th Ave S
King County 98198
(206) 878-3301

Edmonds
250 5th Ave N
Snohomish County 98020
(425) 771-0200

Everett
3002 Wetmore Ave
Snohomish County 98201
(425) 257-8400

Federal Way
33325 8th Ave S
King County 98003
(253) 835-6700

Kennewick
211 W 6th Ave
Benton County 99336
(509) 585-4208

Kent
220 4th Ave S
King County 98032
(253) 856-5800

Kirkland
11750 NE 118th St
King County 98033
(425) 587-3400

Lacey
420 College St SE
Thurston County 98503
(360) 459-4333

Lakewood
9401 Lakewood Dr SW
Pierce County 98499
(253) 830-5000

Lynnwood
19321 44th Ave W
Snohomish County 98036
(425) 774-6900

Olympia
601 4th Ave E
Thurston County 98501
(360) 753-8300

Pasco
525 N 3rd Ave
Franklin County 99301
(509) 545-3421

Puyallup
333 S. Meridian
Pierce County 98371
(253) 841-4321

Redmond
8701 160th Ave NE
King County 98073
(425) 556-2500

Renton
1055 S Grady Way
King County 98055
(425) 430-7500

Richland
871 George Washington Way
Benton County 99352
(509) 942-7360

Seattle
2300 SW Webster St
King County 98104
(206) 733-9800

Spokane
1100 W Mallon Ave
Spokane County 99260
(509) 625-4100

Tacoma
930 Tacoma Ave S Rm 3401524 M.L.K. Jr Way
Pierce County 98402
(253) 594-7800

Vancouver
2800 NE Stapleton Rd
Clark County 98660
(360) 487-7355

Walla Walla
54 E Moore St
Walla Walla County 99362
(509) 527-4434

Yakima
200 S 3rd St
Yakima County 98901
(509) 575-6200

WEST VIRGINIA

Charleston
501 Virginia St E
Kanawha County 25301
(304) 348-6480

Huntington
675 10th St
Cabell County 25701
(304) 696-4470

Morgantown
300 Spruce St
Monongalia County 26505
(304) 284-7522

Parkersburg
1 Government Sq
Wood County 26102
(304) 424-8444

Wheeling
1500 Chapline St
Ohio County 26003
(304) 234-3661

WISCONSIN

Appleton
222 S Walnut St
Outagamie County 54911
(920) 832-5500

Beloit
100 State St
Rock County 53511
(608) 364-6801

Brookfield
2100 N Calhoun Rd
Waukesha County 53005
(262) 787-3702

Eau Claire
740 Second Ave
Eau Claire County 54702
(715) 839-4972

Fond Du Lac
126 N Main St
Fond Du Lac County 54935
(920) 322-3700

Franklin
9455 W Loomis Rd
Milwaukee County 53132
(414) 425-2522

Green Bay
307 S Adams St
Brown County 54301
(920) 448-3200

Greenfield
5300 W Layton Ave
Milwaukee County 53220
(414) 761-5300

Janesville
200 US-14
Rock County 53545
(608) 757-8000

La Crosse
400 L Crosse St
La Crosse County 54601
(608) 789-7200

Madison
211 S Carroll St
Dane County 53703
(608) 261-9694

Manitowoc
910 Jay St
Manitowoc County 54220
(920) 686-6500

Menomonee Falls
W156 N8480 Pilgrim Rd
Waukesha County 53051
(262) 532-8700

Milwaukee
749 W State St
Milwaukee County 53201
(414) 933-4444

New Berlin
16300 W National Ave
Waukesha County 53151
(262) 782-6640

Oak Creek
301 W Ryan Rd
Milwaukee County 53154
(414) 762-8200

Oshkosh
4311 Jackson St
Winnebago County 54901
(920) 727-2888

Sheboygan
1315 N 23rd St
Sheboygan County 53081
(920) 459-3333

Superior
1316 N 14th St #150
Douglas County 54880
(715) 395-7234

Waukesha
1901 Delafield St
Waukesha County 53188
(262) 524-3831

Wausau
515 Grand Ave
Marathon County 54403
(715) 261-7800

Wauwatosa
1700 N 116th St
Milwaukee County 53226
(414) 471-8430

West Allis
11301 W Lincoln Ave
Milwaukee County 53227
(414) 302-8000

West Bend
350 Vine St
Washington County 53095
(262) 335-5000

WYOMING

Casper
201 N David St
Natrona County 82601
(307) 235-8278

Cheyenne
2020 Capitol Ave
Laramie County 82001
(307) 637-6500

Laramie
620 Plaza Ct
Albany County 82070
(307) 721-2526

STATE: STATE POLICE-HIGHWAY PATROLS

ALABAMA

Tim Pullin
Chief
301 South Ripley Street
Montgomery 36104
(334) 242-4393

ALASKA

Colonel James Cockrell
Director
5700 E Tudor Rd
Anchorage 99507
(907) 269-5511

ARIZONA

Daniel Lugo
Assistant Director
2102 W Encanto Blvd
Phoenix 85009
(602) 223-2000

ARKANSAS

Colonel Bill Bryant
Director
1 State Police Plz Dr
Little Rock 72209
(501) 618-8200

CALIFORNIA

Joseph A. Farrow
Commissioner
PO Box 942898
Sacramento 94298
(916) 657-7152

COLORADO

Col Scott G. Hernandez
Chief
700 Kipling St Ste 3000
Denver 80215
(303) 239-4403

CONNECTICUT

Colonel Brian F. Meraviglia
Commander
1111 Country Club Rd
Middletown 06457
(860) 685-8190

FIGURE 5.11

FIGURE 5.12

DELAWARE

Colonel Nathaniel McQueen, Jr.
Superintendent
1441 N DuPont Hwy
Dover 19901
(302) 739-5911

FLORIDA

Terry L. Rhodes
Director
Neil Kirkman Bldg
Tallahassee 32399
(850) 488-4885

GEORGIA

Major Tommy Waldrop
Commanding Officer
959 E. Confederate Ave., SE
Atlanta, GA 30316
(404) 624-7000

97

HAWAII

Daniel Fernandez
Administrator
1111 Alakea St 1st Fl
Honolulu 96813
(808) 538-5656

IDAHO

Col Ralph Powell
Director
700 S Strafford Dr
Meridian 83642
(208) 884-7003

ILLINOIS

Leo P. Schmitz
Chief
PO Box 19461
Springfield 62794
(217) 782-7263

INDIANA

Colonel Mark A. French
Chief
100 N Senate Ave
Indianapolis 46204
(317) 232-8241

IOWA

Sgt. Nathan Ludwig
Director
Wallace State Office Bldg
Des Moines 50319
(515) 284-5824

KANSAS

Col Don Brownlee
Superintendent
122 SW 7th St
Topeka 66603
(785) 296-6800

KENTUCKY

Rodney Brewer
Acting Commissioner
919 Versailles Rd
Frankfort 40601
(502) 695-6300

LOUISIANA

Michael D. Edmonson
Superintendent
PO Box 66614
Baton Rouge 70896
(225) 925-6117

MAINE

Colonel Robert A. Williams
Chief
45 Commerce Drive
Augusta 04333
(207) 624-7200

MARYLAND

Colonel William M. Pallozzi
Superintendent
1201 Reistertown Rd
Pikesville 21208
(410) 486-3101

MASSACHUSETTS

Col Richard D. McKeon
Superintendent
470 Worcester Rd
Framingham 01702
(508) 820-2300

MICHIGAN

Col. Kriste Kibbey Etue
Director
333 South Grand Avenue PO Box 30634
East Lansing 48823
(517) 332-2521

MINNESOTA

Colonel Matt Langer
Chief
444 Cedar St Ste 130
St Paul 55101
(651) 297-3935

MISSISSIPPI

Colonel Donnell Berry
Interim Commissioner
PO Box 958
Jackson 39205
(601) 987-1490

MISSOURI

Colonel J. Bret Johnson
Superintendent
PO Box 568
Jefferson City 65102
(573) 751-3313

MONTANA

Colonel Tom Butler
Chief
2550 Prospect Ave
Helena 59620
(406) 444-3780

NEBRASKA

Col Tom Nesbitt
Superintendent
1600 Nebraska Hwy 2
Lincoln 68502
(402) 471-4545

NEVADA

Colonel Dennis S. Osborn
Chief
555 Wright Way
Carson City 89711
(775) 684-4867

NEW HAMPSHIRE

Colonel Robert L. Quinn
Director
10 Hazen Dr
Concord 03305
(603) 271-3636

NEW JERSEY

Col Rick Fuentes
Superintendent
PO Box 7068
West Trenton 08628
(609) 882-2000

NEW MEXICO

Pete N. Kassetas
Chief
PO Box 1628
Santa Fe 87504
(505) 827-3370

NEW YORK

Joseph D'Amico
Superintendent
1220 Washington Ave Bldg 22
Albany 12226
(518) 457-6721

NORTH CAROLINA

Colonel William J. Grey
Commander
4702 Mail Service Ctr
Raleigh 27699
(919) 733-7952

NORTH DAKOTA

Colonel Michael Gerhart
Superintendent
600 E Boulevard Ave Dept 504
Bismarck 58505
(701) 328-2455

OHIO

Colonel Paul A. Pride
Superintendent
1970 W Broad St
Columbus 43218
(614) 466-2990

OKLAHOMA

COL Rick Adams
Chief
PO Box 11415
Oklahoma City 73136
(405) 425-2001

OREGON

Jeff Hershman
Captain
400 Public Sve Bldg
Salem 97310
(503) 378-3720

PENNSYLVANIA

Col Tyree C. Blocker
Acting Commissioner
1800 Elmerton Ave
Harrisburg 17110
(717) 772-6924

RHODE ISLAND

Col Steven G. O'Donnell
Superintendent
311 Danielson Pike
North Scituate 02857
(401) 444-1000

SOUTH CAROLINA

Colonel Michael Oliver
Commander
Law Enforcement Division
5400 Broad River Rd
Columbia 29212
(803) 896-7920

SOUTH DAKOTA

Colonel Craig Price
Superintendent
500 E Capitol Ave
Pierre 57501
(605) 773-3105

TENNESSEE

Col Tracy Trott
Commissioner
1150 Foster Ave
Nashville 37249
(615) 251-5166

TEXAS

Steve McCraw
Director
PO Box 4087
Austin 78773
(512) 424-2000

UTAH

Col Richard A Greenwood
Superintendent
4501 S 2700 W Box 141100
Salt Lake City 84114
(801) 965-4062

VERMONT

Colonel Matthew Birmingham
Director
103 S Main St Waterbury State Complex
Waterbury 05671
(802) 244-8718

VIRGINIA

Lt W Gerald Massengill
Acting Superintendent
PO Box 27472
Richmond 23261
(804) 674-2000

WASHINGTON

John R. Batiste
Chief
11th & Columbia
Olympia 98504
(360) 753-6540

WEST VIRGINIA

Col Jay Smithers
Superintendent
725 Jefferson Rd
S Charleston 25309
(304) 746-2111

WISCONSIN

Stephen Fitzgerald
Superintendent
4802 Sheboygan Ave Hill Farms State Transp Bldg
Madison 53707
(608) 266-3908

WYOMING

Colonel John Butler
Administrator/Patrol Division
5300 Bishop Blvd
Cheyenne 82003
(307) 777-4301

OTHER STATE AGENCIES

ABC Enforcement

Adult Institutions Division of Operations

Alcohol Beverage Control Division

Army National Guard Headquarters

Attorney General

Bureau of Services

Central Bureau of Parole

Conservation Offices

Department of Corrections

Department of Environmental Protection and Energy

Department of Human Services

Department of Military and Veterans Affairs

Division of Civil Rights

Division of Consumer Affairs

Division of Criminal Justice

Division of Gaming Enforcement

Forest Fire Services

Insurance Fraud Division

Marine Services Unit

Office of Aviation

Parkway Administration

Poison Information and Education

Police Training Commission

Racing Commission

State Board of Medical Examiners

State House

State Police Communications Bureau

State Police Explosive Disposal

State Police Laboratories

State Police Training Bureau

State Ranger

Treasury Taxation Office

Turnpike Administration

Youth Correctional Institutions Division of Operations

FEDERAL AND SPECIAL PROGRAMS

Air Force Special Investigation

Alcohol, Tobacco and Firearms

Bridge Commission

College and University Police

Defense Criminal Investigation Service

Defense Investigation Service

Department of Commerce

Department of Defense

Department of Health and Human Services

Department of the Navy

Drug Enforcement Administration

EMS Helicopter Response Program

Explosive Ordinance Detachments

Federal Bureau of Investigation

General Services Administration

Internal Revenue Criminal Investigation Division

Internal Revenue Inspection Service

Military Police

National Insurance Crime Bureau

Office of Emergency Medical Services (Mobile Intensive Care Units)

Port Authority

Railroad Police

U.S. Attorney's Office

U.S. Coast Guard

U.S. Customs Service

U.S. Department of Agriculture

U.S. Department of the Interior

U.S. Department of Labor

U.S. Department of State

U.S. Department of Transportation

U.S. District Court Pretrial Service

U.S. District Court Probation

U.S. Environmental Protection Agency

U.S. Homeland Security/Citizenship and Immigration Services

U.S. Marshals Service

U.S. Nuclear Regulatory Commission

U.S. Postal Inspection Services

U.S. Secret Service

U.S. Securities and Exchange Commission

U.S. Department of Veterans Affairs

Waterfront Commission

Chapter 6

CORRECTIONAL INTERNSHIPS

INTRODUCTION

The corrections portion of the criminal justice system serves several purposes:

1. To punish offenders
2. To rehabilitate the wrongdoer
3. To deter potential offenders
4. To provide a safe environment for the public

FIGURE 6.1

© Joseph Sohm/Shutterstock.com

CHAPTER OUTLINE

This chapter will cover:

1. Correctional Statistics
2. Conditions and Employment
3. Diversity among Corrections Workers
4. Levels of Correctional Employment
5. Privatization of Corrections
6. Special Programs
7. Parole Programs
8. State Corrections Departments
9. Federal and Special Corrections

CORRECTIONAL STATISTICS

The national crime rate has dropped since the early 1990s; however, the number of persons in correctional systems continues to increase. The increase can be examined in the federal, state, and local levels. The Bureau of Justice Statistics reveals the following:

1. The national incarceration rate has more than doubled between 1986 and 1998.
2. U.S. prisons and jails held a record 1.8 million inmates in 1998. This represents a 4.4% increase (or 76,700 inmates) over 1997.
3. The total sentenced population in federal correctional facilities has more than tripled between 1986 and 1998.
4. The number of women in prison has more than tripled between 1985 and 1997, rising to 138,000.
5. The total number of juveniles held in public correctional facilities rose 47% between 1983 and 1995.

CONDITIONS AND EMPLOYMENT

The trends translate into significant employment growth for correctional professionals of all types—from correctional officers to parole and probation officers to social workers. The Bureau of Labor Statistics ranks corrections officers in the top 20 of all occupations for projected numerical job growth between 1996 and 2006. The Bureau predicts that over 100,000 new corrections officers' positions will be created during the ten-year span.

The employment opportunities for correctional officers are expected to be favorable through the year 2006. The need to replace correctional officers who transfer to other occupations or leave the labor force, coupled with rising employment demand, will generate many thousands of job openings each year.

Employment of correctional officers is expected to increase faster than the average for all occupations throughout the year 2006 as additional officers are hired to supervise and control a growing inmate population.

Finally, layoffs of correctional officers are rare because security must be maintained in correctional institutions at all times.

- The total number of prisoners held by the state and federal correctional authorities in by the end of 2014 (1,561,500) had decreased by 1% (15,400).
- This was both the smallest total prison population since 2005 as well as the second largest decline in more than 35 years.
- The federal prison population decreased by 2.5% (5,300 inmates).
- The number of women in prison who were sentenced to serve more than one year increased by 2% (1,900), raising the total from 104,300 in 2013 to 106,200 in 2014. This is the largest number of female prisoners since 2009.
- Females account for approximately 7% of the total prison population.
- There was a decline in the Bureau of Prisons population due to admissions being 5% fewer (2,800) than the previous year.
- Seven states housed at least 20% of their inmate population in private prison facilities.
- 131,300 inmates total were held in private prison facilities in 30 states and the Bureau of Prisons showed a decrease in inmates of 2100 from 2013 to 2014. Therefore, in 2014 there were 2100 less inmates.

- Since 1999–2014, the size of private prison population grew 90% (69,000-131,300).
- 471 people per 100,000 residents of all ages were imprisoned.
- 612 people per 100,000 residents age 18 or older were imprisoned.

DIVERSITY AMONG CORRECTIONS WORKERS

The Bureau of Justice Statistics reveals that of the 347,320 individuals employed in correctional facilities in 1995, 63% or (220,982 individuals), worked in custody and securities.

The male/female distribution statistics for corrections employees are comparable to those in law enforcement. In 1995, females made up 28.9% of the employees in correctional facilities. The federal correctional facilities reveal 22.1% of their workers were females who served in the capacity of custody/security personnel.

African-Americans comprise 29.2% of the correctional institution officers employed nationwide. The Bureau of Labor Statistics states that the corrections professions ranks fourth among occupations held by African-Americans.

Census of State and Federal Correctional Facilities, 2005

http://www.bjs.gov/index.cfm?ty=pbdetail&iid=530

Between the 2000 and the 2005 censuses, the number of correctional employees rose 3%, resulting in a higher inmate-to-staff ratio in the latter year.

While the stock of minimum security facilities grew by 155 and maximum security facilities rose by 40 between 2000 and 2005, the number of medium security facilities declined by 42.

Number of Inmates, Employees, and Inmate-To-Staff Ratios in Correctional Facilities Under State Or Federal Authority, June 30, 2000, And December 30, 2005

http://www.bjs.gov/index.cfm?ty=pbdetail&iid=1684

There are about 445,000 employees who were working in state and federal correctional facilities at year end 2005.

Male employees out numbered female employees by a ratio of 2 to 1.

The largest difference in staff by gender was among correctional officers in federal facilities. In federal facilities, 87% of correctional officers were men and 13% were women.

The smallest difference—52% men and 48% women—was among the total workforce in private facilities.

LEVELS OF CORRECTIONAL EMPLOYMENT

Like law enforcement and courts, corrections are divided into an adult and a juvenile system.

The levels of corrections officers are divided into:

1. State Department of Corrections
2. Federal Department of Corrections
3. County Department of Corrections

The basic information regarding the six common correctional positions will be discussed subsequently.

CORRECTIONAL COUNSELOR

DESCRIPTION

Evaluate prison inmates' cases, examine counseling needs for rehabilitation; develop training and treatment programs (including substance abuse); and prepare case reports for the U.S. Parole Commission.

REQUIREMENTS

- U.S. citizen
- Drug screening
- Not to exceed 37 years of age
- Bachelor's degree and graduate education in behavioral science
- Counseling abilities
- Written and verbal communication skills

CONTACT INFORMATION

Contact your state department of corrections for state employer opportunities. For federal opportunities contact: The Federal Bureau of Prisons (www.bop.gov).

Mid-Atlantic Regional Office: (303) 317-3211
North Central Regional Office: (913) 551-1193
Northeast Regional Office: (800) 787-2749
South Central Region: (800) 726-4473
Southeast Region: (888) 789-1022)
Western Region: (925) 803-4700

National Institute of Corrections
320 First Street NW
Washington, DC 20534
(800) 995-6423
www.nicic.org/inst/

American Correctional Association
4380 Forbes Boulevard
Lanham, MD 20706
(800) 222-5646

CORRECTIONAL OFFICER

DESCRIPTION

Corrections officers are responsible for monitoring arrestees awaiting trial and those who have been imprisoned. The duties include monitoring activities of prisoners, enforcing rules and maintaining order, and inspecting correctional facilities and prisoners for illegal substances. There were 320,000 correctional officers employed in 1996 across the nation.

REQUIREMENTS

- Eighteen years of age
- U.S. citizen
- Possess a high school diploma or equivalent
- No prior felony conviction

The Federal Bureau of Prisons requires one of the following in order to obtain a GS-5 level:

- Bachelor's degree
- Three years' work experience
- Undergraduate experience and work experience that equals that of three years

CONTACT INFORMATION

Contact your state department of corrections for state opportunities.

Federal opportunities can be pursued by contacting the Federal Bureau of Prisons. www.bop.gov. Also see prior section for regions and contact information for regional offices.

PAROLE OFFICER

DESCRIPTION

A parole officer is responsible for the legal custody of offenders after they are released from incarceration. A parole officer makes sure offenders abide by the conditions of their release to parole. Parole officers provide counseling and support to help parolees reenter society. Their duties include the educating offenders on parole guidelines, monitoring parolee behavior by direct contact or indirectly by utilizing modern technology—electronic reporting, phone calls and e-mail.

REQUIREMENTS

- Bachelor's degree or prior experience in parole or probation
- U.S. citizen
- Valid driver's license
- No prior felony convictions
- Written and oral examination
- Background investigation
- Drug screening

CONTACT INFORMATION

American Probation and Parole Association
The Council of State Government:
PO Box 11910
Lexington, KY 40579
(606) 244-8204
www.appa-net.org

US Office of Personnel Management
1900 E. Street NW
Washington, DC 20415
(202) 606-1800
www. Opm-gov
Job Hotline: (912) 757-3000

PROBATION OFFICER

DESCRIPTION

The probation officer is responsible for counseling and rehabilitating offenders without the use of incarceration. Probation officers evaluate crimes and offenders, make recommendations to the court and facilitate a probation agreement between the federal, state or local courts.

REQUIREMENTS

- Bachelor's degree and/or experience in probation
- U.S. citizen
- Driver's license
- Drug screening
- Medical and psychological screening

CONTACT INFORMATION

American Probation and Parole Association
Parole Association
The Council of State Governments
PO Box 11910
Lexington, KY 40579
(606) 244-8204
www.appa -net.org

SOCIAL WORKER

DESCRIPTION

The social worker helps people address and cope with their personal, social and community problems, which can include substance abuse, chronic disease, employment stress, and family dysfunction. Social workers are typically specialized in such as areas clinical/mental, policy and planning, hospital, juvenile, criminal justice (pretrial services) and occupational work.

REQUIREMENTS

- Bachelor's degree in social work from a school accredited by the Council on Social Work Education
- U.S. citizen

WARDEN

The warden is responsible for the administrative and organizational control of a designated prison through the supervision, security, and facilitation of training inmates. Duties may extend outside the institution. Within the institution, duties include enforcing rules and regulations for safety, health, and protection of both inmates and the community.

REQUIREMENTS

- Pass a background investigation
- Interview
- U.S. citizen
- Must not exceed 35 years of age

CONTACT INFORMATION

The federal employment opportunities mandate that you contact the Federal Bureau of Prisons (www.bop.gov).

PRIVATIZATION OF CORRECTIONS

There has been an increase of the privatization of correctional facilities and services. This trend will not affect the overall availability of corrections jobs, but it may impact the working conditions at individual facilities or facilities in certain states or regions.

The number of privately owned and operated correctional facilities has gone from 16,000 in 1978 to 150,000 in 2016. The states that indicate the greatest number of privately owned and operated prisons are Texas and California. The other states that utilize private operators are:

1. Connecticut
2. Mississippi
3. New Mexico

4. Idaho
5. Oklahoma
6. Utah
7. Wisconsin
8. Colorado
9. Montana

SPECIAL PROGRAMS

JUVENILE CORRECTIONS AND DRUG COURTS

The juvenile corrections and drug courts are two sub-fields of the corrections industry that have undergone significant expansion in recent years, leading to new internship opportunities.

The US Office of Juvenile Justice and Delinquency Prevention reflects an increase in the demand for juvenile corrections professionals. The total number of juveniles held in public correctional facilities has increased by 50% since the 1980s. Also juvenile arrests have increased by at least 50% since the mid 1980's.

The drug courts represent a new kind of opportunity for the intern. There are approximately five hundred (drug courts that have been implemented to address the drug problems and to combat substance abuse and related crimes.

PAROLE PROGRAMS

PAROLE AND PROBATION

Parole and probation programs have come under extensive attacks from the public and special interest groups who believe said programs put the general public at risk. The programs have been challenged since they do not effectively rehabilitate convicted criminals. There seems to be an increase of convicted criminals on probation and parole. The numbers of both have exceeded the four million mark. Therefore, the Bureau of Labor Statistics estimates an above average growth in the number of probation and parole officer positions between 1996 and 2008.

The following is a specific list for agencies within New Jersey, for the benefit of the internships at Rowan University.

© Filip Bjorkman/Shutterstock.com

FIGURE 6.2

NEW JERSEY STATE CORRECTIONAL FACILITIES

Albert C. Wagner Youth Correctional Facility
Burlington County
Ward Ave

Bordentown, NJ 08505
(609) 298-0500
http://www.prisonpro.com/content/albert-c-wagner-youth-correctional-facility

Bayside State Prison
Cumberland County
4293 Route 47
Leesburg. NJ 08327
(856) 785-0040
http://www.prisonpro.com/content/bayside-state-prison

East Jersey State Prison
Middlesex County
US Route 1 & Rahway Avenue
Rahway, NJ 07065
(732) 499-5010
http://www.prisonpro.com/content/east-jersey-state-prison

Edna Mahan Correctional Facility for Women
Hunterdon County
30 County Route 513
Clinton, NJ 08809
(908) 735-7111
http://www.prisonpro.com/content/edna-mahan-correctional-facility-women

Garden State Youth Correctional Facility
Burlington County
55 Hogback Rd
Crosswicks, NJ, 08515
(609) 298-6300
http://www.prisonpro.com/content/garden-state-youth-correctional-facility

Mid-State Correctional Facility
Burlington County
Highbridge Road
Fort Dix, NJ 08640
(609) 723-4221
http://www.prisonpro.com/content/mid-state-correctional-facility

Mountainview Youth Correctional Facility
Hunterdon County
31 Petticoat Lane
Annandale, New Jersey 08801
(908) 638-6191
http://www.prisonpro.com/content/mountainview-youth-correctional-facility

New Jersey State Prison
Mercer County
Third Street & Federal Street
Trenton, NJ 08625
(609) 292-9700
http://www.prisonpro.com/content/new-jersey-state-prison

Northern State Prison
Essex County
168 Frontage Road
Newark, New Jersey 07114
(973) 465-0068
http://www.prisonpro.com/content/northern-state-prison

Southern State Correctional Facility
Cumberland County
4295 Route 47 S
Delmont, New Jersey 08314
(856) 785-1300
http://www.prisonpro.com/content/southern-state-correctional-facility

Southwoods State Prison
Cumberland County
215 Burlington Road South
Bridgeton, New Jersey 08302
(856) 459-7000
http://www.prisonpro.com/content/south-woods-state-prison

NEW JERSEY STATE PAROLE BOARDS (OFFICES)

Central Office (Office #2)
171 Jersey Street
Trenton, NJ 08611
(609) 292-4257

District Office #1
114 Prospect Street
Passaic, NJ 07055
(973) 365-0430

District Office #3
8 Reckless Place
Red Bank. NJ 07701
(732) 741-2424

District Office #4
438 Summit Avenue
Jersey City, NJ 07306
(201) 795-8804

District Office #5
124 Halsey Street
Newark, NJ 07102
(973) 648-3278

District Office #6
210 South Broad Street
Trenton, NJ 08625
(609) 292-4383

District Office #7
2600 Mount Ephraim Avenue
Camden, NJ 08101
(856) 614-3700

District Office #8
157 West White Horse Pike
Galloway Township, NJ 08205
(609) 748-4166

District Office #9
124 Halsey Street
Newark, NJ 07102
(973) 648-2168

District Office #10
Bridgeton State Office Building
40 E. Broad St, Suite 101
Bridgeton, NJ 08302-2847
(856) 575-5588

District Office #11
506 Jersey Avenue
New Brunswick, NJ 08901
(732) 937-6253

District Office #12
114 Prospect Street
Ground Floor
Passaic, NJ 07055
(973) 977-4256

NEW JERSEY'S OFFICE OF THE COUNTY PROSECUTOR

Atlantic County
4997 Unami Boulevard
Mays Landing, New Jersey 08330
(609) 909-7800
http://www.acpo.org/index.html

Bergen County
10 Main Street
Hackensack, New Jersey 07601
(201) 646-2300
http://www.bcpo.net/go.php?display_id=100

Burlington County
Courts Facility - 2nd Floor
49 Rancocas Road
Mt. Holly, NJ 08060
(609) 265-5035
http://www.co.burlington.nj.us/262/Prosecutor

Camden County
25 North 5th Street
Camden, NJ 08102
(856) 225-8400
http://camdencountypros.org/

Cape May County
4 Moore Road DN-110,
Cape May Court House, NJ 08210
(609) 465-1135
http://www.cmcpros.net/

Cumberland County
115 Vine St.
Bridgeton, NJ 08302
(856) 453-0486
http://www.co.cumberland.nj.us/content/173/2135/default.aspx

Essex County
Veterans Courthouse
50 West Market Street
Newark, NJ 07102
(973) 621-4700
http://www.njecpo.org/

Gloucester County
70 Hunter St
Woodbury, NJ 08096
(856) 384-5500
http://www.gloucestercountynj.gov/depts/p/prosoffice/

Hudson County
595 Newark Ave.
Jersey City, NJ 07306
(201) 795-6400
http://www.hcpo.org/index.php

Hunterdon County
65 Park Avenue
Flemington, NJ 08822-0756
(908) 788-1129
http://www.co.hunterdon.nj.us/prosecutor/

Mercer County
209 South Broad Street
Trenton, NJ 08650
(609) 989-6351
http://www.mercercountyprosecutor.com/

Middlesex County
25 Kirkpatrick Street - 3rd Floor
New Brunswick, NJ 08901
(732) 745-3300
http://www.co.middlesex.nj.us/Government/Departments/PSH/Prosecutor/Pages/default.aspx

Monmouth County
132 Jerseyville Avenue
Freehold, N.J. 07728
1 (800) 533-7443
http://prosecutor.co.monmouth.nj.us/

Morris County
10 Court Street - 3rd Floor
Morristown, NJ 07960
(973) 285-6200
http://www.morrisprosecutor.org/

Ocean County
119 Hooper Ave
Toms River, NJ, 08754
(732) 929-2027
http://oceancountyprosecutor.org/

Passaic County
401 Grand Street
Paterson, NJ 07505
(973) 881-4800
http://pcponj.org/

Salem County
Fenwick Building - 2nd Floor
87 Market St.
Salem, NJ 08079-0462
(856) 935-7510 x 8333
http://www.salemcountyprosecutor.org/

Somerset County
40 North Bridge Street
Somerville, New Jersey 08876
(908) 575-3300
http://www.scpo.net/

Sussex County
19-21 High Street
Newton, NJ 07860
(973) 383-1570
http://www.sussex.nj.us/Cit-e-Access/webpage.cfm?TID=7&TPID=858

Union County
32 Rahway Avenue
Elizabeth NJ 07202
908-527-4500
http://ucnj.org/prosecutor/

Warren County
413 Second Street
Belvidere, New Jersey 07823
(908) 475-6275
http://www.wcpo-nj.us/

NEW JERSEY'S COUNTY SHERIFF'S DEPARTMENT

Atlantic County
4997 Unami Blvd.
Mays Landing, NJ 08330
(609) 625-7000
http://www.acsheriff.org/

Bergen County
10 Main Street
Hackensack, New Jersey 07601
(201) 336-3500
http://www.bcsd.us/Default.aspx

Burlington County
49 Rancocas Road - Room 210
Mount Holly, NJ 08060
(609) 265-5127
http://www.co.burlington.nj.us/130/Sheriffs-Department

Camden County
Room 100 - Courthouse
520 Market Street
Camden, New Jersey 08102
(856) 225-5470
http://www.camdencounty.com/sheriff/index.html

Cape May County
4 Moore Road, Middle
New Jersey, 08210
(609) 465-1233
http://www.cmcsheriff.net/

Cumberland County
220 North Laurel Street
Bridgeton, NJ 08302
(856) 451-4449
http://www.co.cumberland.nj.us/content/173/2137/

Essex County
50 West Market Street
Newark, NJ 07102
(973) 621-4111
http://www.essexsheriff.com/

Gloucester County
2 South Broad Street
Woodbury, NJ
(856) 384-4600
http://www.gloucestercountynj.gov/depts/s/sheriff/

Hudson County
595 Newark Ave
Jersey City, New Jersey 07306
(201) 795-6300
http://www.hudsoncountysheriff.com/

Hunterdon County
8 Court Street
Flemington, NJ 08822-2900
(908) 788-1166
http://www.co.hunterdon.nj.us/sheriff.htm

Mercer County
175 South Broad Street
Trenton, NJ 08650
(609) 989-6111
http://nj.gov/counties/mercer/officials/sheriff/

Middlesex County
701 Livingston Ave
New Brunswick, NJ 08901
(732) 745-3366
http://www.co.middlesex.nj.us/Government/Departments/PSH/Pages/Office_Sheriff.aspx

Monmouth County
2500 Kozloski Road
Freehold, NJ 07728
(732) 431-6400
http://www.mcsonj.org/

Morris County
P.O. Box 900
Morristown, NJ 07963
(973) 285-6600
http://www.mcsheriff.org/

Ocean County
120 Hooper Ave.
Toms River, NJ 08754
(732) 929-2044
http://www.co.ocean.nj.us/OCsheriff/

Passaic County
435 Hamburg Turnpike
Wayne, NJ 07470
(973) 389-5900
http://www.pcsheriff.org/

Salem County
94 Market Street
Salem County, NJ 08079
(856) 935-7510
http://www.salemcountysheriff.com/

Somerset County
20 Grove St.
Somerville, NJ 08876
(908) 231-7140
http://www.somcosheriff.org/

Sussex County
39 High Street
Newton, NJ 07860
(973) 579-0850
http://www.sussexcountysheriff.com/

Union County
10 Elizabethtown Plaza
Elizabeth, NJ 07207
(908) 527-4450
http://ucnj.org/sheriff/

Warren County
413 Second St.
Belvidere, NJ 07823
(908) 475-6309
http://wcsheriffnjus.ipower.com/home/

NEW JERSEY'S COUNTY PUBLIC DEFENDER

Atlantic County
5914 Main Street, Suite 201
Mays Landing, NJ 08330
(609) 625-9111

Bergen County
60 State Street
Hackensack, NJ 07601
(201) 996-8030

Burlington County
The Washington House
100 High Street 2nd Floor
Mount Holly, NJ 08060
(609) 518-3060

Camden County
101 Haddon Avenue, Suite 8
Camden, NJ 08103
(856) 614-3500

Cape May County
201 South Main Street
Cape May Court House, NJ 08210
(609) 465-3101

Cumberland County
14 East Commerce Street
Bridgeton, NJ 08302
(856) 453-1568

Essex County (Adult)
31 Clinton Street
Newark, NJ 07101
(973) 648-6200

Essex County (Juvenile)
31 Clinton Street, 4th Floor
(973) 648-3470

Gloucester County
65 Newton Ave., Eastwood Prof. Bldg.
Woodbury, NJ 08096
(856) 853-4188

Hudson County
438 Summit Avenue, 5th Floor
Jersey City, NJ 07306
(201) 795-8922

Hunterdon County
84 Park Avenue, Suite G-102
Flemington, NJ 08822
(908) 782-1082

Mercer County
210 South Broad Street, 2nd Floor
Trenton, NJ 08608
(609) 292-4081

Middlesex County
172A New Street
New Brunswick, NJ 08901
(732) 937-6400

Monmouth County
7 Broad Street
Freehold, NJ 07728
(732) 308-4320

Morris County
2150 Headquarters Plaza
Morristown, NJ 07960
(973) 631-6260

Ocean County
236 Main Street
Toms River, NJ 08753
(732) 286-6400

Passaic County
66 Hamilton Street, 3rd Floor
Paterson, NJ 07505
(973) 977-4150

Salem County
199 E. Broadway, 5th Floor
Salem, NJ 08079
(856) 935-2212

Somerset County
75 Veterans' Memorial Drive East
Suite 201, Somerville, NJ 08876
(908) 704-3020

Sussex County
20 East Clinton Street
Newton, NJ 07860
(973) 383-9445

Union County
65 Jefferson Street
Elizabeth, NJ 07201
(908) 820-3070

Warren County
314 Front Street
Belvidere, NJ 07823
(908) 475-5183

Public Defender Management & Administration
PO Box 850
Trenton, NJ 08625
(609) 292-7087

STATE CORRECTIONS DEPARTMENTS

ALABAMA

DEPARTMENT OF CORRECTIONS
PO Box 301501, 101 S Union St, Montgomery
36130-1501
(334) 353-3870
http://www.doc.state.al.us/

DEPARTMENT OF YOUTH SERVICES
PO Box 66, Mt. Meigs 36057-0066
(334) 215-3800
http://dys.alabama.gov/

FIGURE 6.3

ALASKA

DEPARTMENT OF CORRECTIONS
Office of the Commissioner-Juneau
240 Main St, Ste 700, Juneau 99801
(907) 465-4652
http://www.correct.state.ak.us/

DIVISION OF INSTITUTIONS
4500 Diplomacy Dr, Ste 207, Anchorage 99508-5918
(907) 269-7409
http://www.correct.state.ak.us/institutions/

DIVISION OF COMMUNITY CORRECTIONS
4500 Diplomacy Dr, Ste 207, Anchorage 99508-5918
(907) 269-7370
https://www.google.com/#q=alaska+division+of+community+corrections

DIVISION OF FAMILY AND YOUTH SERVICES
PO Box 110635, Juneau 99811-0630
(907) 465-2212
http://dhss.alaska.gov/ocs/Pages/default.aspx

ARIZONA

DEPARTMENT OF CORRECTIONS
1601 W Jefferson, Phoenix 85007
(602) 542-5497
https://corrections.az.gov/

DEPARTMENT OF JUVENILE CORRECTIONS
1624 W Adams, Phoenix 85007
(602) 542-3987
http://www.azdjc.gov/AboutADJC/AboutADJC.asp

ARKANSAS

DEPARTMENT OF CORRECTIONS
PO Box 8707, Pine Bluff 71611-8707
(870) 267-6200
http://adc.arkansas.gov/Pages/default.aspx

DEPARTMENT OF COMMUNITY PUNISHMENT
105 West Capitol, 2nd Floor, Two Union National Plaza, Little Rock 72201
(501) 682-9510
http://www.dcc.arkansas.gov/Pages/default.aspx

DEPARTMENT OF HUMAN SERVICES
Donaghey Plaza W, PO Box 1437, Slot 344, Little Rock 72203-1437
http://humanservices.arkansas.gov/Pages/default.aspx

CALIFORNIA

YOUTH AND ADULT CORRECTIONAL AGENCY
1100 11th St, Ste 4000, Sacramento 95814
(916) 323-6001
http://www.dof.ca.gov/html/Budget_05-06/Budget/5210.pdf

DEPARTMENT OF CORRECTIONS
1515 S St, PO Box 942883, Sacramento 94283-0001
(916) 445-7688
http://www.cdc.state.ca.us

PAROLE AND COMMUNITY SERVICES DIVISION
1515 S St, Rm 212N, Sacramento 95814
(916) 323-0576
http://www.cdcr.ca.gov/Parole/

DEPARTMENT OF THE YOUTH AUTHORITY
4241 Williamsbourgh Dr, Sacramento 95823
(916) 262-1467
http://www.cya.ca.gov

PAROLE SERVICES AND COMMUNITY CORRECTIONS
(916) 262-1363
http://www.cdcr.ca.gov/Parole/Public_Officers_and_Regional_Offices/

COLORADO

DEPARTMENT OF CORRECTIONS
2862 S Circle Dr, Ste 400, Colorado Springs 80906-4195
(719) 579-9580
https://www.colorado.gov/cdoc/

DIVISION OF ADULT PAROLE SUPERVISION
10403 W Colfax, Ste 7000, Lakewood 80215
(303) 238-5967
https://www.colorado.gov/pacific/cdoc/adult-parole

DIVISION OF COMMUNITY CORRECTIONS
12157 W Cedar Drive, Lakewood 80228
(303) 985-9805
https://sites.google.com/a/state.co.us/dcj-community-corrections/home/contact-us

DEPARTMENT OF HUMAN SERVICES
1575 Sherman St, 8th Fl, Denver 80203-1714
(303) 866-5096
http://www.colorado.gov/apps/jboss/cdhs/childcare/lookup/index.jsf

DIVISION OF YOUTH CORRECTIONS
4255 S Knox Ct, Denver 80236-3195
(303) 866-7345
http://www.cdns.state.co.us/dyc/home.html

CONNECTICUT

DEPARTMENT OF CORRECTIONS
24 Wolcott Hill Rd, Wethersfield 06109-1152
(860) 692-7482
http://www.state.ct.us/doc

OFFICE OF ADULT PROBATION
2275 Silas Deane Hwy, Rocky Hill 06067
(860) 529-1316
http://www.jud.ct.gov/directory/directory/adultprob.htm

DEPARTMENT OF CHILDREN AND FAMILIES
505 Hudson St, Hartford 06106
(860) 550-6300
http://www.state.ct.us/dcf

DELAWARE

DEPARTMENT OF CORRECTIONS
245 McKee Rd, Dover 19904
(302) 739-5601
http://www.state.de.us/correct/ddoc/default,htm

BUREAU OF COMMUNITY CORRECTIONS
(302) 739-5601
https://www.denvergov.org/content/denvergov/en/department-of-safety/alternative-corrections/
community-corrections/residential-programs.html

DEPARTMENT OF SERVICES FOR CHILDREN, YOUTH, AND THEIR FAMILIES
1825 Faukland Rd, Wilmington 19805
(302) 633-2500
http://jeffco.us/human-services/family-children-youth/

DISTRICT OF COLUMBIA

DEPARTMENT OF CORRECTIONS
1923 Vermont Ave NW, Washington 20001
(202) 673-7316
https://www.vinelink.com/vinelink/siteInfoAction.do?siteId=9900

SOCIAL SERVICES DIVISION
DC Superior Court, 409 E St NW, Washington 20001
(202) 508-1800

DEPARTMENT OF HUMAN SERVICES
609 H St NE, Washington 20002
(202) 698-4600

FLORIDA

DEPARTMENT OF CORRECTIONS
2601 Blair Stone Rd, Tallahassee 32399-2500
(850) 488-7480
www.dc.state.fl.us

DEPARTMENT OF JUVENILE JUSTICE
2737 Centerview Dr, Knight Bldg, Tallahassee 32399-3100
(850) 921-0904
http://www.dij.state.fl.us

GEORGIA

DEPARTMENT OF CORRECTIONS
Floyd Bldg, Twin Towers E, Ste 866, 2 Martin Luther King Jr Dr SE, Atlanta 30334
(404) 656-6002
gdccommish@dcor.state.ga.us

DEPARTMENT OF JUVENILE JUSTICE
2 Peachtree St, 5th Fl, Atlanta 30303
(404) 657-2401
http://www.doas.state.ga.us/Departments/DJJ

HAWAII

DEPARTMENT OF PUBLIC SAFETY (CORRECTIONS)
919 Ala Moana Blvd, Honolulu 96814
(808) 587-1350
http://www.state.hi.us/icsd/psd/psd.html

COMMUNITY CORRECTIONAL CENTERS DIVISION
Hawaii Community Correctional Center, 60 Punahele St, Hilo 96720
(808) 933-0428

IDAHO

DEPARTMENT OF CORRECTIONS
1299 N Orchard St, Ste 110, Boise 83706
(208) 658-2000
http://www.corr.state.id.us

DEPARTMENT OF JUVENILE CORRECTIONS
400 N 10th, 2nd Fl, PO Box 83720, Boise 83720-0285
(208) 334-5102
http://www.djc.state.id.us

ILLINOIS

DEPARTMENT OF CORRECTIONS
1301 Concordia Ct, PO Box 19277, Springfield 62794-9277
(217) 522-2666
http://www.idoc.state.il.us

COMMUNITY SERVICES DIVISION
1301 Concordia Ct, PO Box 19277, Springfield 62794-9277
(217) 522-2666

DEPARTMENT OF CORRECTIONS
2700 S California Ave, Chicago 60608
(773) 869-2859

ADULT PROBATION DEPARTMENT
69 W Washington, Ste 2000, Chicago 60602
(312) 603-0258

INDIANA

DEPARTMENT OF CORRECTIONS
Indiana Government Center South, 302 W Washington St, Rm E334, Indianapolis 46204-2278
(317) 232-5715
http://www.state.in.us/indcorrection

DIVISION OF JUVENILE SERVICES
(317) 232-1746
http://www.state.in.us/fssa/HTML/PROGRAMS/za.html

IOWA

DEPARTMENT OF CORRECTIONS
420 Keo Way, Des Moines 50309
(515) 242-5703
http://www.sos.state.ia.us/register/r4/r4corre2.htm

DEPARTMENT OF HUMAN SERVICES
Hoover State Office Bldg, Des Moines 50319
(515) 281-5452

KANSAS

DEPARTMENT OF CORRECTIONS
Landon State Office Bldg, 4th Fl, 900 SW Jackson, Topeka 66612-1284
(785) 296-3317
http://www.ink.org/public/kdoc

DIVISION OF COMMUNITY AND FIELD SERVICES
(785) 296-4520

JUVENILE JUSTICE AUTHORITY
Jayhawk Walk, 714 SW Jackson, Ste 300, Topeka 66603
(785) 296-4213
http://www.ink.org/public/kjja

KENTUCKY

DEPARTMENT OF CORRECTIONS
PO Box 2400, Frankfort 40601-2400
(502) 564-4726

ADULT INSTITUTIONS
(502) 564-2220

COMMUNITY SERVICES AND LOCAL FACILITIES
(502) 564-7023

DEPARTMENT OF JUVENILE JUSTICE
1025 Capital Center Dr, 3rd Fl, Frankfort 40601
(502) 573-2738
http://www.jus.state.ky.us/djj

LOUISIANA

CORRECTIONS SERVICES
PO Box 94304, Capitol Station, Baton Rouge 70804-9304
(225) 342-5723

DIVISION OF PROBATION AND PAROLE
504 Mayflower St, Baton Rouge 70802
(225) 342-6609

DIVISION OF YOUTH SERVICES-PROBATION SERVICES
Division of Youth Services, PO Box 94304, Baton Rouge 70804-9304
(225) 342-2642

MAINE

DEPARTMENT OF CORRECTIONS
State House Station 111, Augusta 04333
(207) 287-4360
http://www.state.me.us/corrections/homepage

DIVISION OF PROBATION AND PAROLE
State House Station 111, Augusta 04333
(207) 287-4384

MARYLAND

DEPARTMENT OF PUBLIC SAFETY AND CORRECTIONAL SERVICES
Ste 1000, 300 E Joppa Rd, Towson 21286-3020
(410) 339-5000
http://www.dpscs.state.md.us/doc

DIVISION OF CORRECTIONS
6776 Reisterstown Rd, Ste 310, Baltimore 21215-2342
(410) 285-3300

DIVISION OF PAROLE AND PROBATION
6776 Reisterstown Rd, Ste 305, Baltimore 21215-2349
(410) 764-4274

DEPARTMENT OF JUVENILE JUSTICE
One Center Plaza, 120 W Fayette St, Baltimore 21201
(410) 230-3100
http://www.djj.state.md.us

MASSACHUSETTS

EXECUTIVE OFFICE OF PUBLIC SAFETY
John W. McCormick State Office Bldg, 1 Ashburton Pl, Rm 2133, 21st Fl, Boston 02108
(617) 727-7775

DEPARTMENT OF CORRECTIONS
Central Headquarters, 50 Maple St, Ste 3, Milford 01757
(508) 422-3348
http://www.magnet.state.ma.us/doc/

OFFICE OF THE COMMISSIONER OF PROBATION
One Ashburton Pl, Rm 405, Boston 02108
(617) 727-5300

EXECUTIVE OFFICE OF HEALTH AND HUMAN SERVICES
One Ashburton Pl, Rm 1109, Boston 02108
(617) 727-7600

MICHIGAN

DEPARTMENT OF CORRECTIONS
Grandview Plaza Bldg, PO Box 30003, Lansing 48909
(517) 373-0720

OFFICE OF COMMUNITY CORRECTIONS
PO Box 30003, Lansing 48909
(517) 373-0415

CHILD AND FAMILY SERVICES ADMINISTRATION
(517) 335-6158

MINNESOTA

DEPARTMENT OF CORRECTIONS
1450 Energy Park Dr, Ste 200, St. Paul 55108-5219
(651) 642-0282
http://www.corr.state.mn.us

PROBATION, PAROLE, AND SUPERVISED RELEASE OFFICES
1450 Energy Park Dr, Ste 200, St. Paul 55108-5219
(651) 603-0181

MISSISSIPPI

DEPARTMENT OF CORRECTIONS
723 N President St, Jackson 39202-3097
(601) 359-5600
http://www.mdoc.state.ms.us/mdoc/Default/htm

COMMUNITY SERVICES DIVISION
723 N President St, Jackson 39202
(601) 359-5600

DIVISION OF YOUTH SERVICES
PO Box 352, Jackson 39205
(601) 359-4972
http://www.state.ms.us/dys.html

COMMUNITY SERVICES DIVISION
(601) 359-4955

MISSOURI

DEPARTMENT OF CORRECTIONS
PO Box 236, 2729 Plaza Dr, Jefferson City 65102-0236
(573) 751-2389
http://www.corrections.state.mo.us

DEPARTMENT OF SOCIAL SERVICES
Broadway Bldg, Jefferson City 65101
(573) 751-4815

DIVISION OF YOUTH SERVICES
PO Box 447, 5th Fl, Broadway Bldg, Jefferson City 65102-0447
(573) 751-3324
http://www.dss.state.mo.us/dys.htm

MONTANA

DEPARTMENT OF CORRECTIONS
1539 11th Ave, PO Box 201301, Helena 59620-1301
(406) 444-3930

JUVENILE CORRECTIONS
Department of Corrections, 1539 11th Ave, Helena 59620-1301
(406) 232-1377

NEBRASKA

DEPARTMENT OF CORRECTIONAL SERVICES
PO Box 94661, Lincoln 68509-4661
(402) 471-2654
http://www.corrections.state.ne.us

HEALTH AND HUMAN SERVICES AGENCY-PROTECTION AND SAFETY DIVISION
PO Box 95044, Lincoln 68509-5044
(402) 471-8410

NEBRASKA PROBATION SYSTEM
PO Box 98910, Lincoln 68509
(402) 471-4928

NEVADA

DEPARTMENT OF PRISONS
PO Box 7011, Carson City 89702-7011
(775) 887-3216

DIVISION OF PAROLE AND PROBATION
1445 Hot Springs Rd, Ste 104, Carson City 89710
(775) 687-5040

DIVISION OF CHILD AND FAMILY SERVICES
711 E 5th St, Carson City 99710
(775) 684-4429

YOUTH CORRECTIONS
620 Belrose, Ste C, Las Vegas 89107-2234
(702) 486-5095

NEVADA YOUTH PAROLE BUREAU
620 Belrose, Ste C, Las Vegas 89158
(702) 486-5080
http://www.state.nv.us/defs/page21.html

NEW HAMPSHIRE

DEPARTMENT OF CORRECTIONS
PO Box 1806, Concord 03302-1806
(603) 271-5600
http://www.state.nh.us

DIVISION OF FIELD SERVICES
105 Pleasant St, 3rd Fl, Box 1806, Concord 03302-1806
(603) 271-5652

DEPARTMENT OF YOUTH DEVELOPMENT SERVICES
1056 N River Rd, Manchester 03104-1998
(603) 625-5471

NEW JERSEY

DEPARTMENT OF CORRECTIONS
PO Box 863, Trenton 08625-0863
(609) 292-9340
http://www.state.nj.us/corrections

JUVENILE JUSTICE COMMISSION
840 Bear Tavern Rd, PO Box 107, Trenton 08625-0107
(609) 530-5200

DEPARTMENT OF LAW AND PUBLIC SAFETY
PO Box 107, Trenton 08625-0107
(609) 530-5200

NEW MEXICO

CORRECTIONS DEPARTMENT
PO Box 27116, Hwy 14, Santa Fe 87502-0116
(505) 827-8709
http://www.state.nm.us/corrections

ADULT PRISONS DIVISION
PO Box 27116, Santa Fe 87502-0116
(505) 827-8638

PROBATION AND PAROLE DIVISION
PO Box 27116, Santa Fe 87502-0116
(505) 827-8830

CHILDREN, YOUTH AND FAMILIES DEPARTMENT
PO Drawer 5160, Santa Fe 87502-5160
(505) 827-7602
http://www.cyfabq.cyfd.state.nm.us

JUVENILE JUSTICE DIVISIOIN
(505) 827-7629

JUVENILE REINTEGRATION CENTERS
300 San Mateo Blvd, Ste 410, Albuquerque 87108
(505) 841-2947

NEW YORK

DEPARTMENT OF CORRECTIONAL SERVICES
1220 Washington Ave, Bldg 2, Albany 12226-2050
(518) 457-8134

DIVISION OF PAROLE
97 Central Ave, Albany 12206
(518) 473-9672

OFFICE OF CHILDREN AND FAMILY SERVICES
52 Washington St, Rensselaer 12144-2735
(518) 473-8437
http://www.dfy.state.ny.us

DIVISION OF PROBATION AND CORRECTIONAL ALTERNATIVES
4 Tower Pl, 3rd Fl, Albany 12203
(518) 485-2395

DEPARTMENT OF CORRECTIONS
60 Hudson St, 6th Fl, New York 10013-4393
(212) 266-1212

DEPARTMENT OF PROBATION
115 Leonard St, New York 10013
(212) 442-4523

NORTH CAROLINA

DEPARTMENT OF CORRECTIONS
214 W Jones St, MSC 4201, Raleigh 27699-4201
(919) 733-4926
http://www.doc.state.nc.us

DIVISION OF PRISONS
831 W Morgan St, MSC 4260, Raleigh 27699-4260
(919) 733-3226

DIVISION OF COMMUNITY CORRECTIONS
2020 Yonkers Rd, 4250 MSC, Raleigh 27669-4250
(919) 716-3100

OFFICE OF JUVENILE JUSTICE
410 S Salisbury St, 1801 MSC, Raleigh 27993-1801
(919) 733-3388

NORTH DAKOTA

DEPARTMENT OF CORRECTIONS AND REHABILITATION
PO Box 1898, Bismarck 58502-1898
(701) 328-6390
http://www.state.nd.us/docr

DIVISION OF ADULT SERVICES
(701) 253-3660

FIELD SERVICES DIVISION, ADULT SERVICES
PO Box 5521, Bismarck 58506-5521
(701) 328-6190

DIVISION OF JUVENILE SERVICES
PO Box 1898, Bismarck 58502-1898
(701) 328-6390

OHIO

DEPARTMENT OF REHABILITATION AND CORRECTION
1050 Freeway Dr N, Columbus 43229
(614) 752-1164
http://www.drc.state.oh.us

ADULT PAROLE AUTHORITY
(614) 752-1254

BUREAU OF COMMUNITY SANCTIONS
(614) 752-1188

BUREAU OF ADULT DETENTION
(614) 752-1065

OFFICE OF VICTIM SERVICES
(614) 728-9947

DEPARTMENT OF YOUTH SERVICES
51 N High St, Columbus 43215-3098
(614) 466-8783
http://www.state.oh.us/dys

OKLAHOMA

DEPARTMENT OF CORRECTIONS
3400 Martin Luther King Ave, Oklahoma City 73136-4298
(405) 425-2500
http://www.doc.state.ok.us

DIVISION OF COMMUNITY SENTENCING
2200 N Classen Blvd, Ste 1900, Oklahoma City 73106-5811
(405) 523-3075

DIVISION OF PROBATION AND PAROLE/COMMUNITY CORRECTIONS
(405) 218-4200

OFFICE OF JUVENILE AFFAIRS
PO Box 268812, 3812 N Santa Fe, Ste 400, Oklahoma City 73126-8812
(405) 530-2800
http://www.state.ok.us/~oja

OREGON

DEPARTMENT OF CORRECTIONS
2575 Center St NE, Salem 97301-6637
(503) 945-0920
http://www.doc.state.or.us

BOARD OF PAROLE AND POST-PRISON SUPERVISION (FT)
2575 Center St NE, Salem 97310-0470
(503) 945-0900

OREGON YOUTH AUTHORITY (OYA)
530 Center St NE, Ste 200, Salem 97301-3765
(503) 373-7205
http://www.oya.state.or.us

PENNSYLVANIA

DEPARTMENT OF CORRECTIONS
Box 598, Camp Hill 17001-0598
(717) 975-4860
http://www.cor.state.pa.us

BUREAU OF COMMUNITY CORRECTIONS
PO Box 598, Camp Hill 17001-0598
(717) 731-7147

BOARD OF PROBATION AND PAROLE (FT)
1101 S Front St, Ste 5000, Harrisburg 17104-2537
(717) 787-5100

RHODE ISLAND

DEPARTMENT OF CORRECTIONS
40 Howard Ave, Cranston 02920
(401) 462-2611
http://www.doc.state.ri.us

ADULT PROBATION AND PAROLE
J. Joseph Garrahy Judicial Complex, One Dorrance Plaza, Providence 02903
(401) 458-3033

ADULT CORRECTIONAL INSTITUTIONS
(401) 462-5163

DEPARTMENT OF CHILDREN, YOUTH AND FAMILIES
610 Mt. Pleasant Ave, Providence 02908-1935
(401) 222-5307
http://www.state.ri.us/manual/data/queries/stdept_.idc?id=20

SOUTH CAROLINA

DEPARTMENT OF CORRECTIONS
PO Box 21787, 4444 Broad River Rd, Columbia 29221-1787
(803) 896-8555
http://www.state.sc.us/doc

DEPARTMENT OF PROBATION, PAROLE AND PARDON SERVICES
PO Box 50666, 2221 Devine St, Ste 600, Columbia 29250
(803) 734-9220
http://www.state.sc.us/ppp

DEPARTMENT OF JUVENILE JUSTICE
PO Box 21069, 4900 Broad River Rd, Columbia 29221-1069
(803) 896-9791
http://www.state.sc.us/djj

SOUTH DAKOTA

DEPARTMENT OF CORRECTIONS
3200 E Hwy 34, c/o 500 E Capitol Ave, Pierre 57501-5070
(605) 773-3478
http://www.state.sd.us/state/executive/corrections

TENNESSEE

DEPARTMENT OF CORRECTIONS
Rachel Jackson Bldg, 320 Sixth Ave N, 4th Fl, Nashville 37243-0465
(615) 741-1000
http://www.state.tn.us/correction

COMMUNITY CORRECTIONS
(615) 741-3141

DIVISION OF FIELD SERVICES
Ste 1513 Parkway Towers, 404 James Robertson Pkwy, Nashville 37243-0850
(615) 741-3141

DEPARTMENT OF CHILDREN'S SERVICES
Cordell Hull Bldg, 436 6th Ave N, Nashville 37243-1290
(615) 741-9701
http://www.state.tn.us/youth

TEXAS

TEXAS DEPARTMENT OF CRIMINAL JUSTICE
PO Box 99, Spur 59 off Hwy 75 North, Huntsville 77342-0099
(936) 437-2101
http://www.tdcj.state.tx.us

COMMUNITY JUSTICE ASSISTANCE DIVISION (CJAD)
PO Box 12427, Capitol Station, Austin 78701
(512) 305-9300

STATE JAIL DIVISION
PO Box 13084, Austin 78711
(512) 463-7663

INSTITUTIONAL DIVISION
PO Box 99, Huntsville 77342-0099
(936) 437-2169

PAROLE DIVISION
PO Box 13401, Capitol Station, Austin 78711
(512) 406-5401

PROGRAMS AND SERVICES DIVISION
PO Box 99, Huntsville 77342-0099
(936) 437-2180

TEXAS YOUTH COMMISSION
4900 N Lamar, PO Box 4260, Austin 78765
(512) 424-6001
http://www.tyc.state.tx.us/index.html

JUVENILE PROBATION COMMISSION (TJPC)
PO Box 13547, Austin 78711-3547
(512) 424-6682
http://www.tipc.state.tx.us

UTAH

DEPARTMENT OF CORRECTIONS
6100 S 300 E, Salt Lake City 84107
(801) 265-5500
http://www.cr.ex.state.ut.us

DIVISION OF UTAH CORRECTIONAL INDUSTRIES
PO Box 250. Draper 84020
(801) 576-7700

DIVISION OF ADULT PROBATION AND PAROLE
6100 S 300 E, Salt Lake City 84107
(801) 265-5500

VERMONT

DEPARTMENT OF CORRECTIONS
103 S Main St, Waterbury 05671-1001
(802) 241-2442

DEPARTMENT OF SOCIAL AND REHABILITATION SERVICES
103 S Main St, Osgood Bldg, 3rd Fl, Waterbury 05671-2401
(802) 241-2100

VIRGINIA

DEPARTMENT OF CORRECTIONS
PO Box 26963, 6900 Atmore Dr, Richmond 23261-6963
(804) 674-3119
http://www.cns.state.va.us/doc

DEPARTMENT OF JUVENILE JUSTICE
PO Box 1110, Richmond 23218-1110
(804) 371-0700

WASHINGTON

DEPARTMENT OF CORRECTIONS
PO Box 41100, Olympia 98504-1100
(360) 753-1573
http://www.wa.gov/doc

DEPARTMENT OF CORRECTIONS,
OFFICE OF CORRECTIONAL OPERATIONS
PO Box 41118, Olympia 98504-1118
(360) 753-1502

JUVENILE REHABILITATION ADMINISTRATION
PO Box 45045, Olympia 98504-5045
(360) 902-7804

WEST VIRGINIA

DIVISION OF CORRECTIONS
112 California Ave, Bldg 4, Rm 300, Charleston 25305
(304) 558-2036

DIVISION OF JUVENILE SERVICES
1200 Quarrier St, 2nd Fl, Charleston 25301
(304) 558-6029

WISCONSIN

DEPARTMENT OF CORRECTIONS
PO Box 7925, 149 E Wilson St, Madison 53707-7925
http://www.badger.state.wi.us/agencies/doc

DIVISION OF JUVENILE CORRECTIONS
149 E Wilson St, PO Box 8930, Madison 53708-8930
(608) 267-9507
http://www.badger.state.wi.us/agencies/doc/html/djc.html

WYOMING

DEPARTMENT OF CORRECTIONS
700 W 21st St, Cheyenne 82002-3427
(307) 777-7208
http://www.state.wy.us/~corr/corrections.html

DIVISION OF FIELD SERVICES
700 W 21st St, Cheyenne 82002
(307) 777-7208

DEPARTMENT OF FAMILY SERVICES
Hathaway Bldg, Rm 318, Cheyenne 82002
(307) 777-5994

FEDERAL AND SPECIAL CORRECTIONS

FEDERAL BUREAU OF PRISONS

FEDERAL BUREAU OF PRISONS
320 Fist St NW, HOLC Bldg, Rm 654,
Washington, DC 20534
(202) 307-3250
http://www.bop.gov

COMMUNITY CORRECTIONS AND
DETENTION DIVISION
(202) 514-8585
http://www.kingcounty.gov/courts/detention/
community_corrections.aspx

CORRECTIONAL PROGRAMS DIVISION
(202) 307-3226
https://www.bop.gov/about/agency/org_cpd.jsp

FIGURE 6.4

MID-ATLANTIC (ANNAPOLIS JUNCTION, MD)
Junction Business Park, 10010 Junction Dr, Ste 100-N, Annapolis Junction, MD 20701
(301) 317-3100
http://www.vermeermidatlantic.com/locations/annapolis-junction-md

NORTH CENTRAL (KANSAS CITY)
Gateway Complex Tower II, 8th Fl, 4th & State Ave, Kansas City, KS 66101-2492
(913) 621-3939
http://www.bop.gov/locations/regional_offices/ncro/

NORTHEAST (PHILADELPHIA)
U.S. Customs House, 7th Fl, 2nd & Chestnut Sts, Philadelphia, PA 19106
(215) 521-7300
http://www.phila.gov/prisons/Facilities/Pages/Curran-FromholdCorrectionalFacility.aspx

SOUTH CENTRAL (DALLAS)
4211 Cedar Springs Rd, Ste 300, Dallas, TX 75219
(214) 224-3389
http://www.dallaspolice.net/

SOUTHEAST (ATLANTA)
3800 North Camp Creek Parkway, SW, Bldg 2000, Atlanta, GA 30331-5099
(678) 686-1200
https://www.bop.gov/locations/institutions/atl/

WESTERN (DUBLIN, CA)
7950 Dublin Blvd, 3rd Fl, Dublin, CA 94568
(925) 803-4700
https://www.bop.gov/locations/institutions/dub/

UNITED STATES PENITENTIARY
3901 Klein Blvd, Lompoc, CA 93436
(805) 735-2771

UNITED STATES PENITENTIARY
PO Box 7500, 5880 State Hwy 67 S, Florence, CO 81226
(719) 784-9454

UNITED STATES PENITENTIARY
601 McDonough Blvd SE, Atlanta, GA 30315-0182
(404) 635-5100

UNITED STATES PENITENTIARY
PO Box 2000, 4500 Prison Rd, Rt 5, Marion, IL 62959
(618) 964-1441

UNITED STATES PENITENTIARY
855 Airbase Rd #1, Pollack, LA 71467
(318) 765-0007

UNITED STATES PENITENTIARY
1300 Metropolitan, Leavenworth, KS 66048
(913) 682-8700

UNITED STATES PENITENTIARY
RD #5, Penn Rd, Lewisburg, PA 17837
(570) 523-1251

UNITED STATES PENITENTIARY
Allenwood, PO Box 3500, White Deer, PA 17887
(570) 547-0963

UNITED STATES PENITENTIARY
Beaumont, PO Box 26035, Beaumont, TX 77720-6035
(409) 727-8188

FEDERAL CORRECTION COMPLEX
Admin Bldg, 846 NE 54th Terr, Coleman, FL 33521-8999
(352) 330-3003

FEDERAL CORRECTION COMPLEX
Low, 846 NE 54th Terr, Coleman, FL 33521-8999
(352) 330-3100

FEDERAL CORRECTION COMPLEX
Medium, 811 NE 54th Terr, Coleman, FL 33521-8997
(352) 330-3200

FEDERAL CORRECTION COMPLEX
Administrative, PO Box 36015, Beaumont, TX 77720-6015
(409) 727-8187

FEDERAL CORRECTION COMPLEX
Low, PO Box 26025, Beaumont, TX 77720-6025
(409) 727-8172

FEDERAL CORRECTION COMPLEX
Medium, PO Box 26045, Beaumont, TX 77720-6045
(409) 727-0101

FEDERAL CORRECTION INSTITUTION
565 E Renfroe Rd, Talladega, AL 35160
(256) 315-4100

FEDERAL CORRECTION INSTITUTION
PO Box 7000, Forrest City, AR 72336
(870) 630-6000

FEDERAL CORRECTION INSTITUTION
37900 N 45th Ave, Dept 1680, Phoenix AZ 85027-7003
(623) 465-9757

FEDERAL CORRECTION INSTITUTION
PO Box 820, Swift Trail Rd, RR 2, Safford, AZ 85548
(520) 428-6600

FEDERAL CORRECTION INSTITUTION
8901 S Wilmot Rd, Tucson, AZ 85706
(520) 574-7100

FEDERAL CORRECTION INSTITUTION
5701 8th St, Camp Parks, Dublin CA 94568
(925) 833-7500

FEDERAL CORRECTION INSTITUTION
3600 Guard Rd, Lompoc, CA 93436
(805) 736-4154

FEDERAL CORRECTION INSTITUTION
1500 Cadette Rd, PO Box 7000, Taft, CA 93268
(661) 763-2510

FEDERAL CORRECTION INSTITUTION
1299 Seaside Ave, Terminal Island, CA 90731-0207
(310) 831-8961

FEDERAL CORRECTION INSTITUTION
15115 Nisqualli Rd, Victorville, CA 92392
(760) 246-2400

FEDERAL CORRECTION INSTITUTION
PO Box 6500, 5880 State Hwy 67 S, Florence CO 81226
(719) 784-9100

FEDERAL CORRECTION INSTITUTION
Englewood, 9595 W Quincy Ave, Littleton, CO 80123
(303) 985-1566

FEDERAL CORRECTION INSTITUTION
Rt 37, Danbury, CT 06811-3099
(203) 743-6471

FEDERAL CORRECTIONAL INSTITUTION
3625 FCI Rd., Marianna, FL 32446
(850) 526-2313

FEDERAL CORRECTIONAL INSTITUTION
15801 SW 137th Ave., Miami, FL 33177
(305) 259-2100

FEDERAL CORRECTIONAL INSTITUTION
501 Capital Circle NE, Tallahassee, FL 32301-3572
(850) 878-2173

FEDERAL CORRECTIONAL INSTITUTION
2600 Hwy 301S, Jesup, GA 31599
(912) 427-0870

FEDERAL CORRECTIONAL INSTITUTION
PO Box 4000, 100 US Rt. 40, Greenville, IL 62246
(618) 664-6200

FEDERAL CORRECTIONAL INSTITUTION
2600 S Second St., PO Box 7000, Pekin, IL 61555-7000
(309) 346-8588

FEDERAL CORRECTIONAL INSTITUTION
PO Box 888, Ashland, KY 41105-0888
(606) 928-6414

FEDERAL CORRECTIONAL INSTITUTION
PO Box 3000, Rt. 8, Fox Hollow Road, Manchester, KY 40962
(606) 598-1900

FEDERAL CORRECTIONAL INSTITUTION
PO Box 5050, E Whatley Rd., Oakdale, LA 71463
(318) 335-4070

FEDERAL CORRECTIONAL INSTITUTION
14601 Burbridge Rd SE, Cumberland, MD 21502-8771
(301) 784-1000

FEDERAL CORRECTIONAL INSTITUTION
PO Box 9999, East Arkona Rd., Milan, MI 48160
(734) 439-1511

FEDERAL CORRECTIONAL INSTITUTION
Kettle River Rd, Hwy 123, Sandstone, MN 55072
(320) 245-2262

FEDERAL CORRECTIONAL INSTITUTION
PO Box 1731, 1000 University Dr SW, Waseca, MN 56093
(507) 835-8972

FEDERAL CORRECTIONAL INSTITUTION
PO Box 5050, 2225 Haley Barbour Pkwy, Yazoo City, MS 39194
(601) 751-4800

FEDERAL CORRECTIONAL INSTITUTION
PO Box 280, Hwy 698, Fairton, NJ 08320
(856) 453-1177

FEDERAL CORRECTIONAL INSTITUTION
PO Box 38, Hartford & Pointville, BLDG 5756, Ft. Dix, NJ 08640
(609) 723-1100

FEDERAL CORRECTIONAL INSTITUTION-La Tuna
PO Box 1000, 8500 Doniphan, Anthony, NM-TX 88021
(915) 886-3422

FEDERAL CORRECTIONAL INSTITUTION
PO Box 600, Two Mile Dr, Otisville, NY 10963-0600
(914) 386-5855

FEDERAL CORRECTIONAL INSTITUTION
PO Box 300, Old Ray Brook Rd, Ray Brook, NY 12977
(518) 891-5400

FEDERAL CORRECTIONAL INSTITUTION LOW
PO Box 999, Old Oxford Hwy 75, Butner, NC 27509
(919) 575-5000

FEDERAL CORRECTIONAL INSTITUTION
PO Box 1000, Old NC Hwy 75, Butner, NC 27509-1000
(919) 575-4541

FEDERAL CORRECTIONAL INSTITUTION
PO Box 89, 8730 Scroggs Rd, Elkton, OH 44415
(330) 424-7448

FEDERAL CORRECTIONAL INSTITUTION
Hwy 66 W, PO Box 1000, El Reno, OK 73036-1000
(405) 262-4875

FEDERAL CORRECTIONAL INSTITUTION
PO Box 8000, 27072 Ballston Rd, Sheridan, OR 97378-9601
(503) 843-4442

FEDERAL CORRECTIONAL INSTITUTION
McKean, PO Box 5000, Rt. 59, Big Shanty Rd, Bradford, PA 16701
(814) 362-8900

FEDERAL CORRECTIONAL INSTITUTION
PO Box 1000, RR #276, Loretto, PA 15940
(814) 472-4140

FEDERAL CORRECTIONAL INSTITUTION
Schuylkill, PO Box 730, Interstate 81 & 901 W, Minersville, PA 17954
(570) 544-7100

FEDERAL CORRECTIONAL INSTITUTION
Allenwood, Medium, PO Box 2500, Rt 15, White Deer, PA 17887
(570) 547-7950

LOW SECURITY CORRECTIONAL INSTITUTION
Allenwood, PO Box 1500, Rt., 15 White Deer, PA 17887
(570) 547-1990

FEDERAL CORRECTIONAL INSTITUTION
501 Gary Hill Rd., PO Box 723, Edgefield, SC 29824
(803) 637-1500

FEDERAL CORRECTIONAL INSTITUTION
PO Box 699, 100 Prison Rd., Estill, SC 29918
(803) 625-4607

FEDERAL CORRECTIONAL INSTITUTION
1101 John A. Denie Rd., Memphis, TN 38134-7690
(901) 372-2269

FEDERAL CORRECTIONAL INSTITUTION
PO Box 730, Hwy 95, Bastrop, TX 78602
(512) 321-3903

FEDERAL CORRECTIONAL INSTITUTION
1900 Simler Ave., Big Spring, TX 79720-7799
(915) 263-6699

FEDERAL CORRECTIONAL INSTITUTION
2113 N Hwy 175, Seagoville, TX 75159
(972) 287-2911

FEDERAL CORRECTIONAL INSTITUTION
PO Box 9500, 4001 FCI Rd., Texarkana, TX 75505-9500
(903) 838-4587

FEDERAL CORRECTIONAL INSTITUTION
PO Box 4000, 206 Thornton St., Three Rivers, TX 78071
(361) 786-3576

FEDERAL CORRECTIONAL INSTITUTION (Petersburg)
PO Box 1000, Petersburg, VA 23804-1000
(804) 733-7881

FEDERAL CORRECTIONAL INSTITUTION (Beckley)
PO Box 1280, Beaver, WV 25813
(304) 252-9758

FEDERAL CORRECTIONAL INSTITUTION
PO Box 1000, Greenbag Rd., Morgantown, WV 26507-1000
(304) 296-4416

FEDERAL CORRECTIONAL INSTITUTION
PO Box 500, off County Hwy G, Oxford, WI 53952-0500
(608) 584-5511

FEDERAL PRISON CAMPS

FEDERAL PRISON CAMP
Maxwell Air Force Base, Montgomery, AL 36112
(334) 293-2100

FEDERAL PRISON CAMP
Eglin Air Force Base, PO Box 600, Eglin, FL 32542-7606
(850) 882-8522

FEDERAL PRISON CAMP
110 Raby Ave, Pensacola, FL 32509-5127
(850) 457-1911

FEDERAL PRISON CAMP
Oakdale, PO Box 5060, Oakdale, LA 71463
(318) 335-4466

FEDERAL PRISON CAMP
PO Box 1400, Stebner Rd, Duluth, MN 55814
(218) 722-8634

FEDERAL PRISON CAMP
Seymour Johnson Air Force Base, CB 8004, Bldg 3681, Goldsboro, NC 27533-8004
(919) 735-9711

FEDERAL PRISON CAMP
Allenwood, PO Box 1000, Rt 15, Montgomery, PA 17752
(570) 547-1641

FEDERAL PRISON CAMP
PO Box 1100 Douglas Ave, Yankton, SD 57078
(605) 665-3262

FEDERAL PRISON CAMP
PO Drawer 2197, 1100 Ursuline St, Bryan, TX 77805-2197
(409) 823-1879

FEDERAL PRISON CAMP
PO Box 16300, SSG Sims Rd, Bldg 11636, El Paso, TX 79906-0300
(915) 566-1271

FEDERAL PRISON CAMP
Glen Ray Rd, Box B, Rts 3 & 12, Alderson, WV 24910-0700
(304) 445-2901

FEDERAL DETENTION CENTERS

FEDERAL DETENTION CENTER
1705 E Hanna Rd, Eloy, AZ 85231
(520) 466-4141

FEDERAL DETENTION CENTER
PO Box 019118, Miami, FL 33101-9118
(305) 982-1114

FEDERAL DETENTION CENTER
PO Box 5060, E Whatley Rd, Oakdale, LA 71463-5060
(318) 335-4466

FEDERAL DETENTION CENTER
1200 Texas Ave, Houston, TX 77052-3505
(713) 221-5400

FEDERAL DETENTION CENTER
SeaTac, PO Box 13901, Seattle, WA 98198
(206) 870-5700

U.S. PAROLE COMMISSION

U.S. PAROLE COMMISSION
Central Office, 5550 Friendship Blvd, Ste 420, Chevy Chase, MD 20815-7286
(301) 492-5990

U.S. COURTS

FEDERAL CORRECTIONS OFFICE OF THE U.S. COURTS
One Columbus Circle NE, Washington, DC 20544
(202) 502-1620

U.S. AIR FORCE

CORRECTIONS DIVISION (HQ AFSFC/SPC)
(210) 671-0788

U.S. ARMY

U.S. ARMY CORRECTIONS SYSTEM
Headquarters Department of the Army (SAMO-ODL-O), Deputy Chief of Staff for
Operations & Plans, 400 Army Pentagon, Washington, DC 20301-0400
(703) 695-8481

U.S. NAVY

CORRECTIONS AND PROGRAMS DIVISION (NPC-84)
5720 Integrity Dr, Millington, TN 38055-8400
(901) 874-4442

U.S. MARINE CORPS

CORRECTIONS SECTION
Marine Corps Headquarters (CODE POS-40), Washington, DC 20380-1775
(703) 614-2674[12]

Chapter 7

JUDICIAL INTERNSHIPS

INTRODUCTION

This chapter presents the numerous internship opportunities within the judicial system—the courts. It commences with a view of the judicial system in the United States and the roles of the major players. It then discusses the various careers within the system that might be pursued by students who have a desire to become major players of the criminal justice system.

It is important to note the wide variety of job opportunities available within the judicial system, which is highly complex and adversarial system by nature. Within the criminal courts this adversarial system is played out as the state or government ver-

FIGURE 7.1

© aerogondo2/Shutterstock.com

sus the defendant. The judicial process is so involved and full of loopholes and technicalities that the system demands a substantial number of employees to respond to complex matters.

The chapter will disclose conditions and employment statistics. Also, the roles and functions of the paralegal, court administrator, the criminal case managers and other court positions will be briefly covered.

CONDITIONS AND EMPLOYMENT

The courts represent one of the more volatile areas of the criminal justice system. The court system includes not only one of the most competitive internship categories, but one of the most explosive in terms of overall growth rate—paralegal.

The criminal justice system is very complex and it needs a substantial number of players or participants. Once you are involved in your internship, the jobs may not seem as glamorous as they are frequently depicted in the media, but they are extremely important and provide exceptional career opportunities.

EMPLOYMENT STATISTICS

The forecast demand for paralegals, court administrators and other judicial support personnel is expected to increase a great deal from 2001 to 2010. It should be noted that while the court system must be examined as a uniform industry that responds as a single unit to economic, political and legal trends, in this context we must view each major internship category separately, and especially in the subsequent information.

JUDICIAL INTERNSHIPS

COURT ADMINISTRATOR

DESCRIPTION
Responsible for court administration and management, with regard to casework, court staffing and fiscal matters. Internships can be found at local, state, and federal levels.

REQUIREMENTS

- Bachelor's degree, often requires graduate education
- U.S. citizen

CONTACT INFORMATION

National Center for State Courts
300 Newport Avenue
Williamsburg, VA 23185
(757) 253-2000

U.S. Office of Personnel Management
1900 E. Street NW
Washington, DC 20415
(202) 606-1800
www.opm.gov
Hotline: (912) 757-3000

PARALEGAL

DESCRIPTION

Paralegals assist lawyers in doing much of the background work for cases. Responsibilities include researching laws, prior cases, investigating facts and evidence, writing legal documents and briefs, coordinating communications and maintaining records of all documents.

REQUIREMENTS

- A college degree or a paralegal certificate from a two- or four-year program may be required.
- Collegiate or work-related experience.
- To become a certified legal assistant, applicants must pass a two-day examination administered by the National Association of Legal Assistants.

CONTACT INFORMATION

Contact the local, state or federal courts in your jurisdiction, U.S. Office of Personnel Management or law firms' directories.

U.S. Office of Personnel Management
1900 G. Street NW
Washington, DC 20415
(202) 606 1800
www.opm.gov
www.usajobs.opm.gov
(job listing)
Hotline: (912) 757-3000

CRIMINAL CASE MANAGER

DESCRIPTION

Responsibilities include the investigation of accused as it relates to bail and the amount of bail. Makes recommendation for pre-trial status, and completes the presentence investigation report.

REQUIREMENTS

Bachelor's degree, often requires graduate education for the director of the criminal case manager's office or unit.

CONTACT INFORMATION

National Center for State Courts
300 Newport Avenue
Williamsburg, VA 23185
(757) 253-2000

U.S. Office of Personnel Management
1900 E. Street NW
Washington, DC 20415
(202) 606-1800
www.opm.gov
Hotline: (912) 757-3000

COURT REPORTER

DESCRIPTION

Court reporters work in courtrooms and outside the courtroom for legal and private organizations, documenting proceedings as official transcripts utilizing a stenotype machine or recording machine, which is fed into computer-aided transcriptions.

REQUIREMENTS

- Qualifying examination for state licensing, which includes testing on skills and knowledge, dictation, and transcription.
- Many states require state certification, which is a certified court reporter degree.
- Two- and four-year programs at post-secondary technical and vocational schools.

CONTACT INFORMATION

Contact the local, state or federal court in your jurisdiction. Also check the U.S. Office of Personnel Management hotline at (912) 774-2299.

National Court Reporters Association
8224 Old Courthouse road
Vienna, VA 22182
www.verbatimreporters.com

National Center for State Courts
300 Newport Avenue
Williamsburg, VA 23185
(757) 253-2000
www.ncsc.dni.us

BAILIFF

DESCRIPTION

Bailiffs are officers, usually deputy sheriffs, who are assigned to facilitate the court process. Duties of the bailiffs include maintaining order in the court and assisting in the moving of those involved in the court process, for example, defendants and the jury.

REQUIREMENTS

The bailiffs are sworn officers and will possess all of the regular requirements as for any police officer. Non-sworn bailiffs may require less education or experience than a regular police officer.

CONTACT INFORMATION

Contact the local, state, or federal court in your jurisdiction. Also check with the U.S. Office of Personnel Management hotline at (912) 774-2299.

CLERK

DESCRIPTION

The role of the clerk includes the maintaining of accurate records and ensuring that court schedules are made and enforced. It is the duty of the clerk to see that all records are properly maintained.

REQUIREMENTS

- Bachelor's degree
- Two year education of post-secondary college
- U.S. citizen

CONTACT INFORMATION

National Center for State Courts
300 Newport Avenue
Williamsburg, VA 23185
(757) 253-2000

U.S. Office of Personnel Management
1900 E. Street NW
Washington, DC 20415
(202) 606-1800
www.opm.gov
Hotline: (912) 757-3000

NEW JERSEY SPECIFIC

PUBLIC DEFENDER

Atlantic County
5914 Main Street, Suite 201
Mays Landing, NJ 08330
(609) 625-9111

Bergen County
60 State Street
Hackensack, NJ 07601
(201) 996-8030

Burlington County
100 High Street 2nd Floor
Mount Holly, NJ 08060
(609) 518-3060

Camden County
101 Haddon Avenue, Suite 8
Camden, NJ 08103
(856) 614-3500

Cape May County
201 South Main Street
Cape May Court House, NJ 08210
(609) 465-3101

Cumberland County
14 East Commerce Street
Bridgeton, NJ 08302
(856) 453-1568

Essex County
31 Clinton Street, P.O. Box 46010
Newark, NJ 07101
(973) 648-6200

Gloucester County
65 Newton Ave
Woodbury, NJ 08096
(856) 853-4188

Hudson County
438 Summit Avenue, 5th Floor
Jersey City, NJ 07306
(201) 795-8922

Hunterdon County
84 Park Avenue, Suite G-102
Flemington, NJ 08822
(908) 782-1082

Mercer County
210 South Broad Street, 2nd Floor
Trenton, NJ 08608
(908) 782-1082

Middlesex County
172A New Street
New Brunswick, NJ 08901
(732) 937-6400

Monmouth County
7 Broad Street
Freehold, NJ 07728
(732) 308-4320

Morris County
2150 Headquarters Plaza
Morristown, NJ 07960
(973) 631-6260

Ocean County
236 Main Street
Toms River, NJ 08753
(732) 286-6400

Passaic County
66 Hamilton Street, 3rd Floor
Paterson, NJ 07505
(973) 977-4150

Salem County
199 E. Broadway, 5th Floor
Salem, NJ 08079
(856) 935-2212

Somerset County
75 Veterans' Memorial Drive East
Suite 201, Somerville, NJ 08876
(908) 704-3020

Sussex County
20 East Clinton Street
Newton, NJ 07860
(973) 383-9445

Union County
65 Jefferson Street
Elizabeth, NJ 07201
(908) 820-3070

Warren County
314 Front Street
Belvidere, NJ 07823
(908) 475-5183

CRIMINAL CASE MANAGEMENT

CRIMINAL CASE MANAGEMENT OFFICES

Atlantic County
4997 Unami Blvd.
Mays Landing, NJ 08330
(609) 909-8154

Bergen County
10 Main St., Room 124
Hackensack, NJ 07601
(201) 527-2400

Burlington County
50 Rancocas Road
Mount Holly, NJ 08060
(609) 518-2565

Camden County
101 South 5th Street
Camden NJ, 08103
(856) 379-2200

Cape May County
4997 Unami Blvd.
Mays Landing, NJ 08330
(609) 909-8154

Cumberland County
60 West Broad Street
Bridgeton, NJ 08302
(856) 453-4300

Essex County
50 West Market Street
Newark, NJ 07102
(973) 776-9300

Gloucester County
70 Hunter Streets
Woodbury, NJ 08096
(856) 686-7500

Hudson County
595 Newark Avenue, Room 101
Jersey City, NJ 07306
(201) 795-6704

Hunterdon County
65 Park Avenue
Flemington, NJ 08822
(908) 237-5840

Mercer County
400 South Warren St.
Trenton, NJ 08650
(609) 571-4104

Middlesex County
14 Kirkpatrick Street
New Brunswick, N.J. 08903
(732) 565-5030

Monmouth County
71 Monument Park
Freehold NJ, 07728
(732) 677-4300

Morris County
Washington & Court Streets
Morristown, NJ 07960
(973) 656-4000

Ocean County
120 Hooper Avenue,
Toms River, NJ 08754
(732) 929-4780

Passaic County
77 Hamilton Street
Paterson New Jersey 07505
(973) 247-8337

Salem County
85 Market Street
Salem, NJ 08079
(856) 878-5050

Somerset County
PO Box 3000
Somerville, NJ 08876
(908) 231-7600

Sussex County
43-47 High Street
Newton, NJ 07860
(973) 579-0675

Union County
2 Broad Street
Elizabeth, New Jersey
(908) 659-4600

Warren County
PO Box 900
Belvidere, NJ 07823
(908) 475-6970

COURTS

U.S. SUPREME COURT

Chief Justice, 1 First St NE, Washington, DC 20543
(202) 479-3000

U.S. COURTS

ADMINISTRATIVE OFFICE

Director, 1 Columbus Cir NE, Washington, DC 20544
(202) 273-3000

U.S. DISTRICT COURTS

FIGURE 7.2

ALABAMA – MIDDLE
Chief Judge, PO Box 629, Montgomery, AL 36101
(334) 223-7802

ALABAMA – NORTHERN
Chief Judge, 1729 5th Ave N Rm 882, Birmingham, AL 35203
(205) 278-1800

ALABAMA – SOUTHERN
Chief Judge, 113 St Joseph St, Mobile, AL 36602
(334) 690-2175

ALASKA
Chief Judge, 222 W 7th Ave #41, Anchorage, AK 99513
(907) 271-3198

ARIZONA
Senior Judge, 230 N 1st Ave, Phoenix, AZ 85025
(602) 514-7225

ARKANSAS – EASTERN
Chief Judge, 600 W Capitol Ste 522, Little Rock, AR 72201
(501) 604-5100

ARKANSAS – WESTERN
Chief Judge, PO Box 3487, Fayetteville, AR 72702
(501) 444-7876

CALIFORNIA – CENTRAL
Clerk of Court, 312 N Spring St Rm G-8, Los Angeles, CA 90012
(213) 894-4445

CALIFORNIA – EASTERN
Chief Judge, 650 Capital Mall, Sacramento, CA 95814
(916) 930-4230

CALIFORNIA – NORTHERN
Chief Judge, 450 Golden Gate Ave 16th Fl Rm 16-1111, San Francisco, CA 94102
(415) 522-2000

CALIFORNIA – SOUTHERN
Chief Judge, 940 Front St Courtroom 1, San Diego, CA 92101
(619) 557-6016

COLORADO
Chief Judge, 1929 Stout St, Denver, CO 80294
(303) 844-4627

CONNECTICUT
Senior Judge, 208 US Cthse 141 Church St, New Haven, CT 06510
(203) 773-2105

DELAWARE
Chief Judge, 844 King St Lock Box 27, Wilmington, DE 19801
(302) 573-6155

DISTRICT OF COLUMBIA
Chief Judge, 333 Constitution Ave NW, E Barrett Prettyman Bldg, Washington, DC 20001
(202) 354-3500

FLORIDA – MIDDLE
Chief Judge, 801 N Florida Ave Ste 1730, Tampa, FL 33602
(813) 301-5730

FLORIDA – NORTHERN
Senior US District Judge, 110 E Park Ave, Tallahassee, FL 32301
(850) 942-8853

FLORIDA – SOUTHERN
Chief Judge, 90 NE Fourth St Ste 1155, Miami, FL 33132
(305) 523-5150

GEORGIA – MIDDLE
Chief Judge, PO Box 1014, Macon, GA 31202
(478) 752-3500

GEORGIA – NORTHERN
Chief Judge, 1988 US Cthse 75 Spring St SW, Atlanta, GA 30303
(404) 215-1490

GEORGIA – SOUTHERN
Chief Judge, PO Box 2106, Augusta, GA 30903
(706) 722-6074

HAWAII
Chief Judge, 300 Ala Moana Blvd, Rm C-400, Honolulu, HI 96850
(808) 541-1904

IDAHO
District Judge, 550 W Fort St Fed Bldg MSC 040, Boise, ID 83724
(208) 334-9270

ILLINOIS – CENTRAL
Chief Judge, 122 Fed Bldg 100 NE Monroe St, Peoria, IL 61602
(309) 671-7821

ILLINOIS – NORTHERN
Chief Judge, 219 S Dearborn St Rm 2548, Chicago, IL 60604
(312) 435-5600

ILLINOIS – SOUTHERN
Chief Judge, 301 W Main St, Benton, IL 62812
(618) 435-3779

INDIANA – NORTHERN
Chief Judge, 2145 Fed Bldg 1300 S Harrison St, Ft Wayne, IN 46802
(219) 422-2841

INDIANA – SOUTHERN
Chief Judge, 46 E Ohio St 210 US Cthse, Indianapolis, IN 46204
(317) 299-3600

IOWA – NORTHERN
Judge, 101 First St SE Fed Bldg Rm 304, Cedar Rapids, IA 52401
(319) 286-2330

IOWA – SOUTHERN
Chief Judge, 123 E Walnut St Rm 115, Des Moines, IA 50309
(515) 284-6235

KANSAS
Chief Judge, 500 State Ave Ste 529, Kansas City, KS 66101
(913) 551-6721

KENTUCKY – EASTERN
Chief Judge, 320 Fed Bldg 1405 Greenup Ave, Ashland, KY 41101
(606) 329-2592

KENTUCKY – WESTERN
Chief Judge, 601 W Broadway Rm 247, Louisville, KY 40202
(502) 625-3600

LOUISIANA – EASTERN
Chief Judge, 500 Camp St, New Orleans, LA 70130
(504) 589-7570

LOUISIANA – MIDDLE
Chief Judge, 777 Florida St Ste 313, Baton Rouge, LA 70801
(225) 389-3576

LOUISIANA – WESTERN
Chief Judge, PO Box 1031, Alexandria, LA 71309
(318) 473-7375

MAINE
Chief Judge, 156 Federal St, Portland, ME 04101
(207) 780-3280

MARYLAND
Chief Judge, 101 W Lombard St, Baltimore, MD 21201
(410) 962-0782

MASSACHUSETTS
Chief Judge, 1 Courthouse Way Ste 5170, Boston, MA 02210
(617) 748-9138

MICHIGAN – EASTERN
Chief Judge, 231 W Lafayette Blvd, Rm 730, Detroit, MI 48226
(313) 234-5110

MICHIGAN – WESTERN
Chief Judge, 410 W Michigan, Kalamazoo, MI 49007
(616) 343-7542

MINNESOTA
Chief Judge, 316 N Robert St, St Paul, MN 55101
(612) 664-5000

MISSISSIPPI – NORTHERN
Senior Judge, PO Box 925, Aberdeen, MS 39730
(662) 369-8307

MISSISSIPPI – SOUTHERN
Chief Judge, 245 E Capitol St, Ste 110, Jackson, MS 39201
(601) 965-4963

MISSOURI – EASTERN
Chief Judge, 1114 Market St US Cthse & Custom Hse, St Louis, MO 63101
(314) 539-3202

MISSOURI – WESTERN
Chief Judge, 400 E 9th US Cthse, Kansas City, MO 64106
(816) 512-5600

MONTANA
Chief Judge, PO Box 985, Billings, MT 59103
(406) 247-7011

NEBRASKA
Chief Judge, PO Box 1076, Omaha, NE 68101
(402) 221-3362

NEVADA
Chief Judge, 400 S Virginia St, Ste 708, Reno, NV 89501
(775) 686-5949

NEW HAMPSHIRE
Chief Judge, 55 Pleasant St, Concord, NH 03301
(603) 226-7303

NEW JERSEY
Chief Judge, 402 E State St, Rm 4000, Trenton, NJ 08608
(609) 989-2123

NEW MEXICO
Chief Judge, 333 Lomas Blvd, Albuquerque, NM 87102
(505) 348-2000

NEW YORK – EASTERN
Chief Judge, 225 Cadman Plz E, Brooklyn, NY 11201
(718) 260-2300

NEW YORK – NORTHERN
Chief Judge, US Court & Fed Bldg, 15 Henry St, Binghamton, NY 13902
(607) 773-2892

NEW YORK – SOUTHERN
Chief Judge, 300 Quarropas St, White Plains, NY 10601
(914) 390-4077

NEW YORK – WESTERN
Chief Judge, 2500 US Cthse, 100 State St, Rochester, NY 14614
(716) 263-5894

NORTH CAROLINA – EASTERN
Chief Judge, 306 E Main St, Fed Bldg 217, Elizabeth City, NC 27909
(252) 338-4033

NORTH CAROLINA – MIDDLE
Senior Judge, 223-A Fed Bldg, 251 N Main St, Winston-Salem, NC 27101
(336) 631-5007

NORTH CAROLINA – WESTERN
Chief Judge, 401 W Trade St, 195 Charles R Jonas Fed Bldg, Charlotte, NC 28202
(704) 350-7440

NORTH DAKOTA
District Judge, PO Box 1578, Bismarck, ND 58502
(701) 530-2315

OHIO – NORTHERN
Chief Judge, 201 Superior Ave E, Cleveland, OH 44114
(216) 522-8251

OHIO – SOUTHERN
Chief Judge, 200 W 2nd St, Dayton, OH 45402
(937) 512-1500

OKLAHOMA – EASTERN
Chief Judge, PO Box 2999, Muskogee, OK 74402
(918) 687-2405

OKLAHOMA – NORTHERN
Senior Judge, 224 S Boulder, Rm 210, Tulsa, OK 74103
(918) 581-7966

OKLAHOMA – WESTERN
Chief Judge, 3309 US Cthse, 200 NW 4th St, Oklahoma City, OK 73102
(405) 231-5554

OREGON
Chief Judge, Rm 240 US Cthse, 211 E 7th Ave, Eugene, OR 97401
(541) 465-6773

PENNSYLVANIA – EASTERN
Chief Judge, 601 Market St, Rm 17614, Philadelphia, PA 19106
(215) 597-0692

PENNSYLVANIA – MIDDLE
Chief Judge, PO Box 913, Scranton, PA 18501
(570) 207-5720

PENNSYLVANIA – WESTERN
Senior Judge, US PO & Cthse Rm 803, Pittsburgh, PA 15219
(412) 208-7380

PUERTO RICO
Chief Judge, 150 Carlos Chardon Ave Fed Bldg, San Juan, PR 00918
(787) 772-3130

RHODE ISLAND
Chief Judge, 214B US Cthse One Exchange Terrace, Providence, RI 02903
(401) 752-7060

SOUTH CAROLINA
Senior District Judge, PO Box 835, Charleston, SC 29402
(843) 579-1490

SOUTH DAKOTA
Chief Judge, 400 S Phillips, Rm 202, Sioux Falls, SD 57104
(605) 330-4505

TENNESSEE – EASTERN
District Judge, PO Box 2484, Knoxville, TN 37901
(865) 545-4215

TENNESSEE – MIDDLE
Chief Judge, 824 US Cthse, 801 Broadway, Nashville, TN 37203
(615) 736-2774

TENNESSEE – WESTERN
Chief Judge, 167 N Main St Ste 1157, Memphis, TN 38103
(901) 495-1265

TEXAS – EASTERN
Chief Judge, 300 Willow Jack Brooks Fed Bldg Ste 239, Beaumont, TX 77701
(409) 654-2880

TEXAS – NORTHERN
Chief Judge, 1100 Commerce St 15th Fl, Dallas, TX 75242
(214) 753-2295

TEXAS – SOUTHERN
Chief Judge, PO Box 1060, Laredo, TX 78042
(956) 726-2267

TEXAS – WESTERN
Chief Judge, 200 W 8th St, Austin, TX 78701
(512) 916-5675

UTAH
Senior Judge, 148 US Cthse, 350 S Main St, Salt Lake City, UT 84101
(801) 524-6190

VERMONT
Chief Judge, PO Box 760, Brattleboro, VT 05302
(802) 258-4413

VIRGIN ISLANDS
Chief Judge, 3013 Estate Golden Rock, St Croix, VI 00820-4355
(340) 773-5021

VIRGINIA – EASTERN
Chief Judge, 401 Courthouse Sq, Alexandria, VA 22314
(703) 299-2112

VIRGINIA – WESTERN
Chief Judge, PO Box 2421, Roanoke, VA 24010
(540) 857-5120

WASHINGTON – EASTERN
Chief Judge, PO Box 2208, Spokane, WA 99210
(509) 353-3163

WASHINGTON – WESTERN
Judge, 1010 Fifth Ave, Seattle, WA 98104
(206) 553-2469

WEST VIRGINIA – NORTHERN
Chief Judge, PO Box 791, Wheeling, WV 26003
(304) 233-1120

WEST VIRGINIA – SOUTHERN
Chief Judge, PO Box 351, Charleston, WV 25322
(304) 347-3100

WISCONSIN – EASTERN
Chief Judge, 517 E Wisconsin Ave, 471 US Cthse, Milwaukee, WI 53202
(414) 297-1122

WISCONSIN – WESTERN
Chief Judge, PO Box 591, Madison, WI 53701
(608) 264-5504

WYOMING
US District Judge, PO Box 985, Cheyenne, WY 82003
(307) 634-6072

COURT OF APPEALS

DISTRICT OF COLUMBIA CIRCUIT: WASHINGTON DC
Chief Judge, E Barrett Prettyman Cthse, 333 Constitution Ave NW, Washington, DC 20001
(202) 216-7380

FIRST CIRCUIT: MAINE, MASSACHUSETTS, NEW HAMPSHIRE, PUERTO RICO, RHODE ISLAND
Senior Judge, 1618 John W McCormack PO & Cthse Bldg, Boston, MA 02109
(617) 223-9049

SECOND CIRCUIT: CONNECTICUT, NEW YORK, VERMONT

Senior Judge, PO Box 696, Brattleboro, VT 05302
(802) 254-5000

THIRD CIRCUIT: DELAWARE, NEW JERSEY, PENNSYLVANIA, VIRGIN ISLANDS
Chief Judge, US Cthse, 601 Market St Rm 19613, Philadelphia, PA 19106
(215) 597-9642

FOURTH CIRCUIT: MARYLAND, NORTH CAROLINA, SOUTH CAROLINA, VIRGINIA,
WEST VIRGINIA
Chief Judge, Rm 230 US Cthse, 255 W Main St, Charlottesville, NC 22902
(804) 296-7063

FIFTH CIRCUIT: LOUISIANA, MISSISSIPPI, TEXAS
Chief Judge, US Cthse Rm 11020, 515 Rusk Ave, Houston, TX 77002
(713) 250-5750

SIXTH CIRCUIT: KENTUCKY, MICHIGAN, OHIO, TENNESSEE
Circuit Judge, 640 Fed Bldg, 110 Michigan St NW, Grand Rapids, MI 49503
(616) 456-2551

SEVENTH CIRCUIT: ILLINOIS, INDIANA, WISCONSIN
Chief Judge, 219 S Dearborn St Rm 2788F, Chicago, IL 60604
(312) 435-5806

EIGHTH CIRCUIT: ARKANSAS, IOWA, MINNESOTA, MISSOURI, NEBRASKA, NORTH DAKOTA,
SOUTH DAKOTA
Chief Judge, 311 US Cthse 400 S Phillips Ave, Saux Falls, SD 57104
(816) 512-5800

NINTH CIRCUIT: ALASKA, ARIZONA, CALIFORNIA, GUAM, HAWAII, IDAHO, MONTANA,
NEVADA, NORTHERN MARIANA ISLANDS, OREGON, WASHINGTON
Chief Justice, 400 S Virginia St Ste 708, Reno, NV 89501
(775) 686-5949

TENTH CIRCUIT: COLORADO, KANSAS, NEW MEXICO, OKLAHOMA, UTAH, WYOMING
Senior Circuit Judge, 6012 Fed Bldg, Salt Lake City, UT 84138
(801) 524-5252

ELEVENTH CIRCUIT: ALABAMA, FLORIDA, GEORGIA
Circuit Judge, PO Box 53135, Jacksonville, FL 32201
(904) 232-2496

U.S. DEPARTMENT OF JUSTICE

OFFICE OF ATTORNEY GENERAL
Attorney General, 950 Pennsylvania Ave NW Rm 4545, Washington, DC 20530
(202) 514-2001

U.S. ATTORNEYS

EXECUTIVE OFFICE FOR THE U.S. ATTORNEY
Director, 950 Pennsylvania Ave NW, Washington, DC 20530
(202) 514-2121

ALABAMA – MIDDLE

US Attorney, PO Box 197, Montgomery, AL 36101
(334) 223-7280

ALABAMA – NORTH

US Attorney, 200 Fed Bldg, 1800 5th Ave N, Birmingham, AL 35203
(205) 244-2001

ALABAMA – SOUTH

US Attorney, 63 S Royal St Ste 600, Mobile, AL 36602
(334) 441-5845

ALASKA

US Attorney, Rm 253 Fed Bldg & Cthse, 222 W 7th Ave #9, Anchorage, AK 99513
(907) 271-5071

Assistant US Attorney, 101 12th Ave Box 2 Rm 310, Fairbanks, AK 99701
(907) 456-0245

ARIZONA

US Attorney, Rm 4000 Fed Bldg, 230 N 1st Ave, Phoenix, AZ 85025
(602) 514-7500

1st Assistant US Attorney, 110 S Church Ave Ste 8310, Tucson, AZ 85701
(520) 620-7300

ARKANSAS – EAST

US Attorney, 425 W Capital 5th Fl, Little Rock, AR 72203
(501) 324-5342

ARKANSAS – WEST

US Attorney, PO Box 1524, Fort Smith, AR 72902
(501) 783-5125

CALIFORNIA – CENTRAL

US Attorney, 312 N Spring St 12th Fl, Los Angeles, CA 90012
(213) 894-4600

Chief, Santa Ana Beach, 411 W Fourth St Ste 8000, Santa Ana, CA 92701
(714) 338-3500

CALIFORNIA – EAST

US Attorney, 501 I Ste 10-100, Sacramento, CA 95814
(916) 554-2700

Chief of Criminal Division, 1130 O St Rm 3654, Fresno, CA 93721
(559) 498-7272

CALIFORNIA – NORTH

US Attorney, 450 Golden Gate Ave, San Francisco, CA 94102
(415) 436-7200

CALIFORNIA – SOUTH

US Attorney, 880 Front St Ste 6293, San Diego, CA 92101
(619) 557-5610

COLORADO

US Attorney, 1961 Stout St Ste 1200, Denver, CO 80294
(303) 844-2081

CONNECTICUT

US Attorney, 157 Church St 23 Fl, New Haven, CT 06510
(203) 821-3700

Supervising US Attorney, 450 Main St Fed Bldg Rm 328, Hartford, CT 06103
(860) 947-1101

Supervisor, Rm 309 Fed Bldg, 915 Lafayette Blvd, Bridgeport, CT 06604
(203) 696-3000

DELAWARE

US Attorney, 1201 Market St Ste 1100, Wilmington, DE 19899
(302) 573-6277

DISTRICT OF COLUMBIA

Law Enforcement Coordinator, 555 4th St NW Judiciary Ctr Bldg, Washington, DC 20001
(202) 514-7483

FLORIDA – MIDDLE

US Attorney, 400 N Tampa St Ste 3200, Tampa, FL 33602
(813) 274-6000

Managing Assistant US Attorney, PO Box 600, Jacksonville, FL 32201
(904) 232-2682

Acting Managing Assistant US Attorney, 201 Fed Bldg, 80 N Hughey Ave, Orlando, FL 32801
(407) 648-6700

Managing Assistant US Attorney, 2110 First St Ste 3-137, Fort Myers, FL 33901
(941) 461-2200

FLORIDA – NORTH

US Attorney, 111 N Adams St 4th Fl, Tallahassee, FL 32301
(850) 942-8430

US Attorney, 21 E Garden St, Pensacola, FL 32501
(850) 444-4000

US Attorney, 104 N Main St, Gainesville, FL 32601
(352) 378-0996

FLORIDA – SOUTH

US Attorney, 99 NE 4th St, Miami, FL 33132
(305) 961-9000

Managing Assistant US Attorney, 500 E Broward Blvd, Fort Lauderdale, FL 33394
(954) 356-7255

Managing Supervisor, 500 Australian Ave Ste 400, West Palm Beach, FL 33401
(561) 820-8711

Chief Assistant US Attorney, 505 S 2nd St Ste 200, Fort Pierce, FL 34950
(561) 466-0899

GEORGIA – MIDDLE

US Attorney, PO Box U, Macon, GA 31202
(478) 752-3511

GEORGIA – NORTH

US Attorney, 1800 US Cthse, 75 Spring St SW, Atlanta, GA 30303
(404) 581-6000

GEORGIA – SOUTH

US Attorney, 100 Bull St, Savannah, GA 31401
(912) 652-4422

1st Assistant US Attorney, PO Box 2017, Augusta, GA 30903
(706) 724-0517

HAWAII

US Attorney, 300 Ala Moana Blvd Rm 6-100, Honolulu, III 96850
(808) 541-2850

IDAHO

US Attorney, PO Box 32, Boise, ID 83707
(208) 334-1211

ILLINOIS – CENTRAL

US Attorney, 600 E Monroe St Rm 312, Springfield, IL 62701
(217) 492-4450

US Attorney, 1830 2nd Ave Ste 320, Rock Island, IL 62701
(309) 793-5884

US Attorney, 201 S Vine St Ste 226, Urbana, IL 61801
(217) 373-5875

US Attorney, 100 NE Monroe St, Peoria, IL 61602
(309) 671-7050

ILLINOIS – NORTH

US Attorney, 219 S Dearborn St 5th Fl, Chicago, IL 60604
(312) 353-5300

US Attorney, 308 W State St Rm 300, Rockford, IL 61101
(815) 987-4444

ILLINOIS – SOUTH

US Attorney, 9 Executive Dr Ste 300, Fairview Hts, IL 62208
(618) 628-3700

US Attorney, 402 W Main St Ste 2A, Benton, IL 62812
(618) 439-3808

INDIANA – NORTH

US Attorney, 1001 Main St Ste A, Dyer, IN 46311
(219) 322-8576

Assistant US Attorney, M01 Robert A Grant Fed Bldg, 204 S Main St, South Bend, IN 46601
(219) 236-8287

Assistant US Attorney, 3128 Fed Bldg, 1300 S Harrison St, Fort Wayne, IN 46802
(219) 226-6333

INDIANA – SOUTH

US Attorney, US Cthse 5th Fl, 46 E Ohio St, Indianapolis, IN 46204
(317) 226-6333

IOWA – NORTH

US Attorney, 401 First St SE Ste 400, Cedar Rapids, IA 52401
(319) 363-6333

Chief Assistant US Attorney, 320 6th St Ste 203, Sioux City, IA 51101
(712) 255-6011

IOWA – SOUTH

US Attorney, 110 E Court Ave, US Cthse Annex Ste 286, Des Moines, IA 50309
(515) 284-6257

KANSAS

US Attorney, 1200 Epic Ctr, 301 N Main St, Wichita, KS 67202
(316) 269-6481

Assistant US Attorney, 444 Quincy St Rm 290, Topeka, KS 66683
(785) 295-2850

Assistant US Attorney, 500 State Ave Rm 360, Kansas City, KS 66101
(913) 551-6730

KENTUCKY – EAST

US Attorney, 110 W Vine St Ste 400, Lexington, KY 40507
(859) 233-2661

V PO Box 72, Covington, KY 41012
(859) 655-3200

KENTUCKY – WEST

US Attorney, 510 W Broadway 10th Fl, Louisville, KY 40202
(502) 582-5911

LOUISIANA – EAST

US Attorney, 501 Magazine St 2nd Fl, New Orleans, LA 70130
(504) 680-3000

LOUISIANA – MIDDLE

US Attorney, 777 Florida St, 208 Russell B Long Fed Bldg, Baton Rouge, LA 70801
(225) 389-0443

LOUISIANA – WEST

US Attorney, 300 Fannin St Ste 3201, Shreveport, LA 71101
(318) 676-3600

Assistant US Attorney, 800 Lafayette St Ste 2200, Lafayette, LA 70501
(337) 262-6618

MAINE

US Attorney, PO Box 2460, Bangor, ME 04402
(207) 780-3257

US Attorney, 99 Franklin St 2nd Fl, Bangor, ME 04401
(207) 945-0374

MARYLAND

US Attorney, 6625 US Cthse, 101 W Lombard St, Baltimore, MD 21201
(410) 209-4800

MASSACHUSETTS

US Attorney, 1 Cthse Way, US Cthse Ste 9200, Boston, MA 02210
(617) 748-3100

Assistant US Attorney, 1550 Main St, Rm 310 US Cthse, Springfield, MA 01103
(413) 785-0235

MICHIGAN – EAST

US Attorney, 211 W Fort St Ste 2001, Detroit, MI 48226
(313) 226-9504

Assistant US Attorney, 101 1st St Ste 200, Bay City, MI 48707
(989) 895-5712

Assistant US Attorney, 600 Church St, Flint, MI 48502
(810) 766-5031

MICHIGAN – WEST

US Attorney, PO Box 208, Grand Rapids, MI 49501
(616) 456-2404

Assistant US Attorney, 1930 US 41 W, Marquette, MI 49855
(906) 226-2500

MINNESOTA

US Attorney, 300 S 4th St Rm 600, Minneapolis MN 55415
(612) 664-5600

US Attorney, 316 N Robert St, St Paul, MN 55101
(952) 290-4401

MISSISSIPPI – NORTH

US Attorney, PO Box 886, Oxford, MS 38655
(662) 234-3351

MISSISSIPPI – SOUTH

US Attorney, 188 E Capitol St Ste 500, Jackson, MS 39201
(601) 965-4480

US Attorney, 808 Vieux Marche 2nd Fl, Biloxi, MS 39530
(228) 432-5521

MISSOURI – EAST

US Attorney, US Court & Custom Hse, 1114 Market St Rm 401, St Louis, MO 63101, (314) 539-2200

MISSOURI – WEST

US Attorney, 400 E 9th St 5th St, Kansas City, MO 64106
(816) 426-3122

Deputy US Attorney, 901 St Louis St Ste 500, Springfield, MO 65806
(417) 831-4406

Special Assistant US Attorney, 301 E McCarty Ste 100, Jefferson City, MO 65101
(573) 634-8214

MONTANA

US Attorney, 2929 Third Ave N Ste 400, Billings, MT 59101
(406) 657-6101

Assistant US Attorney, PO Box 3447, Great Falls, MT 59403
(406) 761-7715

Assistant US Attorney, 100 N Park Ave Ste 100, Helena, MT 59601
(406) 449-5370

NEBRASKA

US Attorney, 1620 Dodge St Ste 1400, Omaha, NE 68102
(402) 221-4774

US Attorney, 487 Fed Bldg, 100 Centennial Mall N, Lincoln, NE 68508
(402) 437-5241

NEVADA

US Attorney, 701 E Bridger Ave Ste 800, Las Vegas, NV 89101
(702) 388-6336

US Attorney, 701 E Bridger Ave Ste 600, Las Vegas, NV 89101
(702) 388-6336

NEW HAMPSHIRE

US Attorney, 55 Pleasant St Rm 352, Concord, NH 03301
(603) 225-1552

NEW JERSEY

US Attorney, 970 Broad St, Fed Bldg 7th Fl, Newark, NJ 07102
(973) 645-2700

Assistant US Attorney, 401 Market 4th Fl, Camden, NJ 08101
(856) 757-5026

Assistant US Attorney, 402 E State St Rm 430, Trenton, NJ 08608
(609) 989-2190

NEW MEXICO

US Attorney, PO Box 607, Albuquerque, NM 87103
(505) 766-3341

Branch Chief, 555 S Belshor Ste 300, Las Cruces, NM 88011
(505) 522-2304

NEW YORK – EAST

US Attorney, 1 Pierpont Plz 15th Fl, Brooklyn, NY 11201
(718) 254-7000

Assistant US Attorney
(516) 228-8630

Chief, 825 E Gate Blvd Ste 301, Garden City, NY 11530
(516) 288-8630

NEW YORK – NORTH

US Attorney, 100 S Clinton St, Syracuse, NY 13261
(315) 448-0672

Assistant US Attorney, 445 Broadway, Rm 231 James P Foley US Cthse, Albany, NY 12207
(518) 431-0247

Supervisor Assistant US Attorney, 319 Fed Bldg, 15 Henry St, Binghamton, NY 13901
(607) 773-2887

NEW YORK – SOUTH

US Attorney, 1 St Andrews Plz, New York, NY 10007
(212) 637-2200

Assistant US Attorney in Charge, 300 Quarropas St, White Plains, NY 10601
(914) 993-1900

NEW YORK – WEST

US Attorney, 138 Delaware Ave, Buffalo, NY 14202
(716) 551-4811

Assistant US Attorney in Charge, 100 State St, 620 Fed Bldg, Rochester, NY 14614
(716) 262-6760

NORTH CAROLINA – EAST

US Attorney, 310 New Bern Ave Ste 800 Fed Bldg, Raleigh, NC 27601
(919) 856-4530

NORTH CAROLINA – MIDDLE

US Attorney, PO Box 1858, Greensboro, NC 27402
(336) 333-5351

NORTH CAROLINA – WEST

US Attorney, 227 W Trade St #1700, Charlotte, NC 28202
(704) 344-6222

Senior Litigation Counselor, 100 Otis St Rm 233, Asheville, NC 28801
(828) 271-4661

NORTH DAKOTA

US Attorney, Quentin Burdick Cthse, 655 1st Ave N Ste 250, Fargo, ND 85102
(701) 297-7400

Assistant US Attorney, PO Box 699, Bismarck, ND 58502
(701) 530-2420

OHIO – NORTH

US Attorney, 1800 Bank One Ctr, 600 Superior Ave E, Cleveland, OH 44114
(216) 622-3600

Supervisor Assistant US Attorney, Four Seagate Ste 308, Toledo, OH 43604
(419) 259-6376

Supervisor Assistant US Attorney, 208 Fed Bldg, 2 S Main St, Akron, OH 44308
(330) 375-5716

OHIO – SOUTH

US Attorney, 280 N High St 4th Fl, Columbus, OH 43215
(614) 469-5715

Supervisor Assistant US Attorney, 220 Potter Stewart Cthse, 100 E 5th St, Cincinnati, OH 45202
(513) 684-3711

Senior Assistant US Attorney, 200 W Second St Rm 602, Dayton, OH 45402
(937) 225-2910

OKLAHOMA – EAST

US Attorney, 1200 W Okmulgee, Muskogee, OK 74401
(918) 684-5100

OKLAHOMA – NORTH

US Attorney, 333 W Fourth St Ste 3460, Tulsa, OK 74103
(918) 581-7463

OKLAHOMA – WEST

US Attorney, 210 W Park Ave Ste 400, Oklahoma City, OK 73102
(405) 553-8700

OREGON

US Attorney, 1000 SW 3rd Ave Ste 600, Portland, OR 97204
(503) 727-1000

Assistant US Attorney, 701 High St, Eugene, OR 97401
(541) 465-6771

PENNSYLVANIA – EAST

US Attorney, 615 Chestnut St Ste 1250, Philadelphia, PA 19106
(215) 861-8200

PENNSYLVANIA – MIDDLE

US Attorney, PO Box 309, Scranton, PA 18501
(570) 348-2800

US Attorney, Rm 220 Fed Bldg, 3rd & Walnut Sts, Harrisburg, PA 17108
(717) 221-4482

PENNSYLVANIA – WEST

US Attorney, 633 US PO & Cthse, 7th Ave & Grant St, Pittsburgh, PA 15219
(412) 644-3500

Assistant US Attorney, 100 State St #302, Erie, PA 16507
(814) 452-2906

Assistant US Attorney, Ste 224 Penn Traffic Bldg, Johnstown, PA 15901
(814) 533-4547

PUERTO RICO

US Attorney, Fed Bldg Rm 452 Chardon Ave, Alto Rey, PR 00918
(787) 766-5656

RHODE ISLAND

US Attorney, Ste Ctr 50 Kennedy Dr 8th Fl, Providence, RI 02903
(401) 528-5477

SOUTH CAROLINA

US Attorney, 1441 Main St Ste 500, Columbia, SC 29201
(803) 929-3000

Assistant US Attorney, PO Box 978, Charleston, SC 29402
(843) 727-4381

Assistant US Attorney, 105 N Spring St Ste 200, Greenville, SC 29601
(864) 282-2100

Assistant US Attorney, 401 W Evans St Rm 222, Florence, SC 29503
(843) 665-6688

SOUTH DAKOTA

US Attorney, PO Box 5073, Sioux Falls, SD 57117
(605) 330-4400

Supervisor Assistant US Attorney, 201 Fed Bldg, 515 9th St, Rapid City, SD 57701
(605) 342-7822

Supervisor Assistant US Attorney, 225 S Pierre St Rm 337, Pierre, SD 57501,
(605) 224-5402

TENNESSEE – EAST

US Attorney, 800 Market St Ste 211, Knoxville, TN 37902
(865) 545-4167

Supervisor Assistant US Attorney, 1110 Market St Ste 301, Chattanooga, TN 37402
(423) 752-5140

Supervisor Assistant US Attorney, 103 W Summer St, Greenville, TN 37743
(423) 639-6759

Assistant US Attorney, 208 Sunset Dr Ste 509, Johnson City, TN 37604
(423) 282-1889

TENNESSEE – MIDDLE
US Attorney, 110 9th Ave S Ste A961, Nashville, TN 37203,
(615) 736-5151

TENNESSEE – WEST
US Attorney, Rm 800 Fed Bldg 167 N Main St, Memphis, TN 38103
(901) 544-4231

Supervisor Assistant US Attorney, 109 S Highland Ave Ste 300, Jackson, TN 38301,
(901) 422-6220

TEXAS – EAST
US Attorney, 350 Magnolia St Ste 150, Beaumont, TX 77701
(409) 839-2538

Assistant US Attorney, 110 N College Ave Ste 700, Tyler, TX 75702
(903) 590-1400

Executive Assistant US Attorney, One Grand Ctr Ste 500, Sherman, TX 75090
(903) 868-9454

Assistant US Attorney, 660 N Central Expy Ste 400, Plano, TX 75074
(972) 509-1201

Assistant US Attorney, Ward R Burke Fed Bldg, 104 N 3rd St Rm 001, Lufkin, TX 75901
(936) 639-8671

TEXAS – NORTH
US Attorney, 1100 Commerce St 3rd Fl, Dallas, TX 75242
(214) 659-8600

Executive Assistant US Attorney, 801 Cherry St Ste 1700, Fort Worth, TX 76102
(817) 252-5200

Deputy Criminal Chief, 1205 Texas Ave, Mahon Fed Bldg Ste 700, Lubbock, TX 79401, (806) 472-7351

TEXAS – SOUTH
US Attorney, 910 Travis Ste 1500, Houston, TX 77208
(713) 567-9300

Assistant US Attorney, 600 E Harrison St Rm 201, Brownsville, TX 78520
(956) 548-2554

Assistant US Attorney in Charge, 1100 Matamoras Ste 200, Laredo, TX 78042
(956) 723-6523

Assistant US Attorney, 606 N Carancahua St Ste 1400, Corpus Christi, TX 78476
(361) 888-3111

Assistant US Attorney in Charge, 1701 W Hwy 83 Ste 600, McAllen, TX 78501
(956) 618-8010

TEXAS – WEST

US Attorney, 601 NW Loop 410 Ste 600, San Antonio, TX 78216
(210) 384-7100

Chief Assistant US Attorney, 700 E San Antonio St Ste 200, El Paso, TX 79901
(915) 534-6884

Chief Assistant US Attorney, 816 Congress Ave Ste 1000, Austin, TX 78701
(512) 916-5858

Chief Prosecutor, 400 W Illinois Ste 1200, Midland, TX 79702
(915) 686-4110

Chief Assistant US Attorney, 700 University Parks Dr Ste 770, Waco, TX 76706
(254) 750-1580

Acting Chief Assistant US Attorney, 111 E Broadway 3rd Fl Rm 306, Del Rio, TX 78840, (830) 703-2025

UTAH

US Attorney, 185 S State St Ste 400, Salt Lake City, UT 84111
(801) 524-5682

VERMONT

US Attorney, 11 Elmwood Ave, Burlington, VT 05402
(802) 951-6725

VIRGIN ISLANDS

US Attorney, 5500 Veterans Dr Rm 260, St Thomas, VI 00802
(340) 774-5757

Managing Assistant US Attorney, 1108 King St Ste 201, St Croix, VI 00820
(340) 773-3920

VIRGINIA – EAST

US Attorney, 2100 Jamieson Ave, Alexandria, VA 22314
(703) 229-3700

Managing Assistant US Attorney, 600 E Main St Ste 1800, Richmond, VA 23219
(804) 819-5400

Supervisor Assistant US Attorney, 101 W Main St, World Trade Ctr Ste 8000, Norfolk, VA 23510
(757) 441-6331

VIRGINIA – WEST

US Attorney, PO Box 1709, Roanoke, VA 24008
(540) 857-2250

Managing Assistant US Attorney, PO Box 1098, Abingdon, VA 24212
(540) 628-4161

Managing Assistant US Attorney, 255 W Main St Rm 104, Charlottesville, VA 22902
(804) 293-4283

WASHINGTON – EAST

US Attorney, 920 W Riverside Ave Ste 300, Spokane, WA 99201
(509) 353-2767

Supervisor Assistant US Attorney, 402 E Yakima Ave Ste 210, Yakima, WA 98901
(509) 454-4425

WASHINGTON – WEST

US Attorney, 601 Union St Ste 5100, Seattle, WA 98101
(206) 553-7970

US Attorney, 1201 Pacific Ave Ste 450, Tacoma, WA 98402
(253) 428-3800

WEST VIRGINIA – NORTH

Assistant US Attorney, PO Box 591, Wheeling, WV 26003
(304) 234-0100

Assistant US Attorney, PO Box 190, Elkins, WV 26241
(304) 636-1739

1st Assistant US Attorney, 320 W Pike St #300, Clarksburg, WV 26301
(304) 623-7030

WEST VIRGINIA – SOUTH

US Attorney, PO Box 1713, Charleston, WV 25326
(304) 345-2200

US Attorney, PO Box 1239, Huntington, WV 25714
(304) 529-5799

WISCONSIN – EAST

US Attorney, 530 Fed Bldg, 517 E Wisconsin Ave, Milwaukee, WI 53202
(414) 297-1700

WISCONSIN – WEST

US Attorney, 660 W Washington Ave Ste 200, Madison, WI 53701
(608) 264-5158

WYOMING

US Attorney, PO Box 668, Cheyenne, WY 82003
(307) 772-2124

Assistant US Attorney Criminal Chief, 111 S Wolcott Rm 300, Casper, WY 82601
(307) 261-5434

Assistant US Attorney, 933 Main, Lander, WY 82520
(307) 332-8195

Chapter 8

TRENDS/VISIONS

Technology is changing the scope and breadth of the criminal justice system. The 2016 and plus years will be facing new demands to confront the emerging internship opportunities.

The juvenile corrections trends will vary from state to state, but the overall national demand for juvenile correction officers and social workers will continue to grow.

The drug courts represent a new kind of opportunity for judicial and correctional professionals. The Drug Courts Program Office has awarded more than 50 million dollars to approximately 300 jurisdictions for the planning, implementation or development of drug courts. This can easily be interpreted into an extensive growth for social workers and other judicial and correctional workers who specialize in substance abuse treatment and related programs.

FIGURE 8.1

© Vectorphoto/Shutterstock.com

There is a substantial increase in the jail population for adult and juvenile offenders. This rapid increase has forced the criminal justice system to examine home detention as a practical alternative to incarceration. By keeping the offenders at home, the electronic-monitoring technology has provided a way to ease the overcrowding of the jails and prisons. Electronic monitoring is often used in conjunction with home detention, offering an effective, inexpensive method of supervising probationers.

The demand for the new areas of corrections and related fields are represented in the following types of opportunities:

1. Safety Manager: offers technical advice on or manages occupational safety programs, regulations, and standards.
2. Ombudsman: acts as an unbiased liaison between inmates and facility administration; investigates inmate complaints, reports findings and helps achieve equitable settlements of disputes between the inmates and the correctional administration.

3. Computer Specialist: manages or designs use and maintenance of computer systems. This is an area of great need in the law enforcement, corrections, and judicial fields.

4. Substance Abuse Specialist: manages or designs substance abuse treatments in order to counter the new or designer drugs.

The above are just a few examples of the emerging trends in the criminal justice system.

Technology will continue to play an important role in the operations of public and private sector organizations combating crime. Moreover, advances in technology (e.g., cellular phones) and the lowered cost of using technology will allow more people to use these tools. This, of course, also applies to criminals, as they will be better able to afford the equipment necessary for committing check fraud, identity theft, and counterfeiting documents.

The increase in electronic commerce over the Internet will provide new opportunities for crime. The availability of information on the Internet has already increased the volume of crime.

While the data is not complete, there is a clear trend toward an increase in technology-based crime.

Chapter 9

CRIMINAL JUSTICE DEGREE PROGRAMS

CONTINUING YOUR EDUCATION

The two-year degree or the associate degree will provide the criminal justice major with the opportunity to secure a fulltime position in the field, or after a few years of criminal justice related experience. It is important for the criminal justice major that the student should have career goals that include the completion of the Bachelor of Arts or Science degrees in criminal justice. The criminal justice majors may be interested in the following list of four (4) year degree programs throughout the United States.

FIGURE 9.1

THE FOLLOWING COLLEGES/UNIVERSITIES OFFER THE BACHELOR'S DEGREE IN CRIMINAL JUSTICE

Aims College, Criminal Justice Department, Greeley, CO 80632
(970) 330-8008

Alabama State University, Department of Sociology and Criminal Justice, Montgomery, AL 36101
(334) 229-4120

Alfred University, Criminal Justice Studies, Alfred, NY 14802
(607) 871-2215

Alvernia College, Criminal Justice Department, Reading, PA 19607
(610) 796-8230

American University, Department of Justice, Law and Society, Washington, DC 20016
(202) 885-2956

Appalachian State University, Department of Political Sciences and Criminal Justice, Boone, NC 28608-2107, (828) 262-3085

Arkansas State University, Department of Criminology, Sociology, Social Work, and Geography, Jonesboro, AR 72467-2410 (501) 972-3705

Arizona State University, School of Justice Studies, Tempe, AZ 85287-0403 (602) 965-7085

Arizona State University West, Administration of Justice Department, Phoenix, AZ 85069-7100, (602) 543-6630

Armstrong Atlantic State University, Department of Criminal Justice, Social and Political Science, Savannah, GA 31419-1997 (912) 921-5677

Auburn University, Criminal Justice Department, Auburn, AL 36849 (334) 844-6054

Bakersfield College, Criminal Justice Department, Bakersfield, CA 93306 (805) 395-4481

Ball State University, Department of Criminal Justice and Criminology, North Quad, Muncie, IN 47306 (765) 285-5979

Becker College, Criminal Justice Administration Program, Millbury, MA 01527 (508) 791-9241

Bellevue University, Criminal Justice Administration, Fred H. Hawkins College, Bellevue, NE 68805 (402) 293-2038

Bemidji State University, Criminal Justice Department, Bemidji, MN 56601 (218) 755-2833

Boise State University, Department of Criminal Justice Administration, Boise, ID 83725-1955 (208) 426-4162

Bowling Green State University, Criminal Justice Program, Bowling Green, OH 43403, (419) 372-7778

Buffalo State College, Department of Criminal Justice, Buffalo, NY 14222 (716) 878-6138

Caldwell College, Department of Sociology and Criminal Justice, Caldwell, NJ 07006 (973) 228-4424

California State University, Criminal Justice Department, Sacramento, CA 95819 (916) 278-6437

California State University – Fresno, Department of Criminology, Fresno, CA 93740-0104 (559) 278-5715

California State University – Los Angeles, Department of Criminal Justice, Los Angeles, CA 90032 (323) 343-4618

California State University – Sacramento, Center for Delinquency/Crime Policy Studies, Sacramento, CA 95819
(916) 278-4522

California State University – San Bernardino, Department of Criminal Justice, San Bernardino, CA 92407
(909) 880-5506

Canisius College, Criminal Justice Program, Buffalo, NY 14208
(716) 888-2749

Cedarville College, Department of Criminal Justice and Public Administration, Xenia, OH 45385
(973) 766-7814

Central Arizona College, Criminal Justice Department, Coolidge, AZ 85228
(520) 426-4371

Central Connecticut State University, Department of Criminology, New Britain, CT 06053
(860) 832-3139

Central Connecticut State University, Department of Criminal Justice, New Britain, CT 06053
(860) 832-3142

Central Missouri State University, Criminal Justice Department, Warrensburg, MO 64093
(660) 543-4950

Central Washington University, Department of Law and Justice, Ellensburg, WA 98926-7580,
(509) 963-1779

Chadron State College, Justice Studies Department, Chadron, NE 69337
(308) 432-6463

Charleston Southern University, Criminal Justice Department, Charleston, SC 29423-8087
(843) 863-7131

Chicago State University, Department of Criminal Justice, Chicago, IL 60628
(773) 995-3861

Columbia College, Department of Criminal Justice, Columbia, MO 65216
(573) 474-8960

Columbus State University, Department of Criminal Justice, Columbus, GA 31907
(703) 568-2023

Concordia University – Wisconsin, Criminal Justice Department, Mequon, WI 53097
(414) 243-4223

Delaware Valley College, Criminal Justice Department, Doylestown, PA 18901
(215) 489-2214

Delta College, Criminal Justice Department, University Center, MI 48710
(517) 686-9110

East Carolina University, Criminal Justice Studies, Greenville, NC 27858,
(252) 328-4190

East Tennessee State University, Department of Criminal Justice and Criminology, Johnson City, TN 37614
(423) 439-8662

Eastern Kentucky University, Correctional and Juvenile Justice Studies, Richmond, KY 40475-3102
(606) 622-1155

Eastern Michigan University, Department of Sociology, Anthropology and Criminology, Ypsilanti, MI 48197
(734) 487-3184

Edinboro University of Pennsylvania, Department of Political Science and Criminal Justice, Edinboro, PA 16444
(814) 732-2404

Elmira College, Sociology and Criminal Justice, Elmira, NY 14901
(607) 735-1933

Ferris State University, Criminal Justice Department, Big Rapids, MI 49307
(231) 591-5009

Florence-Darlington Technical College, Criminal Justice Department, Florence, SC 29501
(803) 661-8134

Florida Atlantic University, Criminal Justice Department, Davie, FL 33314
(954) 236-1242

Florida Gulf Coast University, Division of Criminal Justice, Fort Myers, FL 33965-6565
(941) 590-7831

Florida Metropolitan University, Department of Criminal Justice, Tampa, FL 33619
(813) 621-0041

Florida State University, School of Crime and Criminal Justice, Tallahassee, FL 32309-1127
(850) 644-7372

Florida Southern College, Department of Sociology and Criminology, Lakeland, FL 33801-5698
(813) 680-4307

Gannon University, Criminal Justice Program, University Square, Erie, PA 16541
(814) 871-7498

George Mason University, Administration of Justice, Manassas, VA 20110-2203
(703) 993-8313

George Washington University, Forensic Sciences Department, Washington, DC 20052
(202) 994-7320

Georgia State University, Department of Criminal Justice, Atlanta, GA 30302
(404) 651-3689

Grambling State University, Criminology Justice Department, Ruston, LA 71270
(318) 255-6900

Grand Valley State University, School of Criminal Justice, Allendale, MI 49401
(616) 895-2934

Green River Community College, Criminal Justice Department, Auburn, WA 98092-3699
(253) 833-9111

Governors State University, Department of Criminal Justice, University Park, IL 60466
(708) 534-4577

Illinois Central College, Criminal Justice Department, Peoria, IL 61635-0001
(309) 999-4635

Illinois State University, Department of Criminal Justice, Campus Box 5250, Normal, IL 61790-5250
(309) 438-7626

Indiana State University, Department of Criminology, 233 Holmstedt Hall, Terre Haute, IN 47809
(812) 237-2180

Indiana University, Criminal Justice Department, Bloomington, IN 48405
(812) 855-5161

Indiana University of Pennsylvania, Department of Criminology, Indiana, PA 15705
(412) 357-6244

Indiana Wesleyan University, Criminal Justice Department, Marion, IN 46953
(765) 677-2236

Jacksonville State University, Department of Criminal Justice, Jacksonville, AL 36265
(256) 782-5347

John Jay College of Criminal Justice, New York, NY 10019
(212) 237-8654

Johns Hopkins University, Baltimore, MD 21201
(410) 516-0770

Kaskaskia College, Administration of Justice, Centralia, IL 62801
(618) 545-3336

Kean University, Criminal Justice Department, Union, NJ 07083
(908) 527-2508

Kent State University, Criminal Justice Studies, 113 Bowman Hall, Kent, OH 4424-0001
(330) 672-2775

Keuka College, Criminal Justice Program, 319 Hegeman Hall, Keuka Park, NY 14478-0098
(315) 531-6830

Kutztown University, Criminal Justice Department, Kutztown, PA19530
(610) 683-4238

Lake Superior State University, Criminal Justice Department, Sault Ste Marie, MI 49783
(906) 635-2749

Langston University, Criminal Justice and Corrections Department, Langston, OK 73050
(405) 466-3345

Lewis University, Criminal Justice Department, Romeoville, IL 60446
(815) 836-5949

Long Island University, Department of Criminal Justice, Brookville, NY 11548-1300
(516) 299-2468

Long Island University – C.W. Post, Criminal Justice Department, Brookville, NY 11548
(516) 299-2592

Loyola University – Chicago, Criminal Justice Department, Chicago, IL 60611
(312) 915-7570

Lycoming College, Criminal Justice Department, Williamsport, PA 17701
(570) 321-4202

Madonna University, Criminal Justice Department, Livonia, MI 48150-1173
(734) 432-5546

Marist College, Criminal Justice Department, Poughkeepsie, NY 12601
(914) 575-3000

Marquette University, Criminal and Law Studies Program, Milwaukee, WI 53201-1881
(414) 288-5437

Marshall University, Criminal Justice Department, Huntington, WV 25755-2662
(304) 696-3083

Mercer County Community College, Criminal Justice Program, Trenton, NJ 08690
(609) 586-4800

Mercyhurst College, Criminal Justice Department, Erie, PA 16546
(814) 824-2328

Methodist College, Director of Criminal Justice Studies, Fayetteville, NC 28311
(910) 630-7050

Metropolitan State College, Department of Criminal Justice and Criminology, Denver, CO 80217-336
(303) 556-3160

Metropolitan State University, School of Law Enforcement and Criminal Justice, St. Paul, MN 55108
(651) 649-5460

Michigan State University, School of Criminal Justice, East Lansing, MI 48824
(517) 337-1928

Middle Tennessee State University, Criminal Justice Department, Murfreesboro, TN 37132
(615) 898-5565

Minnesota State University, Department of Sociology and Corrections, 113 Armstrong Hall, Mankato, IL 56001
(507) 389-5612

Minnesota State University – Mankato, Political Science and Law Enforcement, Morris Hall 109, Mankato, MN 56001
(507) 389-1018

Minot State University, Department of Criminal Justice, Minot, ND 58707
(701) 858-3140

Mississippi Valley State University, Department of Criminal Justice, Itta Bena, MS 38941
(662) 254-3641

Missouri Valley College, Criminal Justice Department, Marshall, MO 65340-3407
(660) 831-4179

Mitchell College, Criminal Justice Department, New London, CT 06320
(860) 701-5000

Monmouth University, Criminal Justice Department, Withey Hall, West Long Branch, NJ 07764
(732) 571-3600

Morehead State University, Sociology, Social Work, and Criminology, Morehead, KY, 40351
(606) 783-2551

Mount Marty College, Criminal Justice Studies, Yankton, SD 57078
(605) 668-1465

Murray State University, Department of Criminal Justice, Murray, KY 42071
(502) 762-2700

New Hampshire Technical Institute, Criminal Justice Department, Concord, NH 03301-7412
(603) 271-6952

New Jersey City University, Department of Criminal Justice, Jersey City, NJ 07305
(201) 200-3492

New Mexico State University, Department of Criminal Justice, Las Cruces, NM 88003-0001
(505) 646-5376

Niagara University, Department of Criminal Justice, Niagara University, NY 14109-1941
(716) 286-8081

North Carolina Central University, Department of Criminal Justice, Durham, NC 27707
(919) 530-2010

North Carolina Justice Academy, Drawer 99, Salemburg, NC 28385
(910) 525-4151

North Georgia College State University, Department of Political Science and Criminal Justice,
Dahlonega, GA 30597
(706) 864-1908

Northeastern State University, Department of Criminal Justice, Tahlequah, OK 74464
(918) 456-5511

Northeastern University, College of Criminal Justice, Boston, MA 02115
(617) 373-3362

Northern Arizona University, Criminal Justice Department, Flagstaff, AZ 86011-5055
(520) 523-6528

Northern Kentucky University, School of Law, Highland Heights, KY 41099
(606) 572-5253

Northern Michigan University, Criminal Justice Department, Marquette, MI 49855
(906) 227-2660

Northwest State University, Criminal Justice Department, Deridder, LA 70634
(318) 462-1197

Norwich University, Justice Studies Department, Northfield, VT 05663
(802) 485-2368

Old Dominion University, Department of Sociology and Criminal Justice, Norfolk, VA 23529
(757) 683-5931

Park College, Criminal Justice Department, Parkville, MO 64152
(816) 741-2000

Pennsylvania State Atloona, Criminal Justice Program, Atloona, PA 16601-3760
(814) 949-5507

Pennsylvania State University, Crime, Law, and Justice Program, Department of Sociology,
University Park, PA 16802-6207
(814) 863-0275

Pima College East, Justice Studies Program, Tucson, AZ 85709-4000
(520) 206-7865

Portland State University, Division of Administration of Justice, Portland, OR 97207
(503) 725-8090

Radford University, Department of Criminal Justice, Radford, VA 24142,
(540) 831-6148

Ramapo College – New Jersey, Criminal Justice Department, Montvale, NJ 07645
(201) 476-0401

Richard Stockton College of New Jersey, Department of Criminal Justice, College Drive, Pomona, NJ 08057
(609) 652-4625

Rio Salado College, Law Enforcement Programs, Tempe, AZ 85281-6950
(480) 517-8257

Rochester Institute of Technology, Department of Criminal Justice, Rochester, NY 14623
(518) 442-5631

Roger Williams University, School of Justice Studies, Bristol, RI 02806
(401) 254-3394

Rowan University, Law & Justice Studies, Glassboro, NJ 08028
(856) 256-4399

Rutgers University, School of Criminal Justice, Newark, NJ 07102
(973) 353-5073

Saginaw Valley State College, Criminal Justice Department, University Center, MI 48710
(517) 790-4078

Saint Ambrose University, Criminal Justice Department, Davenport, IA 52803
(319) 333-6157

Saint Cloud State University, Criminal Justice Department, St. Cloud, MN 56301-4498
(320) 255-3974

Saint Leo College, Criminology Department, St. Leo, FL 33574-6665
(352) 588-8402

Saint Louis University, Department of Sociology and Criminal Justice, St. Louis, MO 63103
(314) 977-2895

Saint Xavier University, Criminal Justice Dept., Chicago, IL 60657-4845
(773) 298-3162

Salem State College, Department of Criminal Justice, Carlisle, MA 01741
(978) 542-6748

Sam Houston State University, College of Criminal Justice, Huntsville, TX 77341-2296
(409) 294-1637

San Jacinto College North, Criminal Justice Department, Houston, TX 77049-4513
(281) 458-4050

San Jose State University, Administration of Justice Department, San Jose, CA 95192
(408) 924-2940

Seattle University, Department of Criminal Justice, Seattle, WA 98122
(206) 296-5478

Seton Hall University, Department of Criminal Justice, South Orange, NJ 07079
(973) 275-5885

Shippensburg University, Criminal Justice Department, Shippensburg, PA 17257
(717) 477-1770

Simpson College, Criminal Justice Department, Indianola, IA 50125
(515) 961-1583

Snow College, Criminal Justice, Ephraim, UT 84627-1203
(801) 283-4021

Sonoma State University, Department of Criminal Justice, Rohnert Park, CA 94928
(707) 664-3962

South Carolina State University, Criminal Justice Program, Orangeburg, SC 29117-0001
(803) 536-8791/8600

Southeast Missouri State University, Department of Criminal Justice, Cape Girardeau, MO 63701
(573) 651-2541

Southeastern Louisiana University, Department of Sociology, Criminal Justice, and Social Work, 260 D. Vickers Hall, Hammond, LA 70402
(504) 549-2110

Southern Illinois University – Carbondale, Center for the Study of Crime, Carbondale, IL 62901-4504
(618) 453-6371

Southern Oregon University, Department of Criminology, Ashland, OR 97520-5081
(541) 552-6507

Southern University, Department of Sociology and Criminal Justice, Baton Rouge, LA 10051
(504) 771-2011

Southwestern Adventist University, Criminal Justice Department, Keene, TX 76059
(817) 556-4732

State University of New York, School of Criminal Justice, Albany, NY 12222
(518) 442-5317

State University of New York – Brockport, Department of Criminal Justice, Brockport, NY 14420
(716) 395-5501

State University of West Georgia, Department of Sociology, Anthropology, and Criminology, Carrollton, GA 30118
(770) 577-3920

Stephen F. Austin State University, Department of Criminal Justice, Nacogdoches, TX 75962-3064
(409) 468-4408

Sul Ross State University, Criminal Justice Department, Alpine, TX 79832, (915) 837-8166
SUNY College of Brockport, Brockport, NY 14420
(716) 395-2524

Tarleton State University, Criminal Justice Department, Stephenville, TX 76402
(254) 968-9024

Taylor University, Justice Education Department, Ft. Wayne, IN 46807
(219) 456-2111

Teikyo Post University, Criminal Justice Program, Waterbury, CT 06723-2540
(203) 596-4667

Tennessee State University, Department of Criminal Justice, Nashville, TN 37209
(615) 963-5032

Temple University, Crime and Justice Research Institute, Havertown, PA 19083
(610) 789-0908

Texas A & M University – Commerce, Department of Sociology and Criminal Justice, Commerce, TX 75429
(903) 886-5331

Texas A & M University – Corpus Christi, Criminal Justice Department, Corpus Christi, TX 78412
(512) 994-2697

Texas State University – San Marcos, Criminal Justice Department, San Marcos, TX 78666-4616
(512) 245-2174

The Citadel, Department of Political Science and Criminal Justice, Charleston, SC 29409
(843) 953-6786

The College of New Jersey, Department of Law & Justice, Ewing, NJ 08628-0718
(609) 771-2271

Tiffin University, School of Criminal Justice, Tiffin, OH 44883
(800) 968-6446

Truman State University, Justice Systems Program, Kirksville, MO 63501-4221
(660) 785-4667

Tulane University – University College, Criminal Justice Program, New Orleans, LA 70118
(504) 283-4196

University of Alabama, Criminal Justice Department, Tuscaloosa, AL 35487-0320
(205) 553-6885

University of Alabama - Birmingham, Department of Justice Sciences, Birmingham, AL 35294-2060
(205) 553-6885

University of Alaska-Anchorage, Justice Center, Anchorage, AK 99508
(907) 786-1810

University of Albany, School of Criminal Justice, Albany, NY 12222
(518) 442-5224

University of Arkansas – Little Rock, Criminal Justice Department, Little Rock, AR 72204
(501) 569-3195

University of Buffalo, Regional Community Policing Center, Buffalo, NY 14214-3003
(716) 829-3520

University of California – Irvine, Department of Criminology, Law and Society, Irvine, CA 92697-7080
(714) 824-1437

University of Central Florida, Department of Criminal Justice and Legal Studies, Orlando, FL 32816-1600
(407) 823-5944

University of Central Florida – Daytona Beach, Daytona Beach, FL 32120
(904) 255-7423

University of Central Oklahoma, Department of Sociology and Criminal Justice, Edmond, OK 73034-5209
(405) 974-5626

University of Cincinnati, Center for Criminal Justice Research, Cincinnati, OH 45221-0389
(513) 558-0857

University of Colorado – Denver, Department of Criminal Justice, Denver, CO 80217-3364
(303) 556-5995

University of Dayton, Criminal Justice Studies Program, Dayton, OH
(937) 229-4242

University of Florida, Criminology and Law, Gainesville, FL 32611
(352) 392-1025

University of Great Falls, Criminal Justice Department, Bozeman, MT 59715
(406) 587-9474

University of Houston – Downtown, Department of Criminal Justice, Houston, TX 77002-1001
(713) 221-8016

University of Idaho, Department of Sociology and Justice Studies, Moscow, ID 83844
(208) 885-6117

University of Illinois – Chicago, Department of Criminal Justice, Chicago, IL 60607-7140
(312) 355-2469

University of Illinois – Springfield, Criminal Justice Department, Springfield, IL 19243
(217) 786-7586

University of Illinois – Urbana, Police Training Institute, Champaign, IL 61820
(217) 333-7826

University of Louisiana – Lafayette, Criminal Justice Department, Lafayette, LA 70504
(337) 482-6180

University of Louisville, Justice Administration Department, Louisville, KY 40292
(502) 852-0326

University of Maine, Sociology and Criminal Justice Department, Presque Isle, ME 04769
(207) 768-9465

University of Maryland, Department of Criminology, 2220 LeFrak Hall, College Park, MD 20742
(301) 405-4699

University of Massachusetts – Boston, Criminal Justice Program, Boston, MA 02125-3393
(617) 287-6260

University of Massachusetts - Lowell, Department of Criminal Justice, Lowell, MA 01854-3044
(508) 934-4262

University of Memphis, Department of Criminology and Criminal Justice, 405 Mitchell Hall,
Memphis, TN 38152
(901) 678-8155

University of Missouri - Kansas City, Department of Sociology, Criminal Justice, Criminology,
Kansas City, MO 64110
(816) 235-5706

University of Missouri – St. Louis, Department of Criminology and Criminal Justice,
Bonne Terre, MO 63628
(314) 516-5031

University of Nebraska – Kearney, Department of Criminal Justice, Kearney, NE 68849
(308) 865-8510

University of Nebraska - Omaha, Department of Criminal Justice, Omaha, NE 68182
(402) 554-3945

University of Nevada, Criminal Justice Department, Las Vegas, NV 89154-5009
(702) 895-0246

University of Nevada – Reno, Department of Criminal Justice, Reno, NV 89557
(775) 784-6164

University of New Haven, Department of Criminal Justice, West Haven, CT 06516
(203) 932-7376

University of North Carolina, Department of Criminal Justice, Charlotte, NC 28223-0001
(704) 547-2009

University of North Carolina - Charlotte, Department of Criminal Justice, Charlotte, NC 28223
(704) 547-2510

University of North Carolina – Pembroke, Criminal Justice Department, Pembroke, NC 28358
(910) 521-7582

University of North Dakota, Criminal Justice Studies, Grand Forks, ND 58202
(701) 777-4181

University of North Texas, Department of Criminal Justice, Denton, TX 76203-5130
(940) 565-4591

University of Northern Iowa, Department of Sociology, Anthropology and Criminal Justice,
Cedar Falls, IA 50614
(319) 273-2786

University of Saint Thomas, Sociology and Criminal Justice Department, St. Paul, MN 55105
(651) 962-5631

University of Scranton, Department of Sociology and Criminal Justice, Scranton, PA 18510-4605
(570) 941-7476

University of South Alabama, Department of Political Science and Criminal Justice, Humanities Building, # 226, Mobile AL 36688-0002
(334) 460-7095

University of South Carolina, College of Criminal Justice, Columbia, SC
(803) 777-6424

University of South Carolina – Spartanburg, Criminal Justice Department, 800 University Way,
Spartanburg, SC 29303
(865) 503-5606

University of South Dakota, Criminal Justice Studies, Vermillion, SD 57069
(605) 677-5242

University of South Florida, Department of Criminology, Tampa, FL 33815
(813) 974-9708

University of Southern California, Center of Administration of Justice, Tyler Building Room 108,
Los Angeles, CA 90007
(714) 278-2795

University of Tennessee – Chattanooga, Criminal Justice Department, Chattanooga, TN 37403
(423) 875-2166

University of Texas – Arlington, Criminal Justice Department, Ft. Worth, TX 76111
(817) 816-4037

University of Texas – Brownsville, Criminal Justice Department, Brownsville, TX 78520
(956) 983-7407

University of Texas – El Paso, Criminal Justice Program, Vowell Hall, El Paso, TX 79968
(915) 747-7943

University of Texas – San Antonio, Division of Social, Policy Sciences, and Criminal Justice,
San Antonio, TX 78249-0655
(210) 458-5605

University of West Florida, Division of Criminal Justice and Legal Studies, 11000 University Parkway,
Pensacola, FL 32514-5750,
(850) 474-2871

University of Wisconsin, Criminal Justice Department, Milwaukee, WI 53201
(414) 229-2431

University of Wisconsin – Milwaukee, Criminal Justice Program, Milwaukee, WI 53201-0786
(414) 229-6038

University of Wisconsin – Parkside, Department of Criminal Justice, Kenosha, WI 53141-2000
(414) 595-3416

University of Wyoming, Department of Criminal Justice, Laramie, WY 82071-3293
(307) 766-2988

Valdosta State University, Sociology, Anthropology, and Criminal Justice, Valdosta, GA 31602-0001
(912) 333-5943

Victoria College, Criminal Justice Department, Victoria, TX 77901
(512) 572-6426

Virginia Commonwealth University, Department of Criminal Justice, Richmond, VA
(804) 828-1050

Washington State University, Criminal Justice Department, Pullman, WA 99165
(509) 332-0805

Washington State University – Spokane, Criminal Justice Program, Spokane, WA 99202-1662
(509) 358-7952

Wayne State University, Criminal Justice Department, Birmingham, MI 48202
(248) 644-4909

Weatherford College, Criminal Justice Department, Weatherford, TX 76086
(817) 598-6313

Weber State University, Criminal Justice Department, Ogden, UT 84408-1206
(801) 626-6151

West Chester University, West Chester, PA 19382
(610) 436-2630

West Liberty State College, Criminal Justice Department, Wheeling, WV 26003
(304) 232-2839

West Virginia State College, Criminal Justice Department, Institute, WV 25112-1000
(304) 766-3082

Western Carolina University, Department of Criminal Justice, Cullowhee, NC 28723,
(828) 227-2173

Western Connecticut State University, Division of Justice and Law Administration, Danbury, CT 06810
(837) 8514

Western Illinois University, Department of Law Enforcement, One University Circle, Macomb, IL 61455
(309) 298-2251

Westfield State College, Criminal Justice Department, Westfield, MA 01086
(413) 572-5761

Wheeling Jesuit University, Department of Criminal Justice, Wheeling, WV 26003-6243
(304) 243-2567

Wichita State University, Regional Community Policing Institute, Wichita, KS 67260-0135
(316) 978-5896

Widener University, Criminal Justice and Social Science Division, Chester, PA 19013
(610) 499-4525

Winona State University, Department of Sociology and Criminal Justice, Winona, MN 55987
(507) 457-5670

Xavier University, Criminal Justice Department, Cohen Center, Cincinnati, OH 45207-7371
(513) 745-3518

Youngstown State University, Criminal Justice Department, One University Plaza, Youngstown, OH 44555
(330) 742-3279

GRADUATE EDUCATION

Criminal Justice majors must consider graduate education, as should any person nearing completion in an undergraduate program. At Rowan University, the opportunity is great. A student can apply for the "4 + 1" program. If accepted into this program, students take three courses in their senior year that are counted as both undergraduate and graduate credits, thus allowing a student to complete a Master degree in five years, instead of the traditional six years.

Additionally, Rowan University has other interesting programs for continuing education in the study of law. There are partnerships with three law schools, in which, as an undergraduate in your senior year, you can actually attend a course at the law school, counting toward your law studies.

Other universities and colleges offer other helpful programs, with other partnerships to facilitate achieving your educational goals much faster. These programs can also help you decide if a certain field of study (career) is for you.

All Criminal Justice majors are encouraged to take courses in finance, accounting and/or foreign language. Nearly all careers in criminal justice require a background in those categories.

Remember, it is important to gather letters of recommendation from your internship, from professionals you know and from professors. The portfolio, along with your continuing education, will give you the edge over others.

THE FOLLOWING COLLEGES/UNIVERSITIES OFFER M.A. OR M.S IN CRIMINAL JUSTICE

ALABAMA

Auburn University, Public Safety Dept., Montgomery, AL 36117
(334) 844-8888
http://www.auburn.edu/administration/public_safety/

Jacksonville St. Univ., College of CJ, Jacksonville, AL 36265
(205) 782-5335
http://www.jsu.edu/criminaljustice/

University of Alabama, CJ Dept., Tuscaloosa, AL 35487
(205) 348-7795
http://cj.ua.edu/

University of Alabama, CJ Dept., Birmingham, AL 35294
(256) 782-5335

ALASKA

University of Alaska, Justice Ctr., Anchorage, AK 99508
(907) 786- 4608
http://justice.uaa.alaska.edu/

ARIZONA

Arizona St. Univ., School of Justice Studies, Tempe, AZ 85287
(602) 965-7684
https://sst.clas.asu.edu/undergrad/justice-studies-0

Northern Arizona Univ., Sociology, SW & CJ Dept., Flagstaff, AZ 86011
(602) 523-1520
http://catalog.northern.edu/preview_program.php?catoid=3&poid=576&returnto=654
http://www.northern.edu/academics/Documents/proposals/2014/crimjustminor.pdf

ARKANSAS

Univ. of Arkansas, CJ Dept., Little Rock, AR 72204
(501) 569-3195
http://catalog.uark.edu/undergraduatecatalog/collegesandschools/
jwilliamfulbrightcollegeofartsandsciences/criminaljustice/
http://sociology.uark.edu/

CALIFORNIA

California St. Univ., CJ Division, Sacramento, CA 95819
(916) 278-6487
http://www.csus.edu/HHS/CJ/

California St. Univ., CJ Dept, San Bernardino, CA 92407
(714) 880-5506
http://web.csulb.edu/colleges/chhs/departments/criminal-justice/

Claremont Grad. School, Center for Politics & Policy, Claremont, CA 91711
(714) 621-1148
http://cgu.edu/pages/11266.asp

San Jose St. Univ., AOJ Dept., San Jose, CA 95192
(408) 924-2940
http://info.sjsu.edu/web-dbgen/catalog/departments/JS-section-9.html

Univ. of California - Berkeley, Sociology Dept., Berkeley, CA 94720
http://sociology.berkeley.edu/

Univ. of California - Irvine, Program in Social Ecology, Irvine, CA 92717
https://socialecology.uci.edu/

CONNECTICUT

University of New Haven, Public Mgt. & Forensic Science Program, West Haven, CT 06516
(203) 932-7116
http://catalog.newhaven.edu/preview_program.php?catoid=5&poid=733&returnto=663
http://www.newhaven.edu/lee-college/programs/graduate/forensic-science/

DELAWARE

Univ. of Delaware, Sociology & CJ Dept., Newark, DE 19716
(302) 451-2581
http://www.udel.edu/soc/

DISTRICT OF COLUMBIA

George Washington Univ., CJ Dept., Washington, DC, 20052
(202) 994-7319
https://www.gwu.edu/undergraduate-programs-criminal-justice

FLORIDA

Florida International University, CJ Dept., North Miami, FL 33181
(305) 940-5850
http://cj.fiu.edu/

Florida St. University, School of Criminology, Tallahassee, FL 32306
(904) 644-4050
http://criminology.fsu.edu/

University of South Florida, Criminology Dept., Tampa, FL 33620
(813) 974- 2815
http://www.usf.edu/career-services/students/wcidwami-criminology.aspx

GEORGIA

Albany State College, CJ Dept., Albany, GA 31705
(912) 430-4864
http://www.asurams.edu/academics/college-of-science-health-professions/degree-programs/#mscj

Georgia State University, CJ Dept., Atlanta, GA 30303
(404) 651-3515
http://criminaljustice.gsu.edu/

Valdosta State College, Sociology, Anthropology, & CJ Dept., Valdosta, GA 31698
(912) 333-5943
https://www.valdosta.edu/academics/majors-degrees/sociology-and-anthropology.php
https://www.valdosta.edu/academics/majors-degrees/criminal-justice.php

ILLINOIS

Illinois State University, CJ Dept., Normal, IL 61761
(309) 438-7626
http://criminaljustice.illinoisstate.edu/

South Illinois University, Administration of Justice Dept., Carbondale, IL 62901
(618) 453-5701

University of Illinois, CJ Dept., Chicago, IL 60680
(312) 996-5262
http://www.uis.edu/criminaljustice/

Western Illinois University, Law Enforcement Dept., Macomb, IL 61455
(309) 298-1038
http://www.wiu.edu/coehs/leja/

INDIANA

Indiana St Univ., Criminology Dept., Terre Haute, IN 47809
(812) 237-2190
http://www.indstate.edu/cas/ccj

Indiana University, CJ Dept., Bloomington, IN 47405
(812) 855-9880
http://www.indiana.edu/~crimjust/

Indiana University Northwest, School of Public & Environmental Affairs, Gary, IN 46408
(219) 980-6605
http://www.iun.edu/spea/graduate/master-of-public-affairs.htm

KANSAS

Wichita State Univ., AOJ Dept., Wichita, KS 67208
(316) 689-3710
http://webs.wichita.edu/depttools/depttoolsmemberfiles/gradschool/GBCJ.pdf

KENTUCKY

Eastern Kentucky University, School of Law Enforcement, Richmond, KY 40475
(606) 622-3565
http://justice.eku.edu/

University of Louisville, School of Justice Administration, Louisville, KY 40292
(502) 588-6567
http://louisville.edu/justice

LOUISIANA

Grambling St. Univ., CJ Dept., Grambling, LA 71245
(318) 274-2746
http://www.gram.edu/academics/majors/pro-grad-studies/criminal-justice/

Northeast LA Univ., CJ Dept., Monroe, LA 71209
(318) 342-4026
http://www.ulm.edu/criminaljustice/

Southern University, Dept. of Social Sciences, New Orleans, LA 70126
(504) 286-5000
http://www.subr.edu/index.cfm/page/191/n/297

MARYLAND

University of Maryland, Institute of CJ and Criminology, College Park, MD 20742
(301) 405-4703
http://www.ccjs.umd.edu/

MASSACHUSETTS

Northeastern University, College of Criminal Justice, Boston, MA 02115
(617) 437-3327
http://www.northeastern.edu/cssh/sccj/

Westfield State College, CJ Dept., Westfield, MA 01086
 (413) 568-3311
http://www.westfield.ma.edu/academics/criminal-justice-school-massachusetts

Univ. of MA at Lowell, CJ Dept., Lowell, MA 01854
(508) 934-4246
http://www.ccjs.umd.edu/

MICHIGAN

Eastern Michigan Univ., Soc., Anthro. & Criminology Dept., Ypsilanti, MI 48197
(313) 487-0012
http://www.emich.edu/sac/

Michigan St. Univ., School of Criminal Justice, East Lansing, MI 48824
(517) 355-2192
http://cj.msu.edu/

Wayne State University, CJ Program, Detroit, MI 48202
(313) 577- 2705.
http://clas.wayne.edu/crj/

Western Michigan Univ., Sociology, Anthropology & Criminology Dept., Kalamazoo, MI 49008
(616) 387-5281
https://wmich.edu/sociology
http://wmich.edu/anthropology/research
https://wmich.edu/academics/undergraduate/criminal-justice

MINNESOTA

St. Cloud University, CJ Dept., St. Cloud, MN 56301
(612) 255-4101
http://www.stcloudstate.edu/criminaljustice/

MISSISSIPPI

University of Southern Mississippi, CJ Dept., Hattiesburg, MS 39406
(601) 266-4509
https://www.usm.edu/criminal-justice

MISSOURI

University of Missouri, Sociology/AJ Dept., Kansas City, MO 64110
(816) 276-1597
http://sociology.missouri.edu/

NEBRASKA

University of Nebraska, CJ Dept., Omaha, NE 68182
(402) 554-2610
http://www.unl.edu/criminal-justice/

NEW JERSEY

Rowan University, Criminal Justice, Glassboro, NJ 08028
(856) 256-4399
http://www.rowan.edu/colleges/chss/departments/lawjustice/programs/graduate/

Rutgers University, School of Criminal Justice, Newark, NJ 07102
(201) 648-5870
http://rscj.newark.rutgers.edu/prospective-students/masters/

NEW MEXICO

New Mexico St. Univ., CJ Dept., Las Cruces, NM 88003
(505) 646-3316
https://crimjust.nmsu.edu/

NEW YORK

John Jay College of Criminal Justice, CJ Dept., City University of New York, New York, NY 10019
(212) 237-8695
http://www.jjay.cuny.edu/department-criminal-justice

State University of New York, School of Criminal Justice, Albany, NY 12222
(518) 442-5210
http://www.albany.edu/scj/

State University of New York, CJ Dept., Buffalo, NY 14222
(716) 878- 6819
http://www.nccu.edu/academics/sc/socialsciences/criminaljustice/index.cfm

NORTH CAROLINA

North Carolina Central University, CJ Dept., Durham, NC 27707
(919) 560-6280

University of North Carolina, CJ Dept., Charlotte, NC 28223
(704) 547-4776
http://criminaljustice.uncc.edu/

OHIO

Kent State University, CJ Dept., Kent, OH 44242
(216) 672-2775
https://onlinedegrees.kent.edu/programs-courses/graduate/criminology-and-criminal-justice/

University of Cincinnati, CJ Dept., Cincinnati, OH 45221
(513) 556- 5827
http://cech.uc.edu/criminaljustice.html

Youngstown State University, CJ Dept., Youngstown, OH 44555
(216) 742- 3279
http://web.ysu.edu/gen/bcohhs/Department_of_Criminal_Justice_and_Forensic_Sciences_m16.html

OKLAHOMA

Univ. of Central Oklahoma, Sociology & CJ Dept., Edmond, OK 73034
(405) 341-2980
https://www.uco.edu/la/soc-gero-sas/degrees/degree-programs-soc/index.asp

Oklahoma City University, CJ Dept., Oklahoma City, OK 73106
(405) 521-5045
http://www.okcu.edu/artsci/sociology/

Oklahoma State University, Sociology Dept., Stillwater, OK 74078
(405) 744-6105
http://sociology.okstate.edu/current-students/grad

OREGON

Portland State University, AOJ Dept., Portland, OR 97207
(503) 725- 4014
http://www.pdx.edu/sociology/home

PENNSYLVANIA

Indiana University of PA, Criminology Dept., Indiana, PA 15705
(412) 357-2720
https://www.iup.edu/criminology/

Mercyhurst College, CJ Dept., Erie, PA 16546
(814) 824-2266
http://www.mercyhurst.edu/academics/academic-departments/criminal-justice

Penn. St. University, AOJ Program, University Park, PA 16802
(814) 863-0078
http://www.wb.psu.edu/Academics/Degrees/aoj.htm

St. Joseph's University, Sociology & CJ Dept., Philadelphia, PA 19131
http://www.sju.edu/int/academics/cas/sociology/
https://www.sju.edu/int/academics/cas/criminaljustice/cjmajor.html

SOUTH CAROLINA

University of South Carolina, College of Criminal Justice, Columbia, SC 29208
(803) 777-7097
http://artsandsciences.sc.edu/crju/

TENNESSEE

East Tennessee St. University, CJ and Criminology Dept., Johnson City, TN 37614
(615) 929-6807
http://www.etsu.edu/cas/cj/

Univ. of Memphis, CJ Dept., Memphis, TN 38152
(901) 678-2737
http://www.memphis.edu/cjustice/

Middle Tennessee St. University, CJ Dept., Murfreesboro, TN 37132
(615) 755-4135
http://www.mtsu.edu/programs/criminal-justice/

University of Tennessee, CJ Dept., Chattanooga, TN 37403
(615) 755-4135
https://www.utc.edu/criminal-justice/

TEXAS

Sam Houston State Univ., College of Criminal Justice, Huntsville, TX 77341
(409) 294-1631
http://www.shsu.edu/academics/criminal-justice/departments/criminal-justice-and-criminology/

Texas St. Univ. – San Marcos, CJ Dept., San Marcos, TX 78666
(512) 245-2174
http://www.cj.txstate.edu/

University of Texas at Arlington, CJ Dept., Arlington, TX 76019
(817) 273-3318
http://www.uta.edu/criminology/

VIRGINIA

Virginia Commonwealth Univ., Justice & Risk Mgt. Dept., Richmond, VA 23284
(804) 367-1050
https://procurement.vcu.edu/our-services/insurance-risk-management/

WASHINGTON

Washington State University, Program in CJ, Pullman, WA 99164
(509) 335-2544
https://crmj.wsu.edu/

Washington State University, CJ Program, Spokane, WA 99204
(509) 456-3275

WEST VIRGINIA

Marshall University, CJ Dept., Huntington, WV 25755
(304) 696-3196
http://www.marshall.edu/isat/cjc/

WISCONSIN

Marquette University, Criminology & Law Dept., Milwaukee, WI 53233
(414) 288-6838
http://bulletin.marquette.edu/undergrad/helenwayklinglercollegeofartsandsciences/
socialandculturalsciences/criminologyandlawstudies_crls/

University of Wisconsin, CJ Dept., Milwaukee, WI 53201
(414) 229-6030
https://www.uwplatt.edu/criminal-justice

THE FOLLOWING UNIVERSITIES OFFER THE PH.D. IN CRIMINAL JUSTICE

Arizona State University, School of Justice Studies,
Tempe, AZ 85287
(602) 965-7684
http://sjsi.asu.edu/?q=phd

Sam Houston St. University, College of
Criminal Justice, Huntsville, TX 77341
(409) 294-1631
http://www.shsu.edu/programs/
doctorate-of-philosophy-in-criminal-justice/

Claremont Graduate School, Center for
Politics & Policy, Claremont, CA 91711
(714) 521-1148
http://cgu.edu/pages/10826.asp

FIGURE 9.2

State University of NY- Albany, School of
Criminal Justice, Albany, NY 12222
(518) 442-5210
http://www.albany.edu/scj/phd_program_of_study.php

Florida State University, School of Criminology, Tallahassee, FL 32306
(904) 644-4050
http://criminology.fsu.edu/degrees/graduate-programs/doctoral-program/doctoral-degree-requirements/

Univ. of California–Irvine, Program in Social Ecology, Irvine, CA 92717
(714) 856-6094
http://cls.soceco.uci.edu/pages/phd-program

Indiana University, Dept. of CJ, Bloomington, IN 47405
(812) 855-9325
http://www.indiana.edu/~crimjust/graduate_d_advising.php?nav=graduate

Indiana Univ. of Pennsylvania, Dept. of Criminology, Indiana, PA 15705
(412) 357-2720
https://www.iup.edu/criminology/grad/criminology-phd/default.aspx

University of Cincinnati, Dept. of Criminal Justice, Cincinnati, OH 45221
(513) 556-5827
http://cech.uc.edu/criminaljustice/programs.html?cid=18PHD-CJ

John Jay College of CJ, 444 West 56th St., New York, NY 10019
(212) 237-8695
http://www.jjay.cuny.edu/doctoral-programs

University of Delaware, Dept. of Sociology & CJ, Newark, DE 19716
(302) 451-2581
http://www.udel.edu/soc/

Michigan State Univ., School of CJ, East Lansing, MI 48824
(517) 355-2192
http://cj.msu.edu/programs/doctorate/

University of Nebraska, CJ Dept., Omaha, NE 68182
(402) 554-2610
http://www.unl.edu/criminal-justice/graduate-degree-programs

University of Maryland, Dept. of Criminology and CJ, College Park, MD 20742
(301) 405-4703
http://www.ccjs.umd.edu/graduate/landingtopic/phd-program

Penn. State Univ., Sociology/AOJ Dept., University Park, PA 16802
(814) 863-0078
http://sociology.la.psu.edu/graduate/programs

Univ. of Missouri-St. Louis, Dept. of Crim./CJ, St. Louis, MO 63121
(314) 553-5031
http://www.umsl.edu/gradschool/gradprograms/Doctoral.html

Portland State University, CJ Program, Portland, OR 97207
(503) 229-4014
http://online.ccj.pdx.edu/lpppc-bsccj/?Access_Code=PSU-BSCCJ-
GOOGLE&kwd=portland%20state%20criminology&gclid=Cj0KEQiAyIayBRDo4v-
jdqJrgxZ0BEiQAhOYCYAmz2MVR2IwMSwioQPEDOFU4ET14bkrjFWHxUgWJpYgaAtab8P8HAQ

Rutgers University, School of CJ, Newark, NJ 07102
(201) 648-5870
http://rscj.newark.rutgers.edu/current-students/phd/

Temple University, CJ Dept., Philadelphia, PA 19122
(215) 204-7918
http://www.cla.temple.edu/cj/graduate/phd-graduates/

Chapter 10

CONCLUSION

No matter how well prepared you are, seeking an internship is difficult. You must be extremely patient, especially when you are pursuing state and federal governmental internships. You will have to wait for responses to initial inquiries, interviews, and final decisions.

As you move along your career path, be aware that the assessment of your personal needs, your skills, and your geographical limitations may change as you gain experience and as your personal situation changes. You should periodically assess your career to determine if your personal needs are being met.

The most important aspect of the internship selection is that you must be able to live with yourself and with the daily issues of justice, fairness, and punishment. You must always examine your values and the behavior you exhibit in the workplace. It may be difficult to complete a criminal justice internship because of the internal complex legalities, peer pressure, and the observation of individuals functioning at their worst. If you possess the attitude, philosophy, personal drive, and if you can cope with the myriad emotions and frustrations inherent in this field, then a criminal justice career can be very rewarding in terms of the assistance you will provide to fellow citizens in need.

In deciding which internship is best suited for you and your needs, you must consider educational requirements, background limitations, and experience requirements.

Take the time to learn from your internship. The very skills you test and refine now perhaps will someday create the opportunity to transfer to another career.

A career path is no longer a straight line. Everyone starts off with thoughts of the perfect job. However, this is just a guess. Often someone starts working at a certain job and then they realize maybe it is not so perfect for them. Life-long careers may not be the norm any longer. In the past, a person would stay in one job for 30 years or more. Times have changed; people switch careers three to four times and hold an average of seven jobs. Therefore, being adaptable and willing to accept change, even in one's chosen career, is a necessity.

When one is set on a career path, in particular a path that requires much education, it is difficult to imagine having to change that path. Taking the first steps in altering your path is very ominous, and feels full of risk. Change is scary and not easily acceptable. The proper development and subsequent implementation of systematic steps in changing the career path will reduce the anxiety and produce success. Much can be learned from the internship and lessons from that experience will carry over in this new endeavor. In fact, creating a "career path mindset."

Developing a career path mindset will keep you focused at your current job, while you simultaneously remaining flexible and able to move in a new direction as opportunity presents itself. View every job as a chance to enhance the two most important aspects of a career path mindset: networking and transferable skills.

Transferable skills are the strengths and abilities that will directly affect your new career by using those same skills from the old career or from life experiences. In fact, you have been acquiring transferable skills since childhood. Schoolwork, athletics, internships, part-time employment, class projects, campus and community activities all provide you with skills. Therefore, having a sense of positive energy and bringing forward those things you worked so hard for such as teamwork, leadership, and problem solving skills will benefit both your employer and you.

Networking is often referred to as "It is not what you know, but who you know." Networking occurs every time you interact with people, participate in community events, volunteer work or in countless other forms of social interaction. Focus on building relationships. With each relationship comes a chance to discover the next step in your career path, a step that might not traditionally have been available.

You may have spent much time volunteering, researching, shadowing, and basically paying your dues in the career path you originally chose. That time, though, is not wasted. You can always network and explore a new career path you seek. The process of the internship is repeated. The life lessons and all the time, money, and energy are now put to another test. Take the leap and remember everything is not wasted; transfer it all to the new career. Showcase your innate talent.

Life is dynamic. Trying something new can fail. Learning is a process. One cannot learn if one does not take the opportunity to do so. Therefore, the valuable lessons from your internship can (and will) come back into play. Bill Gates said that jobs are fixed solutions to a changing problem. So having the ability to learn, pivot, and be flexible (just as you did in your internship) will be instrumental in your success.

Finally, internships are an excellent way to discover if a specific area of criminal justice is a good fit for you. An internship is an opportunity to receive supervised, practical on-the-job training in specific areas of the criminal justice system.

We encourage you to pursue your internship with all best wishes and we hope that the completion of the internship coincides with your future endeavors.

USEFUL LINKS

http://www.golawenforcement.com/CriminalJusticeInternships.htm

https://www.atf.gov/careers/internships

http://www.bop.gov/jobs/students.jsp

https://www.fletc.gov/fletc-college-intern-program

http://discovercriminaljustice.com/

http://www.criminaljustice.com/careers/

http://www.eastbrunswick.org/content/204/299/309/319/3283.aspx

http://www.cjpf.org/internship/

https://www.atf.gov/careers/internships

http://www.justice.gov/opa/internships

http://www.justice.gov/legal-careers/department-justice-pathways-programs

http://ojp.gov/about/jobs.htm

http://www.bls.gov/oes/current/oes333051.htm

http://www.bls.gov/ooh/Protective-Service/Private-detectives-and-investigators.htm

http://www.bls.gov/oes/current/oes211092.htm

http://www.bls.gov/oes//current/oes194092.htm

http://www.ncis.navy.mil/careers/interns/pages/default.aspx

http://www.justice.gov/legal-careers/volunteer-legal-internships

INTERNSHIP OPPORTUNITIES

Alice Paul Institute
https://www.alicepaul.org/

American Cancer Society of South Jersey
https://www.cancer.org/

Bayshore Center
https://bayshorecenter.org/

Bridgeton Main Street Association
https://www.getbridgeton.com/

Camden County Council on Alcohol and Drug Abuse
http://www.camdencounty.com/

Center for Historic American Building Arts (CHABA)
http://www.historicbuildingarts.org/HistoricBuildingArts/HOME.html

Clayton Accounting
http://claytonnj.com/public/departments/

Cooper's Ferry Partnership
https://www.coopersferry.com/

Food and Water Watch
https://www.foodandwaterwatch.org/state/new-jersey

Histiocystosis Association
https://www.histio.org/

Hopeworks
https://hopeworks.org/

Hospace Compassus
https://www.compassus.com/locations/new-jersey/willingboro?tab=location_overview

Law Office of Hoffman and DiMuzio
https://www.hoffmandimuzio.com/

Literacy NJ
https://literacynj.org/

Meals on Wheels
https://www.scmealsonwheels.org/

Mullica Hill Art Center
https://www.mullicahillartcenter.com/

Multicultural Arts Exchange
https://globalphiladelphia.org/organizations/multicultural-arts-exchange-0

The Museum of American History at Deptford
http://www.southjerseymuseum.org/

NJ Conservation Foundation
https://www.njconservation.org/

New Jersey Council for the Humanities
https://njhumanities.org/

Rowan Center for Holocaust and Genocide Studies
https://chss.rowan.edu/centers/RCHGS/index.html

Rowan Office of Academic Transition and Support Programs at Rowan University
https://sites.rowan.edu/student-success/

Rowan Radio Corporation of America Heritage Museum
https://www.lib.rowan.edu/campbell/spaces-collections/rca-heritage-program-museum

Rowan Women's Center in the Office of Social Justice, Inclusion, and Conflict Resolution
https://sites.rowan.edu/sjicr/

Silent Noise Publishing Group
http://www.silentnoisepublishing.com/

Sourland Conservancy
https://www.sourland.org/

Southern NJ Development Council
http://snjdc.org/

The Food Bank of South Jersey
https://foodbanksj.org/

This list, by no means exhaustive, offers an example of the range of internship opportunities available to Rowan students.

INTERNSHIP OPPORTUNITIES FOR FALL 2018 AND SPRING 2019

NAME	PARTY-DISTRICT	COUNTY
Senator Jeff Van Drew / **Assemblyman Bob Andrezejzak /** **Assemblyman Bruce Lamp** https://sites.rowan.edu/academic-affairs/_docs/rippac_docs/van-drew-andrzejczak-and-land---dist-1.pdf	D-1	Cumberland / Cape May / Atlantic
Senator Chris Brown https://sites.rowan.edu/academic-affairs/_docs/rippac_docs/dist-2---brown.pdf	R-2	Atlantic
Assemblyman Vince Mazzeo / **Assemblyman John Armato** https://sites.rowan.edu/academic-affairs/_docs/rippac_docs/mazzeo-and-armato---dist-2.pdf	D-2	Atlantic
Senator Steve Sweeney / **Assemblyman John Burzichelli /** **Assemblyman Adam Taliaferro** https://sites.rowan.edu/academic-affairs/_docs/rippac_docs/dist-3---sweeney,-burzichelli-and-taliaferro.pdf	D-3	Cumberland / Gloucester / Salem
Senator Fred Madden / **Assemblyman Paul Moriarty /** **Assemblywoman Gabriella Mosquera** https://sites.rowan.edu/academic-affairs/_docs/rippac_docs/dist-4---madden,-moriarty-and-mosquera.pdf	D-4	Camden / Gloucester
Senator Nilsa Cruz-Perez / **Assemblywoman Patricia Egan Jones /** **Assemblyman Arthur Barclay** https://sites.rowan.edu/academic-affairs/_docs/rippac_docs/cruz-perez-egan-jones-and-barclay---dist-5.pdf	D-5	Camden
Senator Jim Beach https://sites.rowan.edu/academic-affairs/_docs/rippac_docs/dist-6---beach.pdf	D-6	Camden
Assemblyman Louis Greenwald / **Assemblywoman Pamela Lampitt** https://chss.rowan.edu/_docs/dist-6-greenwald-lampitt.pdf	D-6	Camden
Senator Troy Singleton https://sites.rowan.edu/academic-affairs/_docs/rippac_docs/dist-7---singleton.pdf	D-7	Burlington
Assemblyman Herb Conaway https://sites.rowan.edu/academic-affairs/_docs/rippac_docs/dist-7---conaway.pdf	D-7	Burlington

Assemblywoman Carol Murphy https://sites.rowan.edu/academic-affairs/_docs/rippac_ docs/murphy---dist-7.pdf	D-7	Burlington
Senator James Holzapfel / **Assemblyman Gregory McGuckin /** **Assemblyman David Wolfe** https://sites.rowan.edu/academic-affairs/_docs/rippac_ docs/dist-10---holzapfell,-wolfe,-and-mcguckin.pdf	R-10	Ocean
Senator Vin Gopal / **Assemblywoman Joann Downey /** **Assemblyman Eric Houghtaling** https://sites.rowan.edu/academic-affairs/_docs/rippac_ docs/dist11-gopal-downey-and-houghtaling.pdf	D-11	Monmouth
Senator Samuel Thompson https://sites.rowan.edu/academic-affairs/_docs/rippac_ docs/dist-12---thompson.pdf	R-12	Monmouth / Middlesex/ Burlington / Ocean
Assemblyman Dan Benson https://sites.rowan.edu/academic-affairs/_docs/rippac_ docs/benson---dist-14.pdf	D-14	Mercer / Middlesex
Assemblyman Wayne DeAngelo https://sites.rowan.edu/academic-affairs/_docs/rippac_ docs/dist-14---deangelo.pdf	D-14	Mercer / Middlesex
Assemblyman Roy Freiman https://sites.rowan.edu/academic-affairs/_docs/rippac_ docs/dist-16---freiman.pdf	D-16	Hunterdon / Mercer Middlesex / Somerset
Assemblywoman Nacy Pinkin https://sites.rowan.edu/academic-affairs/_docs/rippac_ docs/dist-18---pinkin.pdf	D-18	Middlesex
Assemblywoman Annette Quijano https://sites.rowan.edu/academic-affairs/_docs/rippac_ docs/dist-20---quijano.pdf	D-20	Union
Senator Nicholas Scutari https://sites.rowan.edu/academic-affairs/_docs/rippac_ docs/scutari---dist-22.pdf	D-22	Union
Assemblyman Erik Peterson https://sites.rowan.edu/academic-affairs/_docs/rippac_ docs/peterson---dist-23.pdf	R-23	Hunterdon/ Somerset / Warren
Assemblyman John McKeon https://sites.rowan.edu/academic-affairs/_docs/rippac_ docs/dist-27---mekeon.pdf	D-27	Essex / Morris

Assemblywoman Angela McKnight
https://sites.rowan.edu/academic-affairs/_docs/rippac_
docs/dist-31---mcknight.pdf

D-31   Hudson

Senator Paul Sarlo
https://sites.rowan.edu/academic-affairs/_docs/rippac_
docs/sarlo---dist-36.pdf

D-36   Bergen / Passaic

Assemblyman Clinton Calabrese
https://sites.rowan.edu/academic-affairs/_docs/rippac_
docs/dist-36---calabrese.pdf

D-36   Bergen / Passaic

Senator Gerald Cardinale
https://sites.rowan.edu/academic-affairs/_docs/rippac_
docs/dist-39---cardinale.pdf

R-39   Bergen

Assemblyman Robert Auth
https://sites.rowan.edu/academic-affairs/_docs/rippac_
docs/dist-39---auth.pdf

R-39   Bergen

Senator Kristine Corrado
https://sites.rowan.edu/academic-affairs/_docs/rippac_
docs/dist-40---corrado.pdf

R-40   Bergen / Passaic

Assemblyman Christopher DePhillips
https://sites.rowan.edu/academic-affairs/_docs/rippac_
docs/dist-40---dephillips.pdf

R-40   Bergen / Passaic

Assemblyman Kevin Rooney
https://sites.rowan.edu/academic-affairs/_docs/rippac_
docs/dist-40---rooney.pdf

R-40   Bergen / Passaic

OTHER ORGANIZATIONS AND ELECTED OFFICIALS OFFERING INTERNSHIPS

NAME	LOCATION
Acrisure Insurance (Broker for government entities) (paid) https://sites.rowan.edu/academic-affairs/_docs/rippac_docs /acrisure-insurance.pdf	Woodbridge
Advocacy & Management Group (contract lobbyists) (paid) https://sites.rowan.edu/academic-affairs/_docs/rippac_docs /advocacy-and-management-group.pdf	Trenton
Bergen County Freeholder Tracy Zur https://sites.rowan.edu/academic-affairs/_docs/rippac_docs/bergen -county-freeholder-zur.pdf	Hackensack
Bergen County Government https://sites.rowan.edu/academic-affairs/_docs/rippac_docs/bergen -county-government.pdf	Hackensack

Burlington County Republican Committee
https://sites.rowan.edu/academic-affairs/_docs/rippac_docs/burlington
-county-gop.pdf

Mt. Holly

Congressional Leadership Fund (Republican campaigns)
https://sites.rowan.edu/academic-affairs/_docs/rippac_docs/congressional
-leadership-fund.pdf

Mt. Laurel

Cooper Health Administration
https://sites.rowan.edu/academic-affairs/_docs/rippac_docs/cooper-health
-administration.pdf

Camden

Elizabeth (City) Goverment (paid)
https://sites.rowan.edu/academic-affairs/_docs/rippac_docs/city-of-elizabeth
-government.pdf

Elizabeth

Governor Phil Murphy
https://sites.rowan.edu/academic-affairs/_docs/rippac_docs/governor
-phil-murphy.pdf

Trenton

Greener by Design (energy & environment consulting)
https://sites.rowan.edu/academic-affairs/_docs/rippac_docs/greener-by-design.pdf

New Brunswick

Hugin for US Senate (Republican campaign)
https://sites.rowan.edu/academic-affairs/_docs/rippac_docs/hugin-for
-us-senate-campaign.pdf

Mountainside

Jersey City Division of Community Development
https://sites.rowan.edu/academic-affairs/_docs/rippac_docs/jersey
-city-division-of-community-development.pdf

Jersey City

MacArthur for Congress (Republican campaign)
https://sites.rowan.edu/academic-affairs/_docs/rippac_docs/macarthur
-for-congress.pdf

Mt. Holly /
Toms River

Monmouth County Clerk Kristine Honlon
https://sites.rowan.edu/academic-affairs/_docs/rippac_docs/monmouth
-county-clerk-kristine-honlon.pdf

Freehold

NJ Assembly Democratic Office
https://sites.rowan.edu/academic-affairs/_docs/rippac_docs/nj-assembly
-democratic-office.pdf

Trenton

NJ Assembly Republican Office
https://sites.rowan.edu/academic-affairs/_docs/rippac_docs/nj-assembly
-republican-office.pdf

Trenton

NJ Board of Public Utilities (energy policy & regulation)
https://sites.rowan.edu/academic-affairs/_docs/rippac_docs/nj-board-of
-public-utilities.pdf

Trenton

NJ Business & Industry Association (paid)
https://sites.rowan.edu/academic-affairs/_docs/rippac_docs/nj-business
-and-industry-association.pdf

Trenton

NJ Chamber of Commerce (paid)
https://sites.rowan.edu/academic-affairs/_docs/rippac_docs/nj-chamber
-of-commerce.pdf

Trenton

NJ Democratic Party
https://sites.rowan.edu/academic-affairs/_docs/rippac_docs/nj-democratic
-party.pdf

Trenton

NJ Department of Higher Education
https://sites.rowan.edu/academic-affairs/_docs/rippac_docs/nj-department
-of-higher-education.pdf

Trenton

NJ Food Council (supermarket trade association) (paid)
https://sites.rowan.edu/academic-affairs/_docs/rippac_docs/nj-food-council.pdf

Trenton

NJ Gasoline, Convenience & Automotive Association
https://sites.rowan.edu/academic-affairs/_docs/rippac_docs/nj-gasoline
-convenience-and-automotive-assoc.pdf

Wall Twp.

NJ Hospital Association
https://sites.rowan.edu/academic-affairs/_docs/rippac_docs/nj-hospital
-association.pdf

Princeton

NJ League of Conservation Voters
https://sites.rowan.edu/academic-affairs/_docs/rippac_docs/nj-league-of
-conservation-voters.pdf

Princeton

NJ League of Municipalities (paid)
https://sites.rowan.edu/academic-affairs/_docs/rippac_docs/nj-league-of
-municipalities.pdf

Trenton

NJ Republican Party
https://sites.rowan.edu/academic-affairs/_docs/rippac_docs/nj-republican-party.pdf

Trenton

NJ Senate Democratic Office
https://sites.rowan.edu/academic-affairs/_docs/rippac_docs/nj-senate
-democratic-office.pdf

Trenton

NJ Senate Republican Office
https://sites.rowan.edu/academic-affairs/_docs/rippac_docs/nj-senate
-republican-office.pdf

Trenton

NJ State Laborers PAC (union) (paid)
https://sites.rowan.edu/academic-affairs/_docs/rippac_docs/nj-state
-laborers-pac.pdf

Trenton

NJ Tech Council
https://sites.rowan.edu/academic-affairs/_docs/rippac_docs/nj-tech-council.pdf

New Brunswick

Novo Nordisk (pharmaceutical company) (pays up to $7,000)
https://sites.rowan.edu/academic-affairs/_docs/rippac_docs/novo-nordisk.pdf

Plainsboro

Pallone for Congress (Democratic campaign)
https://sites.rowan.edu/academic-affairs/_docs/rippac_docs
/pallone-for-congress.pdf

Long Branch

Princeton Public Affairs Group (contract lobbyists) (paid)
https://sites.rowan.edu/academic-affairs/_docs/rippac_docs
/princeton-public-affairs-group.pdf

Trenton

SEIU 1199 (healthcare worker union) (paid) https://sites.rowan.edu/academic-affairs/_docs/rippac_docs/seiu-1199.pdf

Woodbridge / Iselin

Sherrill for Congress (Democratic campain)
https://sites.rowan.edu/academic-affairs/_docs/rippac_docs
/sherrill-for-congress.pdf

Morristown

Surfrider Foundation (environmental advocacy)
https://sites.rowan.edu/academic-affairs/_docs/rippac_docs
/surfrider-foundation.pdf

From your home

US Congressman Donald Norcross
https://sites.rowan.edu/academic-affairs/_docs/rippac_docs
/us-congressman-donald-norcross.pdf

Cherry Hill

US Senator Bob Menendez
https://sites.rowan.edu/academic-affairs/_docs/rippac_docs
/us-senator-bob-menendez.pdf

Barrington / Newark

US Senator Cory Booker
https://sites.rowan.edu/academic-affairs/_docs/rippac_docs/us
-senator-cory-booker.pdf

Camden

Valley National Bank (corporate social responsibility) (paid)
https://sites.rowan.edu/academic-affairs/_docs/rippac_docs
/valley-national-bank.pdf

Wayne

Van Drew for Congress (Democratic campaign)
https://sites.rowan.edu/academic-affairs/_docs/rippac_docs
/van-drew-for-congress.pdf

Atlantic County /
Cape May County /
Cumberland County

PROF JOBS

https://sites.rowan.edu/oca/profsjobs1.html

SIGN IN FOR PROF JOBS

https://rowan-csm.symplicity.com/students/index.php?signin_tab=0

MANY POLICE DEPARTMENTS, SHERIFF DEPARTMENTS AND PROSECUTOR OFFICES, NJ COURTS

https://www.internships.com/new-jersey

https://www.indeed.com/q-Summer-Internship-l-New-Jersey-jobs.html

https://www.linkedin.com/jobs/summer-intern-jobs-new-jersey?pageNum=0&position=1

https://www.glassdoor.com/Job/new-jersey-summer-internship-jobs-SRCH_IL.0,10_IS39_KO11,28.htm

https://www.monster.com/jobs/q-summer-intern-jobs-l-new-jersey.aspx

https://www.careerjet.com/summer-internship-jobs/new-jersey-393.html

https://www.nj.gov/oag/dcj/Undergraduate-Law-Internship.html

https://www.justice.gov/crt/volunteer-and-paid-student-internships

https://www.fbijobs.gov/students/undergrad

https://www.theiacp.org/iacp-internships

https://www.google.com/search?client=firefox-b-1-d&q=criminal+justice+internships+nj&sa=X&biw=1360&bih=607&ibp=htl;jobs&ved=2ahUKEwiO3LqmpLTgAhUEuVkKHdFtCpUQp4wCMAB6BAgCEAs#htidocid=NPIW3dhnC8TJL1pFAAAAAA%3D%3D

https://www.njsp.org/recruiting/internship-opportunities.shtml

https://www.state.nj.us/parole/recruitment.html

https://www.njhomelandsecurity.gov/internships/?rq=internships

https://www.gtpolice.com/programs/community-relations/internship-program/

https://www.eastbrunswick.org/Internship

http://www.jointheportauthority.com/pages/internship-program

https://www.njsacop.org/content.asp?contentid=47

https://www.justice.gov/usao-nj/employment-and-internships

https://www.dhs.gov/homeland-security-careers/fletc-college-intern-program
FLETC-Interns@dhs.gov

https://www.dhs.gov/homeland-security-careers/cbp-explorer-program
francis.x.stack@dhs.gov

https://www.usmarshals.gov/district/nc-m/general/internship_application.pdf

https://www.dea.gov/domestic-divisions/new-jersey
https://nbcjm.rutgers.edu/images/stories/Program/PDF/News/DEABrochure.pdf

https://www.atf.gov/careers/internships
internships@atf.gov

https://www.fcc.gov/general/internships-public-safety-and-homeland-security-bureau
PSHSBCyberInternship@fcc.gov
John.Evanoff@fcc.gov

http://www.state.nj.us/parole/docs/InternshipApplicationPacket.pdf
studentinternships@spb.state.nj.us

http://nbcjm.rutgers.edu/images/stories/Jobs/DrugCourtIntern.pdf

http://mercercountyprosecutor.com/employment/

https://www.secretservice.gov/join/diversity/students/

Trenton, New Jersey
609-989-2008

Philadelphia, Pennsylvania
215-861-3300

Egg Harbor Township, New Jersey
609-383-8687

http://www.holmdeltownship-nj.com/291/Internships
tfdurdack@holmdelpolice.org

https://www.ice.gov/careers/internships
ICEPathwaysPrograms@ice.dhs.gov

https://careers.fema.gov/pathways-interns-recent-grads-pmfs
FEMA-PATHWAYS@fema.dhs.gov

https://www.whitehouse.gov/get-involved/internships/apply/
intern_application@whitehouse.gov

http://www.dia.mil/Careers/Students/Academic-Semester-Internship-Program/

https://www.intelligencecareers.gov/icstudents.html?Agency=NSA

https://www.usajobs.gov/Help/working-in-government/unique-hiring-paths/students/

https://www.amu.apus.edu/career-services/internships-and-fellowships/federal.htm

https://nbcjm.rutgers.edu/images/stories/Jobs/PatersonPDInternship.pdf

https://nbcjm.rutgers.edu/images/stories/Jobs/LegalServicesNJ.pdf

https://nbcjm.rutgers.edu/images/stories/Jobs/DeptofHealth.pdf

https://nbcjm.rutgers.edu/images/stories/Jobs/Somerset_PD_Internship_Opportunity_b0440.pdf

https://www.njcourts.gov/public/volunteer/volunteer.html

http://www.co.ocean.nj.us/OC/JuvServices/frmInternships.aspx

https://academics.rowan.edu/chss/departments/lawjustice/career/LawJusticeRowan
UniversityGloucesterCountyPoliceDepts.html

https://academics.rowan.edu/chss/departments/lawjustice/career/LawJusticeRowan
UniversityCamdenCountyPoliceDepts.html

http://www.mercercounty.org/departments/personnel/job-opportunities/
mercer-county-internship-program

https://www.njsp.org/recruiting/internship-opportunities.shtml

http://internsolutions.net/students/

https://sjvolunteers.org/

https://www.nj.gov/corrections/SubSites/OTS/OTS_BSWMSW_FieldPlacement_InternshipOpps.html

https://www.mcsonj.org/about-us/internship-opportunities/

https://www.njpt.uscourts.gov/internship-program

https://www.bop.gov/jobs/students.jsp

https://www.afsc.org/volunteers-interns-fellows

https://www.njhomelandsecurity.gov/internships/

http://www.amazondelivers.jobs/about/students/#internships

https://careers.kohls.com/internships

http://www.co.hunterdon.nj.us/personnel/jobs.htm

https://www.youtern.com/

https://www.ncja.org/ncja/about-ncja/internships

VOLUNTEER OPPORTUNITIES

Department of Corrections—Tutor Prison Inmates

Internship Opportunities & Resources

Central Intelligence Agency (C.I.A.)

https://www.fbi.gov/about-us/otd/internships

Federal Law Enforcement Training Center

Homeland Security

Immigration and Customs Enforcement (I.C.E.)

New Jersey State Parole Board Internship Program

http://www.nj.gov/oag/dcj/Undergraduate-Law-Internship.html

Student Name: _____ Date: _____

Course Section: _____

STUDENT INTERNSHIP AGREEMENT

The student will initial by each paragraph below

_____ I agree to conduct myself in the program according to the requirements within the syllabus and with policies established in the program. I agree to be under the authority of the Internship Coordinator/Faculty and a designated supervisor at the internship site.

_____ I understand that, the internship program has risks, and I release and hold harmless the State of New Jersey and Rowan University, or the employees of either, for any damages or injury (including death) that might result from my participation in the internship program, except in the case of willful misconduct or gross negligence.

_____ I understand that Rowan University reserves the right to terminate my participation in the program at any time should my actions, in the sole discretion of the Rowan University, be determined to be detrimental to the program.

_____ I agree to comply with the rules and codes of conduct outlined by Rowan University and the sponsor agency.

_____ I agree to fulfill the hours required and act in a professional manner at all times while going to, coming from and while at the internship site.

Signed: _____

Date: _____

Student Name: _____ Date: _____

Course Section: _____

INTERNSHIP SCHEDULE

The internship schedule will serve as a guide for the students to complete the three (3) credits (150 hours) or the six (6) credits (300 hours) course(s). The student will be required to complete a minimum of ten (10) to fifteen (15) hours per week at the assigned or approved criminal justice agency or related organization(s).

1. Internship Application (see Appendix A)
   Please fully complete the following information and write legibly.

   Full Name: _____ Social Security #: _____

   Date of Birth: _____

   Driver's License Number and State: _____

   Current status year in the university/college: _____

   Current phone number: _____

   Current address: _____

   Permanent address: _____

   _____

   _____

   _____

   Start date: _____ Ending date: _____ for internship.

Review the following and sign the acknowledgment:

1. A background check will be conducted and I agree to the release of any such information necessary to complete the background check.
2. A drug screen will be conducted. Random drug screening may occur and I agree to be drug free for the duration of the internship.
3. I agree to hold information observed during the internship as confidential. I understand there may be criminal and civil penalties, including University discipline, should I be found in breach of my confidentiality agreement.
4. I agree to act professionally, dress accordingly, follow all reasonable instructions, and comply with University and agency policies.
5. I understand the use of social media will be restricted according to University and agency policy during the internship.
6. I will follow the attendance policy and follow the rules/guidelines set by the University and the agency.

Signed: _____

Date: _____

APPENDIX A: INTERNSHIP APPLICATION

Please fully complete the following information and write legibly.

Full Name: _____ Social Security #: _____

Date of Birth: _____

Driver's License Number and State: _____

Current status year in the university/college: _____

Current phone number: _____

Current address: _____

Permanent address: _____

_____

_____

_____

Start date: _____ Ending date: _____ for internship.

Review the following and sign the acknowledgment:

1. A background check will be conducted and I agree to the release of any such information necessary to complete the background check.
2. A drug screen will be conducted. Random drug screening may occur and I agree to be drug free for the duration of the internship.
3. I agree to hold information observed during the internship as confidential. I understand there may be criminal and civil penalties, including University discipline, should I be found in breach of my confidentiality agreement.
4. I agree to act professionally, dress accordingly, follow all reasonable instructions, and comply with University and agency policies.
5. I understand the use of social media will be restricted according to University and agency policy during the internship.
6. I will follow the attendance policy and follow the rules/guidelines set by the University and the agency.

Signed: _____

Date: _____

Student Name: _____ Date: _____

Course Section: _____

APPENDIX B: AGENCY BACKGROUND INVESTIGATION FORM

Misrepresentation or misstatement of fact is sufficient cause for the rejection of an applicant or removal from the position. _____ APPLICANT INITIALS

Name: _____

Address: _____

City: _____ State: _____ Zip Code: _____

Alias/Nicknames: _____

Maiden Name or Name Change: _____

Date of Birth: _____ Social Security Number: _____

Telephone Number: (H): _____

(W): _____

E-Mail Address: _____

Marks/Scars/Tattoos: _____

Facebook Account Name: _____

Other Social Media Account Names: _____

_____

Arrests: _____

Convictions: _____

Driver's License Number And State: _____

Moving Violations: _____

- Certain infractions, arrests, convictions, University discipline, associations, or other such history which would preclude one from access to confidential information; law enforcement, judicial, correctional facilities; or other disqualifying information may make a student ineligible for certain internships.
- Some agencies require a more in-depth investigation
- To be considered for the "approved" pool of students for the Gloucester County Law Enforcement initiative, a more in-depth investigation may be required.
- Some agencies require a drug screen.

By signing below the student agrees to the background investigation and holds harmless any and all agencies in providing information.

Signed: _____

Date: _____

The Internship Required Checklist

1. Internship Coordinator's Letter to Agency(s) discussing required course credits and mandatory hours
2. Letter of Confirmation
3. The student must obtain letter of confirmation from the agency
4. Internship Agreement
5. The agreement must be completed by student and agency

Student Name: _____ Date: _____

Course Section: _____

Original forms ONLY for submission. No copies will be accepted.

APPENDIX C: INTERNSHIP AGREEMENT

Between the Law and Justice Studies Department of Rowan University and Agency _____

_____

The Law and Justice Studies Department of Rowan University designates _____ (Agency) as an approved internship placement providing a rich blend of practical laboratory experiences yielded by the criminal justice agency or related agency.

The Law and Justice Studies Department and the _____ Agency commit themselves to cooperative efforts as described below, in provision of supervised educational internship experiences.

This agreement becomes effective on _____, remains in force for a period _____ of _____ year(s), and renews itself annually, unless either the Law and Justice Studies Department or the _____ Agency indicates a need for a review or change.

Any adjustments to the agreement will be included in a written addendum.

In the event of unforeseen circumstances which significantly affect the student's educational plan, each party with inform the other in writing, so that the appropriate changes in their agreement may be made within a reasonable amount of time (14 days), to assure sufficient time for planning.

The Law and Justice Studies Department Agrees to:

1. Design learning outcomes and cooperate with the agency supervisor to ensure the expectations of the internship are met.
2. Provide candidates who have been screened and recommend those students to be placed at the agency should the student not find an internship opportunity on their own.
3. Communicate all educational requirements that are necessary for the agency to effectively evaluate the intern.
4. Provide consultation to appropriate staff of the agency in the general development of its internship program.
5. The Faculty/Coordinator of the Internship Program will serve as the Internship Consultant to the agency who will:
   a. Coordinate efforts for academic success between the agency and the department.
   b. Be available to review the intern progress via the forms submitted by the agency and the student at certain intervals throughout the internship.
   c. Ensure the student is aware of policies concerning the internship.
6. Provide opportunities for appropriate evaluations of the agency as a setting of student learning.
7. Provide a copy of the department's course syllabus.

227

The Agency Agrees to:

1. Attempt to the meet the objectives of the department as detailed in the course syllabus.

2. Accept the conditions stipulated in the course syllabus.

3. Involve the students in meaningful agency programs by utilizing appropriate assignments or tasks.

4. Allow students to use their work product for academic discussion with the Faculty/Coordinator of the Internship Program, keeping in mind confidentiality and any rules of the agency.

5. Assure that each supervisor or designated representative will have adequate time within his/her work schedule to:

   a. Satisfy the educational objectives of the students through development of learning opportunities.

   b. Prepare for regularly scheduled conferences with students.

   c. Discuss with the Faculty/Coordinator of the Internship Program at periodic intervals the learning opportunities and student performance.

   d. Prepare reports and evaluation as required by the department.

6. Permit the use of facilities by students of the department during the period of the placement, including space for students in an area sufficiently private for carrying on the assigned work or activity.

7. Assure that the Faculty/Coordinator of the Internship Program is advised of policy and service changes and developments which may affect student learning or the department's curriculum.

8. Inform the Faculty/Coordinator of any early or immediate problems that may develop concerning a student's progress or performance.

9. Observe the University calendar with respect to student holiday and vacation periods.

10. Adhere to course objectives:

    a. _____

    b. _____

    c. _____

    d. _____

    e. _____

FOR THE AGENCY:

BY: _____

DATE: _____

FOR THE UNIVERSITY:

ROWAN UNIVERSITY LAW AND JUSTICE STUDIES DEPARTMENT

BY: _____

FACULTY/COORDINATOR OF INTERNSHIP PROGRAM

DATE: _____

Student Name: _____ Date: _____

Course Section: _____

APPENDIX D: WAIVER AND RELEASE AGREEMENT TO INTERNSHIP COORDINATOR

The student will initial by each paragraph below

I, _____ am a student at Rowan University, and have agreed to participate in the Law and Justice Internship Program from _____ until _____. In consideration for being permitted to participate in the program, I hereby attest that:

I agree to conduct myself in the program according to the requirements within the syllabus and with policies established in the program. I agree to be under the authority of the Internship Coordinator/ Faculty and a designated supervisor at the internship site.

I understand that, the internship program has risks, and I release and hold harmless the State of New Jersey and Rowan University, or the employees of either, for any damages or injury (including death) that might result from my participation in the internship program, except in the case of willful misconduct or gross negligence.

I understand that Rowan University reserves the right to terminate my participation in the program at any time should my actions, in the sole discretion of the Rowan University, be determined to be detrimental to the program.

I agree to comply with the rules and codes of conduct outlined by Rowan University and the sponsor agency.

I agree to fulfill the hours required and act in a professional manner at all times while going to, coming from and while at the internship site.

Signed: _____

Date: _____

Student Name: _____ Date: _____

Course Section: _____

Original forms ONLY for submission. No copies will be accepted.

APPENDIX E: WAIVER AND RELEASE AGREEMENT TO AGENCY

The student will initial by each paragraph below

I, _____ am a student at Rowan University, and have agreed to participate in the Law and Justice Internship Program from _____ until _____. In consideration for being permitted to participate in the program, I hereby attest that:

I agree to conduct myself in the program according to the requirements within the syllabus and with policies established in the program. I agree to be under the authority of the Internship Coordinator/Faculty and a designated supervisor at the internship site.

I understand that, the internship program has risks, and I release and hold harmless the State of New Jersey and Rowan University, or the employees of either, for any damages or injury (including death) that might result from my participation in the internship program, except in the case of willful misconduct or gross negligence.

I understand that Rowan University reserves the right to terminate my participation in the program at any time should my actions, in the sole discretion of the Rowan University, be determined to be detrimental to the program.

I agree to comply with the rules and codes of conduct outlined by Rowan University and the sponsor agency.

I agree to fulfill the hours required and act in a professional manner at all times while going to, coming from and while at the internship site.

Signed: _____

Date: _____

Student Name: _____ Date: _____

Course Section: _____

Original forms ONLY for submission. No copies will be accepted.

APPENDIX F: INTERNSHIP AGREEMENT

Between the Law and Justice Studies Department of Rowan University and Agency _____
_____

The Law and Justice Studies Department of Rowan University designates _____ (agency) as an approved internship placement providing a rich blend of practical laboratory experiences yielded by the criminal justice agency or related agency.

The Law and Justice Studies Department and the _____ Agency commit themselves to cooperative efforts as described below, in provision of supervised educational internship experiences.

This agreement becomes effective on _____, remains in force for a period _____ of _____ year(s), and renews itself annually, unless either the Law and Justice Studies Department or the _____ Agency indicates a need for a review or change.

Any adjustments to the agreement will be included in a written addendum.

In the event of unforeseen circumstances which significantly affect the student's educational plan, each party with inform the other in writing, so that the appropriate changes in their agreement may be made within a reasonable amount of time (14 days), to assure sufficient time for planning.

The Law and Justice Studies Department Agrees to:

1. Work cooperatively with the agency in designing appropriate learning experiences and to actively participate with the student and the Internship Supervisor or Agency site manager in the decision-making concerning the educational appropriateness, timing and the reasonableness of the internship experiences.
2. Respect the autonomy of the agency to set its own program as a service delivery system.
3. Interview, screen, select, and recommend students to be placed at the agency, and to make alternate plans for placement of student(s) in the event that such planning becomes necessary.
4. Formulate and execute all educational decisions concerning the student such as grades, credits, hours completed within the agency, and the curriculum in general.
5. Provide consultation to appropriate staff of the agency in the general development of its internship program.
6. The faculty/coordinator of the Internship Program will serve as the Internship Consultant to the agency who will:
   a. Serve as the principal liaison between the department and the agency during each academic semester.
   b. Be available for the agency as need may be concerning the relationships between the agency and the department.
   c. Have periodic communication to review the student(s) progress.
   d. Discuss policies and procedures of the Internship Course.
7. Provide opportunities for appropriate evaluations of the agency as a setting of student learning.
8. Provide a copy of the department's course syllabus.

The Agency agrees to:

1. Accept the policy of the department that students are assigned in accordance with the provisions of the Federal Civil Rights Act.

2. Adhere to the objectives of the department as contained in its course syllabus.

3. Accept the conditions stipulated in the course syllabus.

4. Involve the students in meaningful agency programs by utilizing appropriate assignments or tasks.

5. Allow students to use their work product for academic discussion with the Faculty/Coordinator of the Internship Program, keeping in mind the agency policy for confidentiality and any other related rules.

6. Assure that each supervisor will have adequate time within his/her work schedule to:

    a. Satisfy the educational objectives of the students through development of learning opportunities.

    b. Prepare for regularly scheduled conferences with students.

    c. Discuss with the Faculty/Coordinator of the Internship Program at periodic intervals the learning opportunities and student performance.

    d. Prepare reports and evaluation as required by the department.

7. Permit the use of facilities by students of the department during the period of the placement, including space for students in an area sufficiently private for carrying on the assigned work or activity.

8. Assure that the Faculty/Coordinator of the Internship Program is advised of policy and service changes and developments which may affect student learning or the department's curriculum.

9. Inform the Faculty/Coordinator of any early or immediate problems that may develop concerning a student's progress or performance.

10. Provide reimbursement of all student travel expenses on agency business.

11. Observe the University calendar with respect to student holiday and vacation periods.

12. Adhere to course objectives:

    a. _____

    b. _____

    c. _____

    d. _____

    e. _____

FOR THE AGENCY:

BY: _____

DATE: _____

FOR THE UNIVERSITY:

ROWAN UNIVERSITY LAW AND JUSTICE STUDIES DEPARTMENT

BY: _____

FACULTY/COORDINATOR OF INTERNSHIP PROGRAM

DATE: _____

Student Name: _____ Date: _____

Course Section: _____

Original forms ONLY for submission. No copies will be accepted.

APPENDIX G: SUPERVISOR'S EVALUATION FORM

Name of Student _____ Date _____

Placement Area _____

Agency Evaluation of the Student Performance

Overall:

Attendance	Excellent ( )	Good ( )	Fair ( )
Reliability	Excellent ( )	Good ( )	Fair ( )
Peer Relations	Excellent ( )	Good ( )	Fair ( )
Supervisory Relations	Excellent ( )	Good ( )	Fair ( )
Understanding of Position	Excellent ( )	Good ( )	Fair ( )
Initiative	Excellent ( )	Good ( )	Fair ( )

Comments _____

_____

_____

Supervisor Name: _____

Supervisor Email and Phone: _____

Supervisor Signature: _____

The student and the supervisor have discussed the learning outcomes as well as any projects or assignments completed/tasked that are reflected in the comments section.

APPENDIX H: MID-TERM REVIEW: SUPERVISOR'S EVALUATION OF STUDENT INTERN

Instruction to Student: The student must complete this portion of the evaluation form and leave it with his or her supervisor for evaluation. The supervisor should e-mail or fax this evaluation to: university/ college faculty/coordinator.

INTERN: _____

Name of Agency: _____

Name of Department: _____

Name of Supervisor: _____ Title: _____

Normal Placement Hrs _____ to _____ Total hrs/weeks

_____

Description of Duties/Learning Objectives/Projects: _____

_____

_____

_____

To be completed by the Supervisor: The Supervisor will evaluate the student using the ratable areas listed. This information will be utilized by the faculty/coordinator for the guidance of the student. Please check the appropriate box for each category and provide a brief explanation.

ABILITY TO LEARN

( ) Learns very quickly

( ) Learns readily

( ) Average in learning

( ) Rather slow to learn

( ) Very slow to learn

JUDGMENT

( ) Exceptionally mature

( ) Above average

( ) Makes the right decision

( ) Uses poor judgment

( ) Consistently uses bad judgment

QUALITY OF WORK

( ) Excellent

( ) Very good

( ) Average

( ) Below average

( ) Very poor

DEPENDABILITY

( ) Completely

( ) Above average

( ) Usually dependable

( ) Sometimes neglectful

( ) Unreliable

ATTITUDE-APPLICATION TO WORK

( ) Outstanding in enthusiasm

( ) Very interested

( ) Average

( ) Somewhat indifferent

( ) Definitely not interested

RELATIONS WITH OTHERS

( ) Exceptionally well accepted

( ) Works well with others

( ) Gets along satisfactorily

( ) Has difficulty working with others

( ) Works very poorly with others

ATTENDANCE

( ) Regular

( ) Irregular

PUNCTUALITY

( ) Regular

( ) Irregular

OVERALL PERFORMANCE

( ) Outstanding

( ) Very good

( ) Average

( ) Poor

The supervisor must certify the number of hours completed by the student:

I, _____ certify that _____

  Supervisor   Student

Has completed _____ hours.

Signed _____ Date _____

  Supervisor

Supervisor Email and Phone: _____

Student Responses and Comments: _____

_____

Student Name: _____ Date: _____

Course Section: _____

APPENDIX I: THE STUDENT MUST ITEMIZE ALL COMPLETED PROJECTS AND TASKS

The itemized list must be submitted to the supervisor and the Internship Coordinator.

1. _____
   _____
2. _____
   _____
3. _____
   _____
4. _____
   _____
5. _____
   _____
6. _____
   _____
7. _____
   _____
8. _____
   _____
9. _____
   _____
10. _____
   _____

Supervisor Signature: _____

Supervisor Email: _____

Student Responses and Comments: _____

_____

_____

APPENDIX J: AGENCY'S ASSESSMENT OF STUDENT PROJECTS

The agency supervisor will assess the student's completed itemized projects or assignments.

1. _____
_____

2. _____
_____

3. _____
_____

4. _____
_____

5. _____
_____

6. _____
_____

7. _____
_____

8. _____
_____

9. _____
_____

10. _____
_____

Supervisor Signature: _____

Supervisor Email: _____

Student Responses and Comments: _____
_____
_____

Student Name: _____ Date: _____

Course Section: _____

APPENDIX K: FINAL REVIEW: SUPERVISOR'S EVALUATION OF STUDENT INTERN

Instruction to Student: The student must complete this portion of the evaluation form and leave it with his or her supervisor for evaluation. The supervisor should e-mail or fax this evaluation to: university/college faculty/coordinator.

Intern: _____

Name of Agency: _____

Name of Department: _____

Name of Supervisor: _____ Title: _____

Normal Placement Hrs _____ to _____ Total hrs/weeks _____

Description of Duties: _____

_____

_____

_____

To be completed by the Supervisor. The Supervisor will evaluate the student using the ratable areas. This information will be utilized by the faculty/coordinator for the guidance of the student. Please check the appropriate box for each category. Please provide a brief explanation.

ABILITY TO LEARN

( ) Learns very quickly

( ) Learns readily

( ) Average in learning

( ) Rather slow to learn

( ) Very slow to learn

JUDGMENT

( ) Exceptionally mature

( ) Above average

( ) Makes the right decision

( ) Uses poor judgment

( ) Consistently uses bad judgment

QUALITY OF WORK

( ) Excellent

( ) Very good

( ) Average

( ) Below average

( ) Very poor

DEPENDABILITY

( ) Completely

( ) Above average

( ) Usually dependable

( ) Sometimes neglectful

( ) Unreliable

ATTITUDE-APPLICATION TO WORK

( ) Outstanding in enthusiasm

( ) Very interested

( ) Average

( ) Somewhat indifferent

( ) Definitely not interested

RELATIONS WITH OTHERS

( ) Exceptionally well accepted

( ) Works well with others

( ) Gets along satisfactorily

( ) Has difficulty working with others

( ) Works very poorly with others

ATTENDANCE

( ) Regular

( ) Irregular

PUNCTUALITY

( ) Regular

( ) Irregular

OVERALL PERFORMANCE

( ) Outstanding

( ) Very good

( ) Average

( ) Poor

The supervisor must certify the number of hours completed by the student:

I, _____ certify that _____
                        Supervisor   Student

Has completed _____ hours.

Signed _____ Date _____
                        Supervisor

Supervisor Email and Phone: _____

Student Responses and Comments: _____

_____

APPENDIX L: STUDENT INTERN EVALUATION OF THE INTERNSHIP EXPERIENCE

Date: _____

Name: _____

Agency: _____ Location: _____

Describe in detail your assignment with this agency _____

_____

_____

_____

Was the placement meaningful to your personal development? _____

_____

_____

Was the placement meaningful to your professional development? _____

_____

_____

What do you consider the best features of this placement? _____

_____

_____

What do you think could be improved of this agency placement? _____

_____

_____

_____

Did your supervisor provide meaningful input in your evaluation? _____

_____

_____

_____

Was training or orientation available? _____

_____

_____

Does this agency offer potential for employment? _____

_____

_____

What is the likelihood that, if offered, you would accept a permanent position with this agency?
_____

Do you feel that the internship experience could be improved in this agency? If so, why or

why not? _____

_____

_____

Comments: _____

_____

_____

_____

_____

Signed: _____

Date: _____

RESOURCES

AUTHOR. *Academy of criminal justice sciences.* (1999). Los Angeles: Roxbury Publishing Company.

AUTHOR. *American correctional association.* (2000). Lanham, MD: PUBLISHER.

Borzak, Lenore (ed.) (1981). *Field study: A sourcebook of experiential learning.* Beverly Hills, CA: Sage Publishing Company.

Brammer, L.M. (1985). *The helping relationship: process and skills* (3rd Ed.). Englewood Cliffs, NJ: Prentice Hall.

Goldstein A. (ed.) (1975). *Practicum manual: A guide for students, faculty and administrators.* Arlington, VA: National Recreation and Park Association.

Harr, Scott J., & Hess, Karen M. (2000). *Seeking employment in criminal justice and related fields (3rd Ed.).* Belmont, CA: Wadsworth Publishing Company.

Havens, L. (1976). *Participant observation.* New York: J. Aronson.

Jorgensen, D. L. (1989). *Participant observation: A methodology for human studies.* Newbury Park, CA: Sage Publishing Company.

National Directory of Law Enforcement Administrators. (2000). *Correctional institutions and related agencies.* Oregon, WI: Span Publishing, Inc.

Rowan University. (2001). *Rowan University career and academic planning.* Glassboro, NJ: Rowan University.

United States Department of Justice, Law Enforcement Assistance Administration. (1968). *Guideline-participation for internship programs.* G.5500.1A

INDEX

N

Needs, assessment of, 8–9
Networking, for effective internship search, 12–17, 206

O

Ombudsman, 179

P

Paralegal, 147, 148, 149
Parole officers, 107–108, 110
Portfolio, internship
    cover letter, 40
    follow-up letter/e-mail, 43
    interviews, 42
    references, 43–44
    resume, 41–42
Probation officers, 104, 108

R

References, 43–44
Resume
    checklist, 41–42
    formulation of, 41–42
Rowan University, 11, 12
    Law and Justice Studies Department, 3
    Student Patrol Program, 3
    study of law, 195

S

Safety manager, 179
Social media policy, 38
Social workers, 104, 108–109, 179
State police-highway patrols, 96–101
Substance abuse specialist, 180
Syllabus, 23–25
    course description, 23
    course objectives, 23
    general education goals, 24
    requirements and grading, 24–25
    suggested observation, 24

T

Technology-based crime, 180
Transferable skills, 206
Trends/Visions, 179–180

U

United States (U.S.)
    Air Force, 144
    Army, 144
    Attorneys, 164–177
    Court of Appeals, 162–163
    Courts, 144, 155–163
    Department of Justice, 163–177
    District Courts, 156–162
    Marine Corps, 145
    Navy, 145
    Parole Commission, 144
    Supreme Court, 155

W

Wardens, 109